Ricky Nelson
IDOL FOR A GENERATION

Ricky Nelson

IDOL FOR A GENERATION

JOEL SELVIN

CB
CONTEMPORARY
BOOKS
CHICAGO

Library of Congress Cataloging-in-Publication Data

Selvin, Joel.
    Ricky Nelson : idol for a generation / Joel Selvin.
      p.   cm.
    Discography: p.
    Includes bibliographical references.
    ISBN 0-8092-4187-0
     1. Nelson, Rick.   1940–1985.   2. Singers—United States—
Biography.
  I. Title.
    ML420.N3826S4   1990
    782.42166'092—dc20   90-31531
    [B]   CIP
                                                    MN

For Keta
Who makes all possible

Contents

Acknowledgments——————————————xi

1   Prelude——————————————————1

2   The Adventures of Ozzie and Harriet————12

3   Here Come the Nelsons——————————31

4   I'm Walkin'——————————————————60

5   Teenage Idol————————————————91

6   Travelin' Man—————————————————117

7   Hello Mary Lou————————————————136

8   Love and Kisses———————————————158

9   Easy to Be Free————————————————178

10   Garden Party—————————————————198

11   Rick Nelson Now————————————————222

12   The Loser, Babe, Is You————————————245

13   Big Train from Memphis—————————————266

14   Epilogue————————————————————287

Discography——————————————————301

Bibliography——————————————————311

Index————————————————————————319

Acknowledgments

THE PIERCING OF THE VEIL OF PRIVACY that has always surrounded the Nelson family was made possible by a number of
people willing to share their candid recollections that went
beyond the typical "they were just like the TV show." Ozzie
Nelson worked hard to preserve the fantasy image of his
family's real life that he portrayed so successfully on the long-
running TV series, and his policy tends to prevail more than a
decade after his death.

First of all, David Nelson not only shared generous amounts
of his time but helped open doors nobody else could have. He
is a charming, pleasant man, and it was impossible not to be
touched by him, a survivor of a family hammered more heavily by hardships than he would care to admit.

Sharon Sheeley proved a never-ending source of anecdotes
and insight; she cheered my research from the sidelines, and
her caustic humor never failed to puncture any pretensions
encountered. Bruce Belland of the Four Preps provided some
special reminiscences, and Joe Byrne supplied an up-close
look at life on and off the set of "The Adventures of Ozzie and
Harriet."

Forrest Stewart gave a heartfelt interview filled with feelings and memories he hadn't examined in many years. Jimmie Haskell endured inquiries with unfailing good nature. Lorrie Carnall dredged up some painful memories with deep sincerity.

Allen Kemp and Dennis Sarokin provided detailed looks at their days with the Stone Canyon Band, and Oscar Arslanian took time to be helpful in many ways, including introducing me to David Nelson.

James Burton, a great guitarist and a courtly gentleman, shared some detailed recollections of his early years with Rick. John Boylan not only opened up a mysterious period in Rick's life but went to bat for me with other less forthcoming sources. Al Kooper turned out to be an erudite Rick Nelson fan whose interview illuminated far more than just the one album project they did together.

Dorothy and Tuesday Knight worked hard to convince Baker Knight, their ex-husband and father, respectively, to do an interview. He didn't think he had anything to contribute but, of course, ended up giving a most soulful account of his experiences with Rick.

Many other people willingly contributed their time for substantial interviews, including Bunny Robyn, Keith Olsen, Gene Garf, Jerry Fuller, Dorothy Colbert, Julie Pinkert, Randy Meisner, John Beland, Richard Murphy, John Fogerty, Connie Francis, Barney Kessel, Richie Frost, Thurley Burnette, Rocky Burnette, Kim Fowley, Denny Bruce, Rich Frio, Angie Dickinson, Earl Palmer, Gregg Geller, Joe Sutton, Richard Oliver, Skip Young, Chester Golasinski, Georgeanne Crewe, Richard Nader, Aaron Schroeder, Joannie Sommers, Eric Andersen, James Intveld, Alan Bush, Jerry McGee, Art Laboe, Nick Venet, Jerry Cole, Gene Taylor, Will Thornbury, Jay DeWitt White, Phil Savenick, and Dr. David Smith of the Haight-Ashbury Medical Clinic.

Others volunteered information, but with the provision that their anonymity be guaranteed. They know who they are.

The project received valuable assistance and encouragement in its early stages from many people, and it never would have happened without Fabian Forte and Pat Holt especially. Nick Clainos of Bill Graham Presents and Dave Marsh also chipped in some important moral support, and made it obvious the story needed to be told.

Vital assistance in research came from Art Fein of Hollywood, who conducted a number of the interviews and provided consequential logistical and spiritual support, and David Ritchie of Southwest News Services, who decoded a great deal of bureaucratic tangles. John Johnson of the *Los Angeles Times* made efforts far above and beyond the call of duty for a friend, and, as always, his wisdom and guidance helped light the path. Todd Everett of the *Los Angeles Herald-Examiner* was also a big help in many ways. Special thanks to Ian Cooke, Rick Nelson fan and collector extraordinaire, who supplied so many hard-to-find videos and records. Howard Kasten, another Rick Nelson fan, supplied some fine old photos.

Thanks must go too to the *San Francisco Chronicle* for all the opportunities and resources provided to me over the years and to Dr. August Coppola, dean of the School of Creative Arts, San Francisco State University, whose support of my academic career provided crucial support during this project.

Frank Weimann couldn't have been a more supportive agent, and Nancy Crossman of Contemporary Books proved to be both an encouraging editor and sagacious publisher. No set of such acknowledgments could be complete without some totally mysterious contribution being noted. In this case, that honor goes to "country bankruptcy lawyer" Barney Shapiro, whose hospitality and generosity made this book possible.

There's a place where lovers go
To cry their troubles away.
And they call it Lonesome Town,
Where the broken hearts stay.

You can buy a dream or two
To last you all through the years.
And the only price you pay
Is a heart full of tears.

Going down to Lonesome Town,
Where the broken hearts stay.
Going down to Lonesome Town,
To cry my troubles away.

In the town of broken dreams,
The streets are filled with regret.
Maybe down in Lonesome Town,
I can learn to forget.

—"Lonesome Town"
by Baker Knight

Ricky Nelson
IDOL FOR A GENERATION

1

Prelude

DEBBIE FOSTER, A TWENTY-TWO-YEAR-OLD TEACHER at De Kalb Independent School, was playing dolls with her two-year-old daughter, Tiffany, before supper. The child began to cry. A noise was hurting her ears, she said. Suddenly, an enormous roar thundered through the house, and the young teacher went to the bedroom window, thinking some massive truck was raging past the house on the highway.

A giant tire and the white underbelly of a large airplane spitting flames filled the window, barely missing her roof, dropping bits of fire as it headed down toward the Joneses' pasture across the highway, breaking the fence and scaring David Jones's sleeping cows.

David Jones, the saw operator and farmer who lived across the road, was also at home when the DC-3 came out of the sky across Highway 909 and headed his way. For a moment, he thought it would hit his house, and he ran outside, catching sight of sparks spraying from one of the plane's engines and the wings clipping off telephone poles. All he could see inside the plane's windows was black smoke.

The World War II–vintage Douglas DC-3 left Guntersville, Alabama, a little before one o'clock the afternoon of New Year's Eve 1985 on a routine flight to Love Field, Dallas. Although the passengers had to disembark and takeoff was delayed while a fuel line was repaired, the flight otherwise began uneventfully. The seven passengers either slept or read quietly, although the copilot later reported he smelled a whiff of marijuana smoke coming from the passenger cabin at one point. Four hours into the flight, the pilot discovered a problem and began making plans to land in Texarkana, Texas.

The control tower at Texarkana Airport tracked the progress of the stricken plane. An American Eagle commuter plane had the DC-3 in sight; both planes were talking to the tower as the DC-3 made plans to chart a course for Texarkana, when the situation turned desperate.

"Just any field will do," crackled the voice from the DC-3. "We've got a problem here."

"OK one-one-yankee," responded the control tower, "can you make it back to Texarkana?"

"Negative," came the reply. "We got to get on the ground."

Don Ruggles, a helicopter pilot, heard the transmission from his airborne position nearby, as the tower started to route the troubled DC-3 to either Red River County or Mount Pleasant airports.

"We've got . . . uh . . . smoke in the cockpit," said the DC-3.

"One-one-yankee, you're breaking up," said Texarkana. "Can you state the nature of the emergency?"

The American Eagle heard the call. "Said he had smoke in the cockpit, center, relaying," said American Eagle.

"Thank you much, Eagle Express. Ask him if he can make it to Mount Pleasant."

"Douglas seven, eleven yankee, can you make it to Mount Pleasant airport?" relayed the commute flight.

"We don't know where it is. We've lost our chart."

"Right on your tail and seventeen miles is an airport," said American Express.

"Can't do it."

"Eagle Express, tell him the Mount Pleasant airport would be 180 degrees heading and, uh, twenty miles, if he wanted to make it," said Texarkana.

"Negative, we can't do it," replied the DC-3.

"Says he can't make it," relayed the American Eagle. "Have you got anything closer at all, even shorter?"

"That's the closest two airports," said Texarkana.

"Smoke in the cockpit . . . have smoke in the cockpit." Then the DC-3 was quiet.

For the next minute and a half, Texarkana control and the American Eagle discussed rerouting the commuter plane to try to lead the stricken plane to safety. Then Don Ruggles, aboard his helicopter, piped up.

"We have the aircraft in sight," he said. "Looks like he's gone down. You need to call Texarkana for the Air Life helicopter."

Debbie Foster tried to phone the De Kalb Fire Department, but the plane came close enough to her roof to cut her telephone and electrical lines. She rushed her daughter Tiffany to an aunt's house and quickly returned to fight the fires on the side of her house, where molten pieces of metal falling from the sky had started grass fires.

Donald Lewis was riding his tractor in a neighboring field. First he heard the airplane coming down. Then he saw the big, white plane trailing black smoke as it flew below the treetops. He watched the plane bank right and pull up before he lost sight of it. Black smoke poured from somewhere over the rise, and he gunned his John Deere and hurried toward where he saw the plane disappear.

Dean Waters had just finished feeding his thoroughbreds when he saw the fuming fireball. He called his wife, Pat, and the two of them jumped in their pickup truck and headed for the site. Two of their employees made their way across the field by foot. Pat Waters thought the yellow, orange, and blue flames engulfing the airplane sounded like a blowtorch. Another nearby farmer, L. B. Barrett, and his son Randy also arrived on the scene, having seen the plane disappear behind the trees while they were feeding cattle.

One plane engine was still running; the other had stopped. Two separate explosions rang out as the tires blew. Don Ruggles settled his helicopter down on the field, and shortly thereafter the emergency rescue helicopter landed too. The disabled plane's pilot ambled painfully away from the left side of the cockpit, and soon a second, badly burned man emerged from the tall grass on the other side, walking away from the smoking inferno. L. B. and Randy Barrett approached the burning craft and saw an arm hanging out of the front left window. The arm never moved.

The seven passengers were dead; one was Rick Nelson.

In Encino, California, David Nelson was standing in his kitchen, ready to go out to a New Year's Eve party, when the phone rang. "I remember picking up the phone," he said, "and somebody told me my brother had died and then hung up the phone. I never knew who that person was." At first, he didn't believe the caller; he turned on the TV set anyway, and the dreadful news blared out.

He called his mother, Harriet Nelson, but the word had already reached her. She saw the news flash on television. Reeling in shock, she could barely speak. David made the hour-long drive to her home in Laguna Beach and brought her back to his house in the San Fernando Valley. New Year's Eve celebrations were forgotten.

A baffling combination of incandescence and darkness, Rick Nelson when he died was a nearly forgotten figure, working on the peripheries of the music scene. At county fairs and steak-and-lobster houses in small cities, he churned out rote but letter-perfect recitations of the hit songs that had made him one of the all-time top record sellers nearly thirty years before. His genuine contributions to the history of rock music were far behind him, ignored and neglected.

He was broke and badly in debt. He kept vampire hours, rising as the sun set and going to bed at dawn. His children rarely saw him, although they lived in the same rambling mansion in the Hollywood hills, originally built by the dissolute movie star Errol Flynn. His startling good looks were fading, and, even on a postmidnight grocery-shopping trip, he would never leave his house without full makeup.

Many people take charge of their destinies and make things happen. Rick was the sort of person that things happened to. He was the fortunate son who stood still while providence came to him. When life smiled on him, he accepted its gifts gratefully. When his luck ran dry, he never complained.

He grew up the sunniest of California's golden boys, a teenager whose fame and wealth exceeded that of powerful statesmen, lauded scholars, and literary geniuses many years his age. Raised as the celebrated son of an almost mythical American family, Rick Nelson never escaped a life of frustration and defeat despite a youth of unparalleled privilege and glory.

Rick himself was a cipher. His closest friends remembered him fondly but not well, invariably first and foremost recalling Rick as "nice." Other, more pointed details always proved vague or missing entirely. It was as if he had been there in shape but not substance. This shadowy figure bundled together contradictions: warm and remote, witty and dull, fortunate and hapless, confident and shy, proud and docile.

He learned to be cautious around strangers, shy to the point of paranoia, and he grew to read his life from a script. Over the years, he would respond to the questions of interviewers with identical answers, almost word for word, like little speeches he had memorized.

The indomitable Ozzie Nelson never used intimidation to rule his sons. He didn't need to. This compulsive overachiever played the benevolent despot who preserved his dominance through manipulation and the granting of privileges. Their mother balanced their father with nonjudgmental cheerfulness shaded with a wry and occasionally ribald sense of humor. Born into show business, Harriet Nelson too lived from a script. All through her life, she routinely served her guests, apparently without irony, milk and cookies, even though the kitchen was foreign territory for this woman raised in hotel rooms.

Ozzie Nelson so totally dominated the TV series "The Adventures of Ozzie and Harriet," which lasted fourteen years on the country's screens, that no detail proved too small for his attention. He wrote the scripts, directed the shows, and scrupulously supervised the postproduction. "The Adventures of Ozzie and Harriet" began as a weekly radio show in 1944, transferred over to television in 1952, running simultaneously with the radio series for one hectic season, and continued through 1966, as the Nelson family—Ozzie, Harriet, and their two sons, David and Ricky—grew to symbolize middle-class American home life during those innocent years.

Ozzie expected his real-life sons to carry their TV-show images into daily life. He constantly reminded them that the livelihood of the forty cast and crew members depended on their living up to the scripts he wrote for them.

As a teen, Rick grew to hate shooting the TV show through which the nation came to know him, and the result was friction between him and his father. Ozzie Nelson always had specific ideas of the way things were supposed to be, and if Ricky failed to measure up, he quickly let him know. But Ricky couldn't openly express any resentment, so rebellion took subtle forms, like long hair, smoking cigarettes, or fast cars.

And rock & roll.

For Rick, rock & roll offered an escape. Like so many other youths of the 1950s, he heard its clarion call and instinctively understood its message. But his father swarmed all over even that too, prodding his son from singing in the bathroom directly to a recording studio and onto nationwide TV while he was still a gangly amateur. In the process, Rick gave the budding music, at the time widely identified with juvenile delinquency and other social ills of the nation's young, a credibility it could never get from some greasy-haired Memphis truck driver shaking his hips. This was "Little Ricky," after all, the adored scion of the country's model middle-class family. It has been said Ricky smuggled rock & roll into America's living rooms.

Of the first-generation rockers, only Elvis Presley sold more records. But a remarkable, unexpected thing happened to Rick and his music. Although instantly a bestselling recording artist, he also grew into one of the music's true innovators, sculpting a brand of California rockabilly that was not only a deeply etched personal signature but also some of the most intensely wrought rock & roll of the fifties.

Rick had good reason to be proud of his musical accomplishments. His records of the fifties easily stand comparison with the best of the era, and his contributions to the literature of rock music endure. His guitarist, James Burton, wrote himself into the vocabulary of his instrument and, along with Elvis Presley's Scotty Moore and Gene Vincent's Cliff Gallup, became one of the triumvirate of rock guitar's founding fathers, who inspired and instructed generations of musicians to come. The musicianship of Rick's early band was renowned among other musicians. When Bob Dylan first looked for a band to back his electric folk rock, he sought out Rick's old musicians. After leaving Rick, Burton spent many years on lead guitar with Elvis.

But Rick's smoldering good looks and television-star image

marked him as a contrived teen idol in the public mind and put him on the defensive the rest of his life, as he struggled for the recognition and acknowledgment that his accomplishments justly earned. His image was a scar on his work that he could never see without flinching. He wanted to be Carl Perkins, but people always saw him as Fabian.

In inducting Rick Nelson into the Rock & Roll Hall of Fame at a 1987 Waldorf-Astoria banquet before famous musicians and other leaders of the record industry, John Fogerty noticed a bemused hush of skepticism fall over the crowd as he praised Rick as one of music's true innovators. He addressed one remark to no less a pioneer than the founder of Sun Records and the first person to record Elvis Presley.

"I looked over at Sam Phillips," Fogerty later recalled, "and I said, 'Sam, he even gave you a run for the money,' meaning that those records were so valid and such high quality and captured the heart and soul of rockabilly. What I was trying to say is that he could have been putting those records out on Sun. I feel that, and I think there are a lot of musicians who feel that way, especially if you lived through that time. But I got the distinct impression that the audience saw Rick as Frankie Avalon, and that just kills me to this day."

As leader of Creedence Clearwater Revival, Fogerty wrote, sang, and produced nine consecutive top-ten records in the late sixties and carried the torch for fundamental rock & roll as a solo artist through the eighties with rockabilly-style hits like "Rock and Roll Girls" and "Centerfield." He could easily remember what Ricky Nelson singles he bought as a teenager and what cuts were on the albums he owned.

Although they crossed paths briefly a couple of times in their careers, Fogerty never knew Rick. He remained a fan from afar. He considers Rick Nelson one of the primary influences on his life's work.

"What I liked about Rick," he said, "is that it seemed to prove you could make cool records and be at the very core of rock and roll and not have to be crazy to do it."

But among the artists who shaped rock, Fogerty is not alone in appreciating Rick's contributions. No less cynical a spokesman than Bob Dylan can wax rhapsodic about Rick and his music. Dylan, of course, was a major inspiration to Rick later in his career, and Rick consistently did some of the finest interpretations of Dylan songs ever recorded. After Rick's death, Dylan returned the compliment. During his 1986 tour with Tom Petty and the Heartbreakers, Dylan always paused to pay tribute to Rick and sing his 1958 hit "Lonesome Town."

David Nelson spent most of his life in the shadow of his younger brother. In our first meeting, David mentioned "inner anger" he holds about how Rick was treated. But in the extensive interviews that followed, he never found a voice for those pent-up resentments. David Nelson carefully circumscribed everything he said. He was scrupulously guarded in expressing his feelings. There were brief glimmers of anger toward his former sister-in-law, Kris Harmon. But he never connected with any deeply held emotions or tapped into any passion. The most animated he got was when discussing his love of the trapeze.

Apparently the one time he did open up with the press was for a 1971 *Esquire* magazine article by Sara Davidson titled "The Happy, Happy, Happy Nelsons," a forthright piece of journalism he now refers to as "a hatchet job." He was level, straightforward, almost flat; a nice, polite, and charming man, the grown-up version of the young boy he portrayed on his father's television series.

"Maybe it's because it was expected in my father's case and unexpected in my brother's," said David, "but my brother's death hit me much harder than my father's. I had more trouble dealing with my brother's death than I did my father's. I think part of it was that I had a sense of responsibility about

Rick that I didn't have about my father. My father was my old man; he took care of us. I spent so many years taking care of Rick that I felt this loss of not just a brother but somebody I had looked out after and maybe, even to this day, not done the best job that I could have."

In Greek mythology, Icarus was the son of Daedalus. When the two escaped from Crete, Icarus flew too close to the sun on the artificial wings his father made for him. The wax with which his wings were fastened melted, and he fell in a fiery ball into the Aegean Sea. Daedalus survived, but he spent the rest of his life grieving. A palpable sadness lingers too around David Nelson, the older son of Ozzie and Harriet Nelson, whose life was so inextricably bound with his younger brother.

Perhaps because Rick grew up with an all-consuming father who sculpted his identity down to fine-point detail, Rick sought out other controlling influences in his adult life. His wife was another golden child—daughter of America's most famous football hero and the woman who played "the sweetheart of Sigma Chi" in the movies—and they produced stunningly beautiful, abundantly talented children. But Kris Harmon was a domineering, ambitious woman, a profligate spender and status-conscious daughter of Hollywood, who gave only lip service to her generation's rejection of gross material values. Rick may have legitimately not cared about such things, but he followed her lead until their acrimonious divorce, as their eighteen-year marriage dissolved in the bitter waters of drink, drug abuse, and despair.

His manager for the final decade of his life held impressive sway over Rick, an influence that extended far beyond the customary boundaries of manager-client relationships. While there is a tendency for people to paint Greg McDonald as a villain, his actions invariably came at Rick's behest or, at least, with his tacit approval. Rick allowed, encouraged, and apparently wanted McDonald to assume these wide-ranging responsibilities and expertly avoided making decisions for himself, unconsciously re-creating his relationship with his father.

What Rick Nelson did was play rock & roll. In singing his songs onstage, he could experience his finest moments. A career is never in decline when the spotlights are trained on you. Record sales don't matter as long as you can hear the applause. If he was never loose and uninhibited onstage, at least he was free.

He could have given up long before he died. He could have resigned himself to a life of guest shots on "The Love Boat" and celebrity tennis tournaments, making a comfortable existence as one of many faded stars in Hollywood. But he chose to continue to grind it out on the road, playing thousands of shows the last decade of his life, living like a wandering rock & roll troubadour. He never gave up the dream of having hit records again, and he spent his entire adult life on the verge of another comeback.

Since the beginning of civilization, mankind has worshipped the qualities of Adonis. But beauty and youth have always been inextricably bound. The classic form and supple skin give way to time. Rick could dye the gray out of his hair, but he could only disguise the inevitability of aging. Having spent his entire youth in front of the nation, he was condemned to be remembered only as a young idol. The world never wanted Rick Nelson to grow up.

2

The Adventures of Ozzie and Harriet

THE ADVENTURES OF OZZIE AND HARRIET really began on New Year's Eve 1931. The twenty-five-year-old bandleader was ringing out the old at the Grand Ballroom of New York's Edison Hotel when he first laid eyes on a beautiful twenty-one-year-old dancer hosting the proceedings. They didn't speak that night.

Several months later, Ozzie and his cartoonist pal Ham Fisher, creator of "Joe Palooka," club-hopped their way into the Hollywood, a Broadway night club known for emcee Nils T. Granlund (simply N.T.G. to his radio followers) and the droves of pretty chorines employed in the shows. Ozzie, scouting for a female singer to join his band, spotted the dancer from New Year's Eve in the midst of performing a "Tea for Two"–type routine. "It took me about thirty seconds to decide that she was the girl I was looking for," he noted in his 1973 memoirs.

"Do you know who she is?" Ozzie asked Fisher.

"Sure," he replied. "Her name is Harriet Hilliard and you don't stand a chance. She lives with her mother, goes straight home every night and doesn't talk to strangers or sit down at tables with customers."

"You don't understand," Ozzie stammered. "I have a brand new idea and she is just the girl I'm looking for."

"I have news for you," said Fisher. "That's the oldest idea in the world and she's not interested in bandleaders . . . or cartoonists."

Undaunted, Ozzie sent a note backstage, suggesting lunch the following day at Sardi's, the elite diner to the sophisticated theater crowd. She agreed. When Ozzie arrived late, he sheepishly admitted that he had some difficulty finding the restaurant because he had never actually been there before.

"That's OK," said Harriet. "Neither have I."

In a 1940s magazine article, "The Girl That I Married," Ozzie also allowed he auditioned more than twenty singers before running across his future wife. In another interview he gave during the forties, he recollected catching Harriet Hilliard appearing with his singing idol and inspiration, Rudy Vallee, in a short musical film, *Musical Justice*, which he happened to see one day at New York's Paramount Theater prior to the serendipitous encounter at the Hollywood. So the account of their meeting that appeared in his autobiography may well be poetically condensed. Ozzie Nelson rarely reached important decisions without thorough and thoughtful consideration.

Ozzie's parents began their courtship on the stage too. Vocalist George Nelson—billed as "Jersey City's Honey Boy"—and pianist Ethel Orr combined talents for boy-girl duets in local turn-of-the-century vaudeville shows before getting married in 1903. (Rick once described his piano style as "half Ray Charles, half Grandma Nelson.") In 1911 the couple and their two sons, Alfred, age seven, and Oswald, six, settled in Ridgefield Park, New Jersey, where Ozzie would spend the rest of his youth.

"It was a charming little community," he wrote, "bordered

on the west by the Hackensack River, with its shoreline dotted
by boat clubs and swimming holes, and on the east by Over-
peck Creek, which obligingly froze over in winter to provide
ice for small boys to skate on. There were churches of every
denomination and a Boy Scout troop in every church. There
was a movie theater, the Opera House, which was packed
every Saturday afternoon by noisy kids cheering Bronco Billy
and William S. Hart or laughing hysterically at Charlie Chaplin
or Buster Keaton."

Although Ridgefield Park was only seven miles across the
Hudson River from New York City, it might as well have been
thousands of miles for the kind of Norman Rockwell, small-
town upbringing it provided Ozzie Nelson.

George Nelson worked as vice president of a bank, but he
also found time to operate the local amateur vaudeville house,
where young Ozzie and his older brother, Al, accompanied by
their mother on piano, used to perform impressions of the
popular vaudevillians of the day: Van and Schenck, Ada Jones
and Bill Murray, Bert Williams and Al Jolson. An athletic
youngster, Ozzie excelled in football and tennis, two sports
that would stick with him the rest of his life. He became the
youngest Eagle Scout in the country at age thirteen and, in
1920, joined three hundred other scouts on a trip to Europe
for the First International Boy Scout Jamboree in London,
where the troops were reviewed by Boy Scout founder Baden
Powell and Prime Minister Lloyd George.

On the train from London to Paris, one of the scouts traveling with Ozzie and Al developed a small problem—"Let's give
Harry's problem a number," delicately clarified Ozzie, "and
say he was referring to number two"—and found the lines at
the bathrooms too long to accommodate his urgency. Employing time-honored scout inventiveness, the poor fellow relieved
his discomfort in his Boy Scout cap, which was immediately
discarded out the window. "For years later I speculated on a

scene of a Frenchman walking down a railroad track," wrote Ozzie. "Suddenly he spies something. 'Mon Dieu,' he says, 'un chapeau!' Let's hope he looked it over carefully before trying it on."

All his life, Ozzie Nelson drove himself. He never accepted less than the best, from himself or the people around him. He relished accomplishment, reveled in work, and thrived on success.

During his high school years, in addition to playing quarterback on two consecutive championship football teams, Ozzie picked up the banjo when he left off the ukulele and began playing the occasional dance and wedding with a quartet called the Syncopation Four. Beginning a lifetime of compulsive overachieving, Ozzie entered Rutgers University in 1923, where he played three years of varsity football as an undersized five-foot-ten, 160-pound starting quarterback, in addition to competing in lacrosse, diving, and boxing; serving on the student council, debating team, and college humor magazine; belonging to a fraternity; and working occasional musical engagements (although he was turned down after his one and only audition to join the college musical club).

George Nelson died of cancer at age forty-eight, only three months before Ozzie graduated from Rutgers in 1927. That fall the family, including an infant brother, Don, moved back to Jersey City, while Ozzie enrolled in New Jersey Law School. Without any family money to help him, he supported himself by working as football coach at Lincoln High School in Jersey City and commuting nightly to another job, singing with a dance band in City Island, New York, doing his homework on breaks from the bandstand. Despite all this scrapping hard work, his career as an attorney was never to be.

Before graduating from law school, Ozzie landed a job in 1930, leading a band he put together on the spur of the moment. The band broadcast daily on New York's WMCA and got a three-month engagement that summer at the Glen Island Casino in New Rochelle, Westchester County, overlooking Long Island Sound. In the years to come, thousands of young people would come to Glen Island to listen and dance to the big band sounds of Glen Gray and his Casa Loma Orchestra, Tommy and Jimmy Dorsey, Claude Thornhill, Charlie Barnett, and the Glenn Miller band, but it was Ozzie Nelson who first brought dance music to Glen Island. The opening night crowd included such notables from the music world as Paul Whiteman, Vincent Lopez, Fred Waring, Will Osborne, Ted Lewis, Morton Downey, and even Ozzie's hero, Rudy Vallee. The evening inaugurated a nightly coast-to-coast radio broadcast on the CBS network, and record executive Jack Kapp offered the band a contract with Brunswick Records on the spot. Graduation was still two weeks away, but law practice would have to wait.

The band played engagements that fall and winter at the Barbizon Plaza Hotel, Pelham Heath Inn, and the Ritz Tower and, following some one-nighters in ballrooms and several weeks of vaudeville, returned to Glen Island Casino for a second season. The winter of 1932 was spent playing the posh Indian Creek Club in Miami Beach, Florida, and, after some college prom dates, the band was scheduled to return for a third season at Glen Island. Sensing a turning point in the offing for the band's already upward fortunes, Ozzie decided to beef up the sound, adding several musicians, and hit on the idea of teaming himself with a female vocalist for duets.

Harriet Hilliard was born Peggy Lou Snyder. Her father, Roy E. Hilliard, a well-known theatrical director, adopted his last name when he found himself working in a company that already had another Snyder. Her mother, Hazel MacNutt, the daughter of the chief of detectives in Des Moines, Iowa, began working in musical and stock companies at age fourteen. Their only child, Harriet, made her stage debut when she was just six weeks old, when she was carried onstage in a touring company of *The Heir to the Hoorah* and got her first speaking part at age three in *Mrs. Wiggs of the Cabbage Patch*. Her show business career was interrupted at age five, when she was sent to live with relatives and attend school while her parents continued touring, joining them for school vacations and summers. She went to the St. Agnes Academy in Kansas City, a few years behind Joan Crawford.

Harriet returned to the road as a teenager, rejoining her parents in Erie, Pennsylvania (a young Thelma Ritter was also a member of the troupe). At age fifteen, Harriet and her mother moved to New York, so Harriet could study ballet with Chester Hale, who had danced with ballet immortal Anna Pavlova, and Harriet worked with the Capitol Theatre Corps de Ballet. In 1926, the following year, she appeared in her first Broadway production, playing the lead role in *The Blonde Sinner* at the Ziegfeld Roof. Her parents separated the following year. Her mother remained in New York with Harriet, acting as her manager. Her father lived out his life in the Midwest and never knew his grandchildren.

Harriet toured the vaudeville circuit, sang with a group called the California Collegians that featured Fred MacMurray on saxophone, and played New York's prestigious Palace Theater four times, once with Ken Murray, once with Bert Lahr, once—shades of things to come—in a family situation-comedy sketch with Danny Duncan, and once with radio star N.T.G., who hired her to work at his Broadway club.

Her booking at the Hollywood restaurant was originally supposed to be a limited engagement as a specialty dancer for seventy-five dollars a week. But the "limited" engagement stretched out to nearly a year, by which time Harriet was appearing in sketches, acting as mistress of ceremonies, and "doing everything but sweeping out the joint," she said. Harriet earned the heady sum during those Depression times of

$150 a week by the end of the run, when Ozzie and Ham Fisher wandered into the club for a midnight snack.

This princessly sum came as sad news to Ozzie over their lunch at Sardi's, since it was exactly twice the amount he could afford to pay her. She nevertheless told him she would think it over and phone him later at his mother's in New Jersey, where he was staying. The phone call woke Ozzie from his bed around three in the morning, after her show was over, and Harriet said she had talked it over with her mother and some of her friends and decided that it might be a good idea. She also mentioned that she had read Ozzie had been an Eagle Scout, so he must be a nice boy.

"A good friend of mine said, 'Why don't you try it for the summer, Harriet?' " she recalled for the 1987 documentary *A Brother Remembers*. " 'I think he's going to go far, and I'd like to see you hitch your wagon to that star.' "

"Ozzie would always tell people Holly and Harriet joined the band on the same day," said Holly Humphreys, an experienced trumpet player from the Fred Waring band, who came aboard to brighten the brass section at the third Glen Island engagement. "He was a young guy, and he had inexperience written all over him. I thought I could help him and I did. I'd been in name bands and I'd gone out with my first vaudeville act when I was fourteen. So I'd been in many bands, played in pit orchestras. I'd done the whole bit by the time I met him."

Ozzie played it safe with the band's sound, sticking largely to a mainstream, ballroom-dance sound, nothing too adventurous or daring. Jazz historian George Simon offered some lukewarm praise in his book *The Big Bands*. "Everything the band did it did well," he wrote, "but it did little but play middle tempos that featured full ensembles with a good blend, good phrasing, good intonation and, very infrequently, an individual solo."

"We had a little of everything," said Holly Humphreys, "but

that was another way Oz was smart. He aimed at a certain market. If you went into, say, the Park Central Hotel, the people in there weren't in blue jeans and doing the hippity-dip or whatever that dance was called. They were people who wanted to dance, and most of them were thirty-five or over. And he aimed our music at that group. We used to say, 'Oz, shouldn't we play them a little faster?' And he'd say, 'No, sir, we're going to stick to that going-to-the-grocery-store tempo . . . boom-chink, boom-chink, boom-chink.' "

From the middle of June through Labor Day 1932, the band packed the Glen Island Casino every night. The female-singer idea worked out well, and Ozzie and Harriet's duets rapidly became a major feature of the program. Harriet also handled a lot of ballads. "Before the summer was over," wrote Ozzie, "at least a thousand guys had fallen in love with Harriet Hilliard—including me."

"You could hardly help that," said Humphreys. "She was gorgeous and smart and well behaved. And a good singer. Oz had to do a lot of training. He worked with her hard to train her to sing. But she could take direction, that's one thing."

Ozzie definitely ran the show, a benign dictator who ruled with the proverbial velvet glove. "Ozzie used to say, 'Don't ever argue with me,' " said Humphreys. " 'My name's on the show, and if it's bad, that's my fault. Don't ever stop rehearsal and tell me what's wrong. If I say this is the way it goes, let's do it my way and then it's my fault.' Everybody understood that and so did Harriet."

From that fall through New Year's Eve, the band appeared at the Hotel Paramount Grill on Forty-sixth Street and Broadway, with red-hot mama Sophie Tucker headlining the floor show. Spring and summer came to be devoted to one-nighters in ballrooms across the country, the band caroming from date to date like a gypsy caravan, driving by night over the highways in eleven cars and a van, working ceaselessly. "We used to have to plead to get a day off," said Humphreys. "I'm telling you, we'd have to gang up on him."

Collecting cash from the proprietors, Ozzie kept the band's funds stuffed in a suitcase. Since they largely traveled from town to town after jobs and slept during the day, when banks were open, the suitcase—dubbed "the baby" or "nanny goat"—often piled up with proceeds. Once in Indianapolis, following a one-nighter at the Claypool Hotel, Ozzie left "the baby" behind in a greasy spoon where he stopped for a bite after the show. He discovered his mistake on the way out of town, made a panic-stricken about-face, and beat it back to the restaurant. But one of the other band members had already managed to retrieve the suitcase, which happened to contain a little more than $10,000.

In the fall of 1933, the band signed to do its first weekly radio series, "The Bakers' Broadcast," starring comedian Joe Penner, who enjoyed brief but tremendous popularity spouting catchphrases like "Wanna buy a duck?" or "You nasty man, doncha ever doo-ooo that," which convulsed audiences of the time (it was how he said them). This vaulted the group into even greater heights of popularity, and work poured in. Between 1932 and 1938, they took only two two-week vacations. "During the bottom of the Depression, I was making more money as a musician than the president of the United States was," said Humphreys.

Penner left the show after two seasons—his salary climbed from $950 to $8,000 a week that second season—to be replaced by Robert Ripley of "Believe It or Not" fame, but Ozzie, Harriet, and company remained. At this point, things began to happen fast for Ozzie and Harriet, starting with the band's first trip to California, which came about as a result of a joke.

Sandy Wolff, the band's guitarist, kept pushing Ozzie to book dates in California. Ozzie and some of the musicians kidded Wolff about arranging a date for the band at Los Angeles's swanky Cocoanut Grove. Booking agent Sonny Werblin of the fledgling Music Corporation of America, who was hoping to convince Ozzie to let him represent the band, happened to overhear the remark, not knowing they were joking. Werblin went ahead and arranged just such a date. So it was off to Hollywood, zigzagging across the country along the way, playing dates as far apart as Minnesota and Texas.

Driving across Texas after a show, Ozzie asked Harriet to marry him. "I think we've got enough money saved up now," he began.

"He was so formal I thought for a moment he was going to bounce me out of the band," Harriet recalled.

During the previous spring, Harriet had had a screen test for MGM, reading a scene from *The Postman Always Rings Twice*, which came to nothing. During the month-long run at the Grove, however, her agent showed the test to an RKO executive, who immediately offered Harriet the lead role in a movie at the whopping salary of $750 a week. She turned it down. She did not want to stay in Hollywood without Ozzie, who was due back in New York in about two weeks to start an engagement at New York's Lexington Hotel and to begin the radio series with Ripley. She wanted to get married and have a family. She was considering leaving show business altogether.

RKO persisted, upping the ante to a grand $1,500 a week, until Harriet caved in. Ozzie and Harriet returned to the East Coast and were married at Ozzie's mother's apartment in Hackensack, New Jersey, on October 8, 1935. The Sunday before the wedding, the radio series started, and the following Friday the band opened at the Lexington. Two days later, Harriet and her mother got on a plane for Hollywood.

RKO originally intended Harriet for a modestly budgeted drama called *Two O'Clock Courage*, but director Mark Sandrich happened to see her *Postman* screen test and immediately tabbed her to play opposite Randolph Scott in *Follow the Fleet*, starring Fred Astaire and Ginger Rogers, who were currently the top box-office attractions in the movie business. For the next three months, Ozzie and Harriet conducted their honeymoon by long-distance telephone.

Harriet played Ginger Rogers's sister, Connie Martin, an ugly-duckling-turned-swan music teacher who fell for a womanizing, lummox sailor (Randolph Scott). The flimsy plot actually turned on this secondary love interest. While the role did not really supply material for an incendiary film debut, Harriet gave the sympathetic part a warm and endearing portrayal, sang a couple of modest Irving Berlin ballads ("Get Thee Behind Me, Satan" and "Where Are You?"), and earned good notices from critics.

Although she planned to return to New York in time for Christmas, Harriet did not get back until the first week of January, with the daily newspapers dutifully chronicling the couple's Grand Central Station reunion. Within a couple of months, Harriet found an apartment on Seventy-eighth Street, only blocks away from Central Park, and was pregnant. The couple cut an elegant figure on the New York nightlife circuit, taking limousines to clubs where they had nodding acquaintances with many of the regulars, members in good standing of the glitterati of the day.

The customary spring and summer tour wound up at New York's Paramount Theater, by which time Harriet was having trouble fitting into her stage costumes. On the morning of October 24, 1936, Ozzie, Harriet, and her mother took a taxi to New York's Doctor's Hospital, and David Ozzie Nelson was born while Ozzie waited in the coffee shop.

The band's second season on the Ripley show also got underway that October, with vocalist Shirley Lloyd filling in for Harriet, who returned to action in December. In January, however, she headed back out to Hollywood to make two movies, *New Faces of 1937* and *The Life of the Party*. David stayed behind in the care of his father.

With home-movie buff Holly Humphreys behind the camera, Ozzie scripted and acted in a short film for Harriet. Feigning concern over David's bald head, Ozzie consults a "doctor of rugs," played by another member of the band. The short climaxes with the doctor whipping a towel off infant David's head to reveal the youngster in a luxuriant auburn wig Ozzie took off a doll. It was a gag he loved repeating anytime a visitor to the Seventy-eighth Street apartment asked to see the baby.

In September 1937, the Nelsons and band moved to Hollywood at the suggestion of the advertising agency responsible for the radio series. The new series starred Feg Murray, a syndicated newspaper gossip columnist whose "Seeing Stars" became the format for the radio show as well. On his 8mm home-movie camera, Humphreys captured the parade of movie-star guests Murray interviewed—Humphrey Bogart, George Raft, Tyrone Power, John Barrymore, Jr. The famous Irish tenor John McCormack sang with the musicians on one occasion, but mainly the band was relegated to a purely supporting role. With only two days a week devoted to work on the series, Ozzie and Harriet, for once, had plenty of time for a home life at their rented Toluca Lake Tudor-style house. Ozzie joined the nearby Lakeside Golf Club, whose members included Bing Crosby, Bob Hope, Johnny Weissmuller, and a spate of Hollywood linksters. In December the band took a booking at Victor Hugo's, a new Beverly Hills supper club, followed by a run at the Palomar Ballroom. Harriet, busy with another film, *Cocoanut Grove*, skipped both engagements.

Sometime during the spring of 1938, Ozzie learned the radio series would be canceled. It was his English butler who broke the news, perhaps not surprisingly, since servants in Hollywood always have access to the best gossip first. In the middle of August the family packed up and moved back to New York.

In September the band opened at the Strand Theater, their first New York date in more than two years.

During one matinee, David got loose from his nurse backstage. His parents happened to be finishing a specialty song written for them on the occasion of his birth, "The Kid in the Three-Cornered Pants," when two-year-old David wandered out onstage by himself as if he was part of the act. It was the beginning of a lifelong career in show business and the first entrance of a third generation of Nelson performers.

"It was almost like a grocery store," remembered David. "I really felt a part of the band, even though I didn't play an instrument. The band guys were my buddies. I had a lot of fathers. I liked the traveling, and I liked the trains. I thought all that was great. I was very aware that it was all a performance. Life was a performance."

With a young child to mind, Harriet grew tired of the endless life on the road, and in November she was replaced by Rose Anne Stevens, who opened with the band at Chicago's Drake Hotel, a run that closed just in time for Ozzie to return home for Christmas. The first six weeks of 1939 were spent on the theater circuit again, with the band opening an extravagant Billy Rose musical revue in February at his Seventh Avenue supper club, Casa Mañana. Although Ozzie expected the show to run through the summer, Rose closed it down after twelve weeks, and the Nelsons took off for an unexpected two-week vacation in Miami Beach. They used to tell David that he should appreciate having been the only kid they ever knew who went along on his parents' honeymoon.

The rest of the year was spent touring, although Ozzie began to worry about sustaining the momentum without the benefit of regular radio exposure. When the lease on the Seventy-eighth Street apartment expired, the family moved to Brinkeroff Manor, a new complex in Englewood, New Jersey, and installed Harriet's mother in an apartment in the next building. Ozzie's mother and his two brothers, Al and Don, lived within a few blocks, and it was amidst this familial setting that Ozzie and Harriet got the news that David would be expecting a younger brother or sister sometime in April.

The band opened a ten-week engagement at Chicago's Blackhawk Restaurant on Valentine's Day 1940, and it was during this run that Ozzie wrote and recorded a number that would become his band's best-known hit record. Based on the proliferation of dance bands across the country, the prewar build-up of armed forces membership, and the resulting dearth of top-flight musicians, the title said it all: "I'm Looking for a Guy Who Plays Alto and Baritone and Doubles on Clarinet and Wears a Size 37 Suit." Rose Anne Stevens sang the female part on the record. With the baby expected to arrive about the middle of April, Ozzie flew home twice toward the end of the engagement, hoping he might be on hand for the event. But the baby hadn't arrived by the time the date closed on May 1, so he started back out on the road again.

He was playing the Riverside Theater in Milwaukee and sitting in the dressing room on the afternoon of May 8, 1940, following a matinee, when the phone rang with the news. His brother Al informed Ozzie that Harriet had given birth to a healthy baby boy at Holy Name Hospital in Teaneck, New Jersey. They named him Eric Hilliard Nelson, but called him Ricky.

Four days later, between Milwaukee and Memphis dates, Ozzie flew home and took David to the hospital to get their first look at his younger brother, while the obstetrician recorded the moment for posterity with his camera. For the first time, the cast was assembled.

Harriet never had a home of her own. Out on the road, she would thumb through women's magazines and clip out pictures of home furnishings and paste them into a scrapbook she kept. An antique coffee grinder purchased for twenty-five cents in a secondhand store traveled with them wherever they went, symbolizing to her the home they would one day own.

At the end of the summer, Ozzie and Harriet finally decided to settle down and make that home. They bought a new house on the edge of a wooded area in Tenafly, New Jersey, down the road from an eighty-year-old farmhouse, which they also bought and remodeled for Ozzie's mother and younger brother, Don, thirteen years old at the time. In order to spend Christmas at home, they arranged a six-week booking at the Strand beginning around Thanksgiving. Ozzie and Harriet returned home after the last show at the theater Christmas Eve to finish trimming their tree and laying out the presents. Snow covered the ground outside their windows, as strains of "O, Little Town of Bethlehem" wafted in from outside. The King Sisters, along with Alvino Rey and his band, had finished playing at the nearby Rustic Cabin and decided to come caroling at the Nelsons as a surprise.

Everybody came inside for hot chocolate and coffee, and the sisters insisted that Harriet and Ozzie open some of their presents. When Harriet opened a box of lace handkerchiefs and read Ozzie's card aloud—"Just in case I make you cry sometime"—all the women burst into tears.

(Ozzie also once stuffed an unloaded revolver into the pocket of an expensive Persian lamb coat he bought Harriet one Christmas and attached a card reading, "In case you don't like the coat, there's a revolver in the pocket so you can shoot me.")

Humphrey Bogart joined the bill at the Strand that December to plug his latest film. They worked up an act, based on a reel of film clips in which he and his mobster pals all got shot, where Bogart would call upon members of the band to be interviewed as possible new members of his mob. The ensuing wisecracks kept audiences and Bogie alike howling, and he postponed the start of his next picture so he could continue the routine in Philadelphia. He used to enjoy intercepting Ozzie's phone calls in the dressing room, putting on a phony accent and explaining that he was Mr. Nelson's valet and that Ozzie was busy auditioning chorus girls and couldn't come to the phone.

In February 1941 the band played New Orleans during Mardi Gras, and David sat on the lap of the drummer during the matinee shows. David also tumbled into Lake Pontchartrain while riding a bicycle one afternoon and could have drowned, except he managed to pull himself up from the muddy bottom and paddle back to shore. Ozzie wrapped him in a blanket and carried him asleep back to the hotel. He woke up in the elevator long enough to plead with his father, "Don't tell the guys in the band about this—they'll think I'm dumb."

From New Orleans, the group headed west, back again to California, this time for both Ozzie and Harriet to work on a movie called *Sweetheart of the Campus.* What they didn't know was that California was about to become their permanent home.

One-year-old Ricky and Harriet's mother took the train west to join the rest of the family in San Rafael, across the Golden Gate Bridge from San Francisco, where the band was working the Palace Hotel. The week before they closed, the Nelsons were offered a role on the Red Skelton radio show, where Ozzie and the band would provide the music and Harriet would play Red's mother in his "mean widdle kid" skits.

"Ozzie wouldn't take the show without her," said Holly Humphreys. "In fact, we were offered the Bob Hope show, but he wouldn't take it because Bob wanted Dolores [his wife] on the show and Ozzie said, 'No woman goes on the show, no singer goes on the show except Harriet Hilliard.' "

They rented a house in Hermosa Beach for the summer, while Harriet made a couple of movies (*Meet Boston Blackie* and *Canal Zone*), and Ozzie and the band worked at the Casa

Mañana Ballroom in Culver City. In October 1941 the Red
Skelton show started, and their careers were never the same
again.

The show was the crowning touch in a powerhouse Tuesday night lineup on NBC radio: "Fibber McGee and Molly,"
followed by Bob Hope, followed by Skelton. The program
proved to be a great showcase for Harriet, Ozzie, and the band.
Ozzie was soon writing skits for the band and, occasionally,
material for Skelton himself. The show became an immediate
hit.

In November 1941 the Nelsons moved into a house that
would be their home for the rest of their married life. Located
on a dead end of Camino Palmero, just north of Franklin
Avenue and nestled in the bottom of the Hollywood hills, the
two-story, nine-room, colonial-style white house with the
green shutters would become something of a television land-
mark since it was used in the opening shot of every episode of
"The Adventures of Ozzie and Harriet."

"We got stuck here," said Humphreys. "We were actually a
New York band. The war broke out, and by the time we were
ready to go back, you couldn't get train tickets. There was no
way to get back comfortably. Everything was in an uproar out
here. The Japs were going to bomb us. We stayed on through
the start and all of the draft routine. Couple of the guys got
drafted, and we had to take on new people. And then we all
drifted away. We all got that brown suit routine . . . the army.

"They offered Ozzie a commission in the navy. But they
wanted to put him on an aircraft carrier, and he did the
research on it. He had lots of connections, of course, and
people would tell him what the job amounted to. It amounted
to sitting behind a desk on an aircraft carrier, and he didn't
think that would help the war effort much. So I don't know
how it worked, but he stayed out of the shindig and picked up
musicians that were draft-proof, guys that were 4-F but could
still play, and kept the band going."

By the time the band followed Paul Whiteman into the Florentine Gardens in February 1942, the only remaining members from Glen Island days were Humphreys and saxophonist Charlie Bubeck. The Gardens was a nightclub presided over by their old associate, N.T.G. During the early months of 1942, Harriet appeared in a musical for Universal, *Juke Box Jenny*, and Ozzie and the band played in another film, *Strictly in the Groove*, as well as did a small part in a movie called *The Big Street* that starred Henry Fonda and Lucille Ball (who, coincidentally, made one of her early film appearances in *Follow the Fleet*).

The band continued the customary summer theater tour, with the Skelton exposure boosting its appeal. The opening show on the tour took place in June at the Golden Gate Theater in San Francisco, and the reviewer for the *San Francisco Chronicle* noted the connection: "Probably one need go to no great length in describing Nelson's own songs, since they are aired regularly on the Red Skelton program. It should be enough to say that they are part song, part musical sketch, and his presentation of them with Miss Hilliard seems to be what the customers asked for when they stopped at the box office."

During the spring of 1944, Skelton got his own draft notice, spelling an end to his radio series for the time being. The West Coast representative for the advertising agency that produced the show, John Guedel, had created "People Are Funny" with Art Linkletter. Over a lunch with Ozzie at Hollywood's Brown Derby restaurant, Guedel suggested Ozzie might do a show of his own. Ozzie mentioned the possibility of a husband-and-wife show, on which he and Harriet would discuss the problems and events that occur in everyday life, and offered to try his hand at knocking off a pilot script, even though he had never written more than simple bits and sketches before. Two days later, he gave Guedel his work.

"We made the audition from that script," Guedel said, "with scarcely a line changed, and the executive of the advertising agency who heard it went into a rave, calling it one of the best scripts he had ever heard. The show sold itself. The one question asked by every prospective sponsor was could they employ the writer who had done the audition script if they bought the show? I could reassure them on that question and we sold the show to International Silver."

The summer of 1944 was the last time the band toured, doing the typical musical comedy sketches and the special material duets at the same houses across the country, this time, however, with Ozzie's younger brother, Don, playing tenor saxophone. At the end of the tour, the band went back to the West Coast, while Ozzie and Harriet headed to New York to discuss the upcoming radio show with the sponsors. The audition show revolved around Ozzie and Harriet as road-weary musicians who inherited a drugstore. He wanted to drop the drugstore idea and worried that the sponsors might not like it if he did. As it turned out, the drugstore was the one thing about the script the sponsors didn't like.

So, on Sunday, October 8, 1944, Ozzie and Harriet's ninth wedding anniversary, the theme music swelled and announcer Jack Bailey intoned, "The solid silver with beauty that lives forever is International Sterling. From Hollywood, International Silver Company, creators of International Sterling, presents 'The Adventures of Ozzie and Harriet,' starring America's favorite young couple, Ozzie Nelson and Harriet Hilliard."

"The Adventures of Ozzie and Harriet" was on the air. Nobody could have guessed it would last twenty-two years.

3

Here Come the Nelsons

THE SIMPLE, EVERYDAY HUMOR AND EASYGOING WARMTH of the two
principals of "The Adventures of Ozzie and Harriet" had
struck a resonant chord with radio-listening America, and the
show became a hit almost immediately. Ozzie and Harriet
found themselves highly sought-after guest stars on other
radio programs and, between 1945 and 1948, made appearances with Jack Benny, Eddie Cantor, Fred Allen, Al Jolson, Art
Linkletter, Dinah Shore, Tallulah Bankhead, and many others,
including Bing Crosby.

When Crosby let it be known through their mutual publicist, Maury Foladare, that he would entertain a reciprocal
invitation if Ozzie could come up with a storyline suitable for
him and one of his sons, Lindsay, Ozzie jumped at the chance
of landing the country's leading crooner and top box-office
attraction.

Crosby did not allow his sons to frequent the L.A. Tennis
Club, where Ozzie and his sons played regularly. Instead, one
of the tennis club pros, Johnny Faunce, used to give private

lessons to the Crosbys on their own court at the Crosby clan's Toluca Lake manor, and David and Ricky used to go along with Faunce. Lindsay Crosby was only a year younger than David, and the three of them schemed together to have the Nelson boys included on the upcoming program as well.

David and Ricky existed as characters on their parents' show from the start. One running gag involved a deep-voiced man playing Ricky rumbling "Goodnight, Dad," to which Ozzie would invariably say, "We've gotta get that kid's tonsils taken out." A thirteen-year-old actor named Joel Davis played the part of David the first season. The second season Tommy Bernard took the part of David, and Henry Blair played Ricky. Blair was thirteen years old but could pitch his voice to believably sound like a five-year-old. The real David and Ricky would go to the studio and watch the actors portray them, feeling more than a little left out. Mary Jane Croft, who played neighbor Clara Randolph both on the radio show and TV series, used to have a standard wisecrack for anybody who asked if she knew Ricky Nelson: "Are you kidding? I knew him when he was Henry Blair."

Although the Nelsons were reluctant to use David and Ricky on the show, the boys were eager to join the cast. "We knew that once David and Ricky came on the show," wrote Ozzie in his autobiography, "that would be it: they would be professional performers from then on with all the pressures and heartache inherent in our business."

"I didn't really think in terms past the first show," said David. "I thought it would be fun to do it once. I don't think anybody thought, gee, after we do this one show, it's going to be the first of twenty years of doing this. It just became a natural progression of things. The first show we did was the preview; it wasn't an air show. The other actors who played our parts did the air show, even with Lindsay Crosby and Bing."

Years later, Rick himself would remember his show business debut.

"One day there was to be a Christmas broadcast with Bing Crosby and his kids," he said. "Dave and I confronted our father and said 'Hey, what is this? How come the Crosby kids are on it and we aren't?' Eventually, our father let us do our own parts and we came onto the radio and the family show. People just ate it up. The studio audience laughed at everything I said. I was eight years old, very uninhibited, and didn't know what was going on, so I'd make jokes with Dave. We had this bet on the side—a dime or a quarter for every line that the other one goofed up. I'd make faces at him while he read, just to try to make more money. I'd stare at David's fly as he read a line so I could get more money out of him. I was also too short for the mike stands, so I sat at a table [with a mike] and took my shoes off. I hated shoes. I had no idea the audience could see what was going on under the table, but they ate that up too. I used to take the paper clip off my script and get the pages all messed up all over the table. My folks used to worry about me finding the right page at the right time, but I always did. I guess they really sweated."

In the first season, the show leaned on gags for laughs, like most radio shows of the time. But as the series progressed, Ozzie began to orient himself toward humor that developed out of situations, like the show that found Ozzie accepting a dinner invitation from a friend he met at the bus stop, but whose name he couldn't remember and was too embarrassed to ask. He built a stable of characters from his off-air life. He borrowed the names of his actual neighbors, Syd and Katherine Thornbury, for the palsy fictional neighbor, Thorny, of the show, although Ozzie and Syd Thornbury, a wealthy pharmaceutical manufacturer, were hardly buddies. Harriet's mother, Hazel, was added to the cast, played by actress Lurene Tuttle. Emmy Lou came from a composite of four or five teenagers

Ozzie encountered around the swimming pool at the L.A. Tennis Club, first played by Janet Waldo and later by Barbara Eiler, who wound up marrying Ozzie's brother Don, as real life and radio began to blend together for the Nelsons.

By the second season, Ozzie had established his routine. Story meetings would take place Monday evenings in his upstairs office at Camino Palmero. The creative team featured at least five writers, and the conferences would last into the night, with a customary break for ice cream around two or three in the morning. Five quarts of ice cream would arrive, delivered by Schwab's Drug Store, around eleven o'clock. Each writer had his own bowl with his name on it and would serve himself with a silver ladle. The following week, each writer would return with a completed script, and Ozzie would expertly merge them into one master script, which would be previewed before a live audience. Ozzie would make his final editing decisions based on a disc recording of the preview, which he would play at home.

The boys officially joined the cast on February 20, 1949, for an episode titled "Invitation to Dinner." They had played the preview show with the Crosbys the previous December. "Before we had gone more than two or three minutes into the show," Ozzie wrote, "we knew what the decision would be. David and Ricky were knocking off their lines like seasoned veterans and the laughs were rolling in like tidal waves."

"They got such a tremendous reaction," recalled Harriet in 1971, "that we dismissed the actors and the boys took over. When an actor gets his first laugh, he's hooked. It's as if he's tasted blood."

"Rick was pretty small then," said David. "He wouldn't really read, so he memorized his parts for the first year. He refused, though, to go onstage—it was in front of a live audience—unless he had a script. They didn't have a microphone short enough for him, so he would sit at a table. He would have the script and keep his left eye out so when somebody turned the page, he could turn his page. He was always concerned that people would think he was dumb."

Little Ricky clearly relished the laughs he got, hamming it up "like a miniature Jerry Lewis," in David's words, on and off the airwaves. He was a mass of funny faces, wisecracks, slapstick bits, and aggressive younger-brother bids for attention. His father would take him aside after broadcasts when the audience cracked up over his swinging his bare feet beneath his table or humming unself-consciously not quite off-mike as he thumbed through his script pages. "Son, those aren't the kind of laughs we want," he told him. Once, after Ricky adlibbed a punch line, Ozzie laid down the law: "Son, there is no such thing as a child comedian."

Ozzie could be a warm and loving parent, but he was always the director of the show first. It was a distinction his sons learned to make as long as they worked for their father.

As soon as they were added to the weekly series, David, twelve, and Ricky, eight, each started earning $500 a week, which was salted away in a trust fund. Determined his sons would not become spoiled Hollywood rich kids, Ozzie doled out weekly allowances of five dollars for David and fifty cents for Ricky. The show operated on a $10,000 weekly budget, which left about $4,000 after costs for the other two stars, a sumptuous income at a time when the average attorney earned less than $8,000 a year and bread cost fourteen cents a loaf.

Despite the flush of material success, the Nelsons did not indulge in an extravagantly splashy Hollywood lifestyle. A swimming pool was dug in the backyard at Camino Palmero, but otherwise they assiduously practiced what passed in their eyes as a normal, middle-class home life. Ozzie did not drink or smoke; his sole addictions were ice cream and hard work. He kept late hours, getting up around noon and working at home on the show until the predawn hours.

Harriet's role on the show as the quintessential homemaker

was strictly fictional. She always had servants who prepared and served the meals, except for weekends, invariably spent at the family getaway in Laguna Beach. After her years eating at restaurants, on the road with the big band, Harriet knew little about cooking.

Although Ozzie and Harriet didn't partake in the glitzy Hollywood openings or lavish nightlife of the show-business crowd, they did socialize. "They were good friends of Art Linkletter," David recalled. "I'm talking about the people who would come to our house. We had Art and Lois Linkletter, Fred MacMurray and his wife, the Corrells, Charlie Correll of 'Amos 'n' Andy.' They used to go out. On special occasions for us as a family, I remember going out to Don the Beachcomber's. My father liked that. He liked Chasen's. I can remember them getting dressed and going various places. But he didn't really like to finish work, come home, and have to get dressed to go out someplace. He had to make sure that when he walked in, the table was ready and that we didn't have to stand around and wait. That was one of his things. They went to other people's houses for parties. They knew Walt Disney. They knew Edgar Bergen."

David belonged to the Cub Scouts, along with next-door neighbor Will Thornbury, and Harriet and Katherine Thornbury dutifully became den mothers. The boys attended public school at the nearby Gardner Street School, and Grandmother Hilliard, who lived across the street from the school, walked them home in the afternoons. At bedtime, Ozzie would play hide-and-seek with his sons, read them bedtime stories of excerpts from Dickens or Goldsmith, and tuck them away with a nightly ritual of a quartet sing of the Lord's Prayer.

"I felt the responsibility before we started on the show," said David, "for my behavior with sponsors coming over and conducting myself, making sure my hands were washed and my hair was combed for dinner. We started out fairly formal. We would come to dinner with coats and ties with nobody there."

With a demanding, imposing father like Ozzie Nelson, the two sons faced a tough battle in establishing independent identities for themselves, and they took opposite routes. David, unfailingly polite, was the quiet conformist who went along with the program without complaint; Ricky, loud and hyperactive, chafed at the bit. He was the little rebel who could bait his father into outrage, but David would never participate in the resulting screaming matches. "Why don't you just keep your big mouth shut?" he would ask Ricky later, as they lay in their bunk beds.

Ozzie did not shy away from a position as authority figure. He would quiz the boys over dinner about geography and spelling and ask about school, far from their favorite topic of conversation. He ruled the roost, but he avoided handing out the punishments. "He wasn't stern, ever," said David. "The disciplinarian in the family was my mother. My father was the valedictorian of the two-hour lecture. Those were almost worse than a quick swat on the rear end."

The two brothers got into typical scrapes. David and Will Thornbury once covered Rick in green house paint to go with his Indian costume. Ricky pushed David down a hill after David shot him with a slingshot. They could quickly reduce disagreements into heated exchanges of angry "Oh, yeah?" . . . "Yeah!" But they were also close and protective of one another. David woke his parents urgently in the middle of the night when two-year-old Ricky suffered his first asthma attack. While Harriet called the doctor, Ozzie gave him artificial respiration. Ricky was gasping for air and turning blue when the doctor arrived with the oxygen bottle. For the next six years, Ricky slept with an oxygen inhaler beside his bed.

The two boys developed an intense competitiveness with one another. Ricky possessed a quickness of mind and natural grace that made everything come easy. The slower, duller

David could often rely only on being nearly four years older to give him an edge. Conflicts were inevitable.

"They fought a lot," said Will Thornbury, David's best friend and next-door neighbor. "All the time, they were at each other. But again, it was one of those things; no matter how close you were to them, if you started hassling the other one, they were on your throat. They were really close."

Another neighbor, Joe Sutton, remembered that, despite the age difference, Ricky held his own hanging out and playing sports with the older boys. "Ricky was the brashest kid I've ever met," Sutton said. "He was like one of the Dead End boys. He was a wise guy. He thought he was six-foot-five and weighed 240 at age ten. That was his attitude. He wasn't offensively that way; he was just confident. He was a cocky little guy. And he was little, a skinny little guy."

"As a kid, he was not very strong," said Will Thornbury. "He suffered from respiratory problems. He was a skinny kid and inclined to be a bit sickly. But he was quick. He was fast with a barb and the first one in there with a little jab. His mind worked very quickly. He was fun, a fun kid to be around, except that he was three years younger and a pain in the ass."

"I was quote-unquote responsible for him as my younger brother," said David, "but I spent most of the time trying to get away from Rick and be with my own friends, and he would want to come along."

"Ricky was the guy who always tagged along," said Sutton, "but he was good enough as an athlete and as a kid to always be welcome. No one threw him out. And you know when a kid can't cut it, you just cut him out and tell him to go home."

"We used to try and get rid of him all the time," said Thornbury, "throw him over the fence, because he was this kid. But he more than held his own, and it was important for him to do that. There was great rivalry between Ricky and Dave. Ricky seemed to be testing everybody. I think he was really bugged that he hadn't been born three years earlier, and so he determined he was going to make up for it. And he did. No question about it."

Music grabbed hold of the more cerebral Ricky even in his youth, the beginning of his great obsession. His father remembered him lying next to a heater listening for hours to classical music from a large console radio. At age eight, he got a set of drums and, for a while, took lessons from jazz great Louis Bellson. He practiced in a room specially soundproofed for the endeavor. "I used to hear this little trap set and brushes," said Will Thornbury, "and he would be playing these brushes all the time to the music of Erroll Garner, strangely enough. He was also very hip in that area."

There were also skating lessons at the Polar Palace, and Ricky proved especially adept at speed skating. "All along the way we had a lot of lessons like that," said David. "We had horseback-riding lessons. Dorothy Poynton, who had won a medal in the Olympics, was a diving coach who came over and taught me how to dive. Part of the procedure of growing up in those days was to be proficient in those areas, not so much to my father, but to my mother's way of thinking."

But what the family did best together was work. Ozzie knew he had a gold mine in his cottage industry, fashioning a mythic American family out of his real one. If the two young boys felt the pressure of living up to roles created for them by an omniscient, obsessive father, there was also no escape. Anything the boys did could wind up in the show. If David learned how to do a standing back flip off the diving board, Ozzie would find a way to work it into an episode. They lived their parts, falling into the routine as soon as just one outsider showed up. Harriet expounded her theory of cottage economy, undoubtedly originally promulgated by her husband, to a reporter.

"It's a principle as old as families," she said. "In the Middle

Ages, a blacksmith's or toolmaker's helpmate kept his forge hot and the children learned the trade at their father's knee. In early America, families linked hands to work a farm, run a village store or small business. Warm companionship developed through striving toward the same goal. These days, cottage economy has all but disappeared. If modern kids are sassy, lack responsibility, treat home strictly as a stopover between dates, and have no respect for earning money, it may be because the old-times ties that bound have been broken. With the Nelsons they have become a firm anchor to happiness."

Ozzie was too smart not to see the potential for his family show on video. With television bursting on the scene as mid-century approached, he decided to take a test run at combining visual images with the format of his family radio show. Producer Aaron Rosenberg approached him about doing a movie based on the series. Brother Don had joined the team of radio writers while still studying at USC. In fact, it was Don Nelson who authored Ricky's famed catchphrase "I don't mess around, boy," a strutting little rejoinder that feisty bantam Ricky employed time and time again on radio, much to the delight of the show's many fans.

Ozzie, Don, and another radio show scenarist, Bill Davenport, put together a movie script for Universal Pictures in 1951. At last Ozzie had a job; he worked for an H. J. Bellows Advertising Agency in the movie and saved the big account as well as captured the bad guys (who kidnapped Ricky) in the final scene.

In addition to the four Nelsons, the cast of *Here Come the Nelsons* featured a young actor who had just changed his name from Roy Fitzgerald to Rock Hudson, alongside character actors like Gale Gordon, Jim Backus, and Sheldon Leonard. Ozzie also wanted to use an actress he had seen, but she turned out to be signed to another studio, so they made the movie without Marilyn Monroe. The 1952 release was directed by Fred de Cordova, who would become one of television's most durable producers with "The Tonight Show Starring Johnny Carson."

"I thought that it would be kinda fun," said David, "but it was scary in a way, mostly after I saw myself in dailies for the first time. You always have an inflated opinion of what you look like until you really see yourself. I was right at an age where that was becoming important. I was devastated when I first saw myself. I wanted to go off into the hills of Tennessee or someplace."

In part, David's dismay may have had roots in the taunts of his younger brother, who delighted in calling David "fatty." David returned the insult by calling Ricky "fang," a reference to his off-center front tooth, but Ricky's jibes may have stung more.

Ronnie Rondell, son of a veteran stuntman and David's stand-in, befriended David during the shooting, and the two would borrow a studio limo during lunch and practice driving on the back lot, well before David reached the legal age for a learner's permit.

With his eye on television, Ozzie counted himself pleased with the results. "It seemed to come off amazingly well," he wrote, "especially those scenes involving the boys. Most importantly, from our standpoint, however, was that it demonstrated to us that our type of comedy projected just as well on the screen as it did on radio and that the transition from radio to television would not be too difficult."

"The Adventures of Ozzie and Harriet" came to television at eight o'clock, Friday, October 3, 1952, on sixty-two ABC-TV stations. *Variety* singled out Ricky in the show-business bible's review of the first episode: "It became increasingly apparent that Ricky, 12, is being groomed as the star of the family. He was cute only in spots, which was more the fault of the writing than his own talents at wringing a laugh from a line. David, the older, is used mostly as a foil for Ricky."

The early shows frequently consisted of little more than rewritten versions of scripts already used on the radio, but Ozzie adapted rapidly to the demands of television. He built up a backlog of scripts, and if Harriet was filmed coming down the stairs for one episode, he would have her change her dress and repeat the action for inclusion in a later show, without having to change the lights or camera positions. With the shows initially budgeted at $14,000 apiece—not counting story cost and performers' salaries—cutting such corners counted. After renegotiating their ten-year contract with ABC, the Nelsons were receiving almost $300,000 a year, with the boys getting $1,100 a week for their television duties, which went directly into the trust funds without either touching a penny.

"The knack is not to get rattled and cost conscious when you're having trouble," Ozzie told the *New York Times*, already sounding like a veteran only a month after the first show aired. "We take our time and do it the best way we know how. Of course, being so close to the writing of the scripts and being fortunate to be ahead on them, it is easy for me to double up and take advantage of a similar scene in the next story by swinging into it as long as the camera set-up and the lights are right. We are lucky in this respect because we don't change the set every time as other shows do, and Harriet and the boys know how to respond almost by instinct."

His insatiable drive for excellence led Ozzie to break new technical ground for those early days of television. Not happy with the flat look of the show's camera work, Ozzie changed cameramen in the middle of the first season. Impressed with the cinematography on a current movie, *A Place in the Sun*, he contacted the man responsible, cinematographer William Mellor, who would win an Academy Award for his work on that film. Although union scale for cameramen ran around $400 a week, Mellor earned $750 working on movies. Ozzie offered him $1,000 a week and guaranteed him forty weeks' work. Furthermore, he instructed Mellor to put together an entire production team that would represent the best behind-the-scenes talent Hollywood could offer. The producer ABC assigned to the show, Leo Peppin, had to put his job on the line to get the higher-ups to agree, but by the start of the second season, Ozzie had assembled a crew capable of giving his television sitcom all the production values of a major motion picture.

In fact, Ozzie later thought the only technical advance left for TV was a wide-screen set, so, in preparation for the future, he shot all his episodes in motion-picture aperture, despite the difficulties that posed for blocking the sets and for actors and actresses knowing where their entrance marks were.

At first, the boys worked only on Saturdays, so they wouldn't miss school, while the rest of the cast shot around their parts during the week. Not that they would have minded being absent. Neither of his sons inherited Ozzie's intellectual predilections, and they didn't care for school. Ricky didn't see the need, anyway, he said, since he could already read scripts well enough and figured that was what he would probably be doing for the rest of his life.

But when David started playing quarterback at Hollywood High School—he showed considerable talent at football and made the YMCA Junior High All-Star team while attending Bancroft Junior High—their work days switched to Mondays and Wednesdays, and a private tutor, Randolph Van Scoyk, was hired to work on the set. Since game days came on Friday, David's parents decided the weekend's rest was too important. For Ozzie, the old Rutgers quarterback, football came second only to work.

The family grew fascinated with the new medium. Dinners moved into the living room, as they ate off TV trays in front of the television, before Ozzie went upstairs to work through the night. In addition to the abundant work he did at home, he put in long hours at the studio. He stuck his nose into every part of the production, personally supervising even the smallest details, and ended up staying at the studio hours after the rest of the family went home.

"Sometimes he would have dinner after we had finished," said David, "because he would come home real late, like nine-thirty, quarter to ten. Those days he was doing the sound-track, mixing the laughs and the music, which he was very on top of. He used to drive the people at the sound company crazy. It was always, 'God, here comes Ozzie again.' He really truly was a perfectionist. He used to say, 'I care about this show, and if you don't care about your job as much as I care about mine, then I want to use somebody else.' "

Crew members once gave Ozzie a framed plaque containing honorary membership cards in every union represented in the company, a tribute to his ubiquitous involvement in every phase of the production.

At the studio, rambunctious Ricky came to be called "the little terror," riding his bike around the set, squeezing the horn. When crew members teased him about his severe crew cut, he wisecracked that he was training to be president of the Fuller Brush Company. He used to practice hiding from the tutor, instead of studying between takes.

At the start of the second season, Ricky, now acting with the assurance of a practiced show-business hand, gave an interview to the *Los Angeles Times* outside the Camino Palmero house, while he tried on a new pair of roller skates. "I think the first requirement for a young actor, or any actor for that matter, is to lose his self-consciousness and be himself," the thirteen-year-old told the reporter. "People who are ill at ease and self-conscious are people who are thinking too much of themselves and worrying about the impressions they are making on others. The best actors love themselves in their parts and read their dialogue as naturally as possible.

"A very important thing for young actors to remember is to listen to the director and play the scene exactly as he wants it played. This is especially true when, as in the case of our show, the director happens to be your father. Dad has an old rule he learned back in his football days at Rutgers. He always says it's a good man who takes his coaching.

"There is one possible exception to this rule and that is when a young actor is given lines that no boy or girl of his age would say. I think in cases like this it is perfectly proper for the youngster to call this to the attention of the director. I have often watched television shows and felt terribly sorry for the boys and girls struggling to make lines sound real when they seemed to have been written by someone who was never a child.

"My mother gave me some good advice some years ago when she said 'Son, there is no such thing as a child comedian. If you want to be funny, try to be funny by being natural rather than by trying to act like an adult.' That to my mind is the first rule in all acting, on and off the stage. Be natural. Be yourself."

With that, he scooted off down the street on his skates, spilling into a heap on the sidewalk as he tried to turn the corner.

In 1953 Ricky got a part in the MGM movie *The Story of Three Loves*, in which he played a young boy who wished to grow up so he could fall in love with his governess. His wish was granted, and he became Farley Granger, who wooed the governess, played by Leslie Caron. It gave him the opportunity to act alongside some of the movie business's biggest names, as the cast also included Ethel Barrymore, Kirk Douglas, James Mason, and Pier Angeli, and he earned an award as the country's top child actor for his part. But it was not an entirely

satisfactory experience for Ricky, since it required that he get
up at six in the morning, while David got to sleep. "Never
again, boy," he said. "The money isn't worth it."

For the second season, Ozzie began to pull together the
familiar elements and strong ensemble that would mark the
series for its many remaining years. Don DeFore continued to
play next-door neighbor Thorny. Lyle Talbot and Mary Jane
Croft were Joe and Clara Randolph. (Jim Backus, who played
Joe in the movie, probably would have continued on TV had
he not already been committed to "I Married Joan.") Frank
Cady, who played a number of characters during the first
season, settled in as Doc in the second. Jack Wagner, someone
else who played a variety of roles the first year, got a permanent job as soda jerk at the malt shop. The adult sidekicks of
Ozzie and Harriet became known on the set as "Ozzie's
posse," and the shows continued to focus on their exploits the
second season, with David and Ricky providing mostly comic
relief.

Ricky played a smart mouth, vaguely insolent and uppity.
He and David crabbed at each other, but Ricky always had the
last jab. His wisecracks were fairly tame, but coming out of his
young mouth in his squeaky voice, they invariably served as
the show's most pungent punch lines. The one canned laugh
that Ozzie used for every joke throughout the show's history
always punctuated his saucy comebacks.

Ricky: "Could I borrow some money, Pop? I want to buy
some comic books."

Ozzie: "OK, here's your allowance, but I wish you'd raise
your literary standards."

Ricky: "I wish you'd raise my allowance."

Some other characters disappeared altogether, like Emmy
Lou and the Dipples. Announcer Vern Smith stopped doing
voice-over narration during the show and simply read the
weekly introduction. Pacing of the plots also picked up. Per-

haps most important of all, Ozzie became the show's official producer with the start of the second season.

The Nelsons' television home was redecorated, although it remained basically the same. The set that was built on stage five of General Service Studios, the production facility at the corner of Las Palmas and Santa Monica boulevards, closely resembled the Nelsons' own home at Camino Palmero, merging the family's genuine identity and the TV version further. General Service was a haven for independent television productions like "I Love Lucy," "The Bob Cummings Show," "The George Burns and Gracie Allen Show," and "Our Miss Brooks." Located across the street from Bancroft Junior High, first David and later Ricky could walk to work from school.

At Hollywood High, David excelled in athletics. He played football all three years, pitched baseball, went out for swimming, and ran high hurdles in track. He broke up a no-hitter by future baseball hall-of-famer Don Drysdale, pitching for Van Nuys in the citywide championship Dorsey Tournament. "I never saw the ball," said David. "It was one of those bloop singles. We lost the game. We had no business being in the Dorsey Tournament with our team. We just squeezed in."

Being on television apparently had little effect on how David was treated—or how he acted—at high school. Bruce Belland, who sang with a group called the Four Preps and eventually joined the "Ozzie and Harriet" cast, went to Hollywood High with David.

"David acted so absolutely normal," said Belland. "It was smart to go to Hollywood High. In the fifties, it was a great, wonderful, legendary school. So many of the kids were regulars in the business—Norma Jean Nielson who was a regular on 'Father Knows Best,' Sally Kellerman, the Four Preps—we were all in school and doing stuff. So they weren't as freakish as they'd be in school in Des Moines. I had a class with David, and he would leave at one o'clock every day to go down for the afternoon shooting. So he never took any afternoon classes. But then at one point he wanted to play on the junior varsity football team, so his dad rearranged the whole shooting schedule. I would watch him out there, getting knocked around with all the other guys, throwing jock straps in the locker room, just acting like one of the guys."

David also belonged to a Hollywood High School social club called the Elskers. Anyone with any social standing at all belonged to one of these clubs, whose members wore identifying jackets and sat at specified tree wells during lunch. The clubs were not officially recognized but were a prominent part of the social landscape nonetheless. Initiations could be rather cruel. Pledges were frequently dropped off in remote areas and forced to make their way back home without help.

When his turn came, David called on studio professionals. The special effects department built David a false heel in his shoe, where he hid some money and was able to call for help. It was largely considered good, old-fashioned fun, but one member's parents complained to the school that year about the hazing and the club was suspended from campus. Ozzie, ever the conservative, tradition-bound sportsman, took up the cause. "My father went in and argued the case for the Elskers and won," said David.

Taking one last opportunity to do something together as a family besides work, Ozzie decided to take everybody to Europe in the summer of 1954, after David graduated from high school and before he entered college. Ozzie had not been overseas since his Boy Scout trip of 1920. He also planned to take tapes of the show to the BBC in England to see whether there was any interest in airing the show over there. Business was never far from Ozzie's mind. Passage was booked on a Swedish-American liner, *Kungsholm*.

David, who didn't want to leave his high school girlfriend for the summer, was reluctant to go, but he didn't have a choice. In New York the boys talked their father into taking his first trip to the top of the Empire State Building, David sporting a home-movie camera that Eastman Kodak gave his parents.

The tubby liner made a rough crossing, with everybody in the family feeling the effects. Ricky enjoyed himself, becoming the ship's Ping-Pong champ and sitting in every night with the ship's orchestra to play drums.

One day Ozzie gathered the family on deck for a talk. "I told them the 'ugly American' image so many Europeans have is not a true picture of Americans," he recalled. "I said 'let's be the one family who will make people think Americans aren't so bad. Let's be considerate, thoughtful and adaptable.' "

Ozzie may have had good intentions, but his resolve wavered almost as soon as the boat docked. Landing in Sweden, the Nelsons experienced a brief panic on their own, far away from home. In the United States, Ozzie said, "there was always a Mr. Ass Kisser to meet us at the airport, take care of our arrangements and see us off." As they listened to the Swedish dockworkers speaking to each other in an incomprehensible tongue, they couldn't help but wonder, "Where's Mr. Ass Kisser?" But a chauffeur from the hotel, speaking perfect English, mysteriously appeared, whisked the family through customs, and was hired for the remainder of their stay in Sweden. From that point on, Ozzie wired ahead to every city they went, requesting an "American-speaking" chauffeur.

As a small boy, Ozzie used to hear his Grandmother Nelson speak of Lysekil, a summer vacation village where her father owned a hotel and she learned to swim as a young girl, and Ozzie decided to make a visit to his ancestral roots. Once lodged in the Lysekil hotel, however, he learned that virtually nobody in the small town spoke English. They visited with some distant cousins, who didn't speak a word of English, and headed off for Paris via Denmark. In Paris the family engaged in a whirlwind tour of the typical tourists' sights. Their chauffeur took Ricky to lunch at his home and cried when the family left.

They rode the famous Blue Train to the South of France, where the family landed in the beachside resort of Juan-les-Pins, a swinging spot with lots of water skiing and girls in bikinis, daring aquatic fashion in those days and largely unseen outside the Côte d'Azur. Ozzie amused the family by trying out his schoolboy French. At the Eden Roc, a private beach club in nearby Cap d'Antibes, they ran into actress Rhonda Fleming, and Ozzie and the boys had such a good time, they outvoted Harriet and canceled a planned week in Rome to extend their stay at the beach before heading to London. In England Ozzie's efforts to interest the BBC in the show met with little success. Executives didn't think the trivial trials and tribulations of an American family would hold much interest for British audiences.

Also in London, Ricky experienced his first sexual encounter. Sex education had never been a strong part of their home life, although Ozzie was always proud that he and Harriet were the first couple on television to sleep in a double bed. "The first news I got about the birds and the bees," David remembered, "was from Will Thornbury next door, when I was seven. His explanation was a disaster. I resolved not to ever let it happen to me. All I knew about girls was that they were bad football players." He came home one day to find a book placed prominently on his bed.

"It was called *The Egg and I* or something," he said. He showed the book to his brother. "Do you know what you have to do when you get married?" he asked.

"I knew about it," recalled Ricky. "I don't know whether I was for it, but I wasn't shocked."

The night before they left to return to America, the two boys and a more worldly American friend cruised the streets of

London in search of prostitutes. Ricky, who turned fourteen a month before leaving for Europe, kept turning down the girls. "I was scared to death," he later remembered. "Finally, the two guys parked the car, went out and got a woman and brought her back. She opened the door and grabbed my hand. She was really nice to me. I didn't want to leave. The guys had told her I was a young French water skier and she kept wishing me luck. When we got back to the hotel, though, I couldn't look my mom in the face. I remember thinking 'She knows.' "

"I remember him walking off with this girl his arm could barely reach around," chuckled David.

The party made the return trip on the maiden voyage of the SS *United States*, which set a new transatlantic speed record in the process.

Back home, Ricky entered Hollywood High and David went off to USC. "I couldn't wait to get out on my own," said David, who moved into an apartment close to campus. He belonged to a fraternity, and, of course, Ozzie worked that into the show too. In fact, "The Kappa Sig Party," an episode where David throws a fraternity party at the Nelsons' home with his parents and younger brother promising—but failing—to stay out of the way, introduced a new character to the ensemble, who would become a fixture on the show for the next decade.

Skip Young grew up in the San Fernando Valley, and his father had been a big-band jazz musician. Skip entered the navy and at first served overseas as a photography technician. His father's friend Bob Hope, however, wangled a transfer for Young to special services in San Diego, where he began his show business career with another young naval officer and actor-to-be, Dean Jones. After leaving the service, Young found himself acting in old-fashioned melodramas at Knott's Berry Farm, where he was working when his agent called him for an interview on the "Ozzie and Harriet" set. Although Young had never acted in front of cameras before, Ozzie immediately found him perfect for the part of Chubby, the fraternity brother who hovered around the kitchen, constantly stuffing himself with food.

The day of the shooting, Young found himself lost in a sea of people he didn't know. In addition to the regulars, the cast that day also included such young veterans playing fraternity brothers as Johnny Wilder (who played Little Beaver as a child actor on radio's "Red Rider") and Dwayne Hickman from "The Bob Cummings Show."

"Suddenly John Wilder comes up and says, 'You're Skip Young?' " Young recalled, "and I said, 'Yeah.' He said, 'Do you want to go out to lunch with us? We're going to go out to Tiny Naylor's for lunch.' He took me with Dave and Rick and Dwayne over to Tiny Naylor's for lunch. I didn't have much to say. They'd ask me questions about my career and background, and I'd tell them a little bit about this and that. But that was one of the most impressive things in my life. Years later, after I'd been with the show for ten years, every so often a new young actor would come aboard, and I could tell just from the look on his face that he was just as lost as I was. So I would do the same thing that John Wilder did for me. It got to be a kind of a thing where we never let a new actor, who was probably already so scared he couldn't stand straight, be left alone. It got to be a real tradition in the show."

Ozzie liked his portly presence and squeaky voice. He called him back to play a delivery boy, then again to be a bellboy in a hotel scene. The third time, in an episode called "David and the Hot Dog Stand," Young became one of David's fraternity brothers and picked up a first name, Wally. When Ozzie decided to build a show around Wally and his father, he thought about giving the characters the last name of Dipple. Young asked him if instead he could use his own real last name (*Young* was a stage name), and Wally Plumstead was created. He would become one of the most lasting characters on the series outside of the family. Somewhere along the way Wally picked up a girlfriend, Ginger, who was played by several different actresses, until Charlene Salerno nailed down the part.

"Wally was really the moocher," said Young. "And he's a fatso. And he's always mooching money off the guys. And he's always putting together these deals that he gets himself in trouble with, and they have to bail him out. And he's always fooling around, so to speak, with other girls, but he doesn't want Ginger to know. There were all these things that just began to build."

The fraternity life as portrayed on the show was drawn more from Ozzie's memories of his own days at Rutgers than David's own fraternity at USC. But then life as reflected in "The Adventures of Ozzie and Harriet" was really fashioned more after Ozzie's own youth, New Jersey in the 1920s. Ricky and David never hung out at a malt shop, preferring drive-ins like Tiny Naylor's, and the whole small-town ambience of the TV show was quite at odds with the Hollywood lifestyle the younger Nelsons knew.

Ricky did not cut a wide swath through Hollywood High School, where he started in the fall of 1954. The only evidence of his time there in the school yearbooks is his presence in the team picture of the sophomore B football squad. He made the photo but missed the season because of a broken hand. "He was not revered as some special entity because of his status in the industry," said actor Mike Farrell of TV's "M*A*S*H," who went to Hollywood High a couple of years behind Ricky. "After all, it was not that far from the norm at Hollywood High."

"I just never liked school," Rick told Bill Bentley of the *L.A. Weekly* twenty-five years later. "I really didn't. It always smelled of pencils. I enjoyed playing sports and stuff. I played some football and that kind of stuff. But I really didn't care. I think it was getting up in the morning. I had one class I flunked, I think it was English. My dad's going 'How can you flunk English?' I was late. I never made it. I think I was present there, like, ten days."

Bruce Belland, who was a couple of years ahead of Ricky, remembered them flunking a typing class together. "We screwed around a lot in that class," he said. "We were always playing tricks on the teacher and throwing our voices, throwing a spitball and then going back to typing. Terrible juvenile delinquent stuff. So we both got D's in typing, which is real hard to do."

When Ricky entered Hollywood High, he fully expected to follow his brother into the Elskers. When David belonged, the club members spent many weekends playing basketball or swimming in the Nelsons' backyard, and Ricky knew many of the older Elskers already. He took it hard when he was mysteriously blackballed from the club. "I know that really hurt him," said David. "He revolted at that time and started hanging with a group of guys in motorcycle boots and black leather jackets."

"It was really degrading to me," remembered Rick, "because they were all, like, friends of mine. I vowed to myself I'd get back at these guys, and I did."

The club's rejection brought about a change in Ricky. Once an outgoing wisecracker, he began to effect the look and attitude of a blue-jean rebel. He began running around with a far less savory crowd, including members of a tough, greasy car club called the Rooks. He tattooed his initials in India ink on his hand and another design on his wrist. He coated his hair in Brylcreem and combed it into a waterfall over his forehead.

"I was really out of control then, with the Rooks," he remembered fifteen years later. "We would cruise Hollywood Boulevard and choose off people we thought we could beat up. We were arrested for stealing construction lanterns. We thought we were really bad. Most of the guys did end up in jail—they went on to bigger things, like armed robbery. That's when my character became different from the TV role. But it wasn't that different. I was a nice greaser."

His parents were alarmed. Juvenile delinquency was a phrase that struck fear in the hearts of parents of fifties American teens, and this image was far from desirable for the member of a wholesome, sunny TV show like "Ozzie and Harriet." His parents took steps. "They started paying a little more attention," said David. One friend was banished. "They didn't think he was a very good influence on Rick, so they straightened that situation out pretty quick," said David.

Most of Rick's friends came from the tennis world. He got his first racket when he was nine years old and won his first trophy when he and his partner were runners-up in the eleven-and-under division of a city tournament at Altadena. By the time he got to Hollywood High, his room was crowded with similar awards. Perhaps he didn't excel at football like his brother, but at age fifteen, Ricky was rated fifth in the state for juniors and competed in tournaments in Michigan, Illinois, and Minnesota. He represented Hollywood High in interscholastic matches, and not only did he and his partner, Bruce Campbell, win all of their matches, neither of them ever lost a set in either singles or doubles in league competition. Perhaps even more important, on a good day he could trim his father on the court. As his popularity on the show grew, he began to draw enormous crowds of autograph seekers whenever he played in competition.

In 1956 he and partner Allen Fox reached the semifinals of the National Indoor Junior Championship and were matched against players two years older. Rick worked very hard on his game and got very aggressive. His strong forehand made up for his weaker backhand, and he liked to take the game to the net. Win or lose, tennis was one of the challenges in life that he faced on his own merits. He could take his lumps and did very well.

He met Forrest Stewart playing Ping-Pong at a tennis tournament in Ojai, California. Stewart was a couple years older than Ricky, and their backgrounds couldn't have been more dissimilar. Stewart came from a poor family in Pasadena. His single mother worked as a waitress, and Stewart took to tennis as a way out. Somehow he and Ricky struck up a friendship immediately.

Stewart and Ricky became constant companions, although Stewart always wondered how close they really were. "I don't know if Rick knew how to have a real relationship with a person," Stewart said. "Who did he have one with? I don't know if he had one with anybody. I was as close to him as anyone could have been. We were shadows of each other for four or five years. We essentially never helped each other as people. We didn't do anything for each other. He certainly wasn't better for me being there, and I wasn't better for him being there. I was just there, first of all, because I had a driver's license and he didn't. He had a learner's permit, and that was one of the reasons for Ozzie supporting the relationship. I was kind of wholesome, at least on the surface, because I was a good tennis player and I was a college student, as opposed to some of the guys he was hanging around before I knew him. He was supposed to be hanging around with some real shady characters. He was fourteen and getting in trouble. He had tattoos on his hands.

"Ozzie saw this rebellious nature, and he panicked. So he was trying to get him in this wholesome atmosphere, and he thought tennis, tennis players. He was kind of in the back, manipulating the situation."

With his father representing something of an indomitable force, Rick narrowed down the arenas of conflict to smaller terms, like smoking cigarettes or haircuts.

"His dad wanted a nice, clean-cut haircut," said Stewart, "and he let his sideburns grow and wanted his hair long. He'd come in for the television show and his dad would say, 'God-dammit, I told you to cut your hair.' And he'd say, 'I did cut it.' And they'd go at each other about the haircut. His dad wanted him to go to the tutor and become more educated, and Ricky didn't want to be involved with the tutor. He was always hiding from Van Scoyk, the tutor.

"He rebelled against the L.A. Tennis Club, which is where his dad played tennis. He just did the opposite of what his dad was. He stopped playing tennis completely.

"Around the tennis club, Ricky Nelson was just another kid. He wasn't a movie star or anything else, and he was treated like that. He was made fun of, and he was treated like any kid was. If I did something stupid, somebody would make fun of me. We were kids around there," Stewart said.

Fast cars figured in the picture. Teenage California was built on the mobility cars provided. Drive-ins became the social centers, and every 1950s teen cherished the notion of not having to borrow Dad's car but of actually owning his own, something David and Ricky could easily afford.

David started out with motorcycles, dirt racing in the desert, and Ozzie, of course, fashioned a TV script around David's motorcycle. He worked his way up to hot rods like his 1941 Ford and a Mercury. Ricky's first car was a blue Chevy Bel-Air. The two used to race down both sides of winding Laurel Canyon. Dangerous as it was, they always ended up at Tiny Naylor's, laughing about their escapade.

David even bought half-ownership in a midget auto racer, which he tried out for the first time on the dirt lot adjacent to the Pan Pacific Auditorium. Two days later his partner entered him in the races for real at the Gardena track, without telling David in advance. He was underage, so his racing license was under a phony name, as he matched his meager skills against

professional race-car drivers. He made about four races before
the cameraman from "Ozzie and Harriet" happened to spot
him at the track and told his father. Ozzie put a quick stop to
that activity.

Their parents bought them a pair of new 1957 Porsches as a
present, a year after James Dean killed himself by crashing his
Porsche on a California highway while traveling at more than
100 mph. There were no Porsche dealers in those days. The
prestigious, expensive cars had to be ordered and were delivered six months later. Ricky owned his only a couple of
months before the night he and Forrest Stewart went to see
the rock & roll movie *The Girl Can't Help It* at a Westwood
theater in his new car.

They met a couple of girls at the movie and showed off the
car, driving them around the hills behind Westwood until
about an hour past midnight. They dropped the girls off and
headed toward home down Sunset Boulevard.

"We were zipping around where it winds on Sunset," Stewart recalled, "and then all of a sudden it straightens out about
three or four blocks before the Beverly Hills Hotel. We were
going down that straightaway—neither of us had the seat belts
on; this car had seat belts—and he opened it up. He was going
about 120 miles per hour. I said, 'Slow down.' I was frightened.
I said, 'Goddammit, slow down.'

"I no sooner said that than the next block the sprinkler
system had flooded the street, and he hit the brakes. He
couldn't tell where the water started and hit the brakes into
the water. The car spun sideways, and it spun into the last
island there on Sunset. We hit the curb broadside on my side
and flew into the air, I don't know how far, and landed. We
turned over eight or nine times, sideways, down the middle
island in the grass.

"The car stopped. It ripped the wheels off the car. We
stopped and I said, 'We must be all right.' And Ricky's sitting

there saying, 'Oh, my leg. My God, my leg.' He's screaming. I just opened the door and got out. I said, 'Are you OK?' I opened the door and got him out. I pulled him over to the side. I stood up, and I'm feeling myself. I'm all right. I couldn't believe it.

"There's ambulances and people coming, and they're all hovered around him. I'm standing up next to a tree. I'm suffering from shock, but I don't know it. A few people recognize who he is. So finally the ambulance guys say, 'Was there anybody else involved?' And I say, 'Yes, I was.' So they say, 'You better get in the ambulance, too.'

"We go to the hospital. Turns out—they x-rayed us—we both had a cracked pelvis, not a bad thing. I had bumps on my head. I had patches of hair that came out. He had similar injuries. He had a bruise on his leg. We were out of the hospital in a couple of days."

Photographs of the demolished car made the newspapers. David remembered the police finding a football helmet in the back and commenting that it was a good thing Rick had been wearing a helmet (he wasn't). They were terribly lucky to escape more serious injury or even being killed. But life had bigger things in store just around the corner for Ricky Nelson, sixteen, than death in a car crash.

4
I'm Walkin'

RICK NELSON ALWAYS TOLD THE SAME STORY about how he made his first record. But like a lot of the stories he told about himself, it was only part of the story.

"I was going with this girl at Hollywood High School," he recounted for the umpteenth time in 1977. "I remember taking her home one night and she didn't really like me that well. I think she liked my car or something. I was taking her home and driving down Laurel Canyon and Elvis's record came on the radio. She did this whole thing about Elvis and I thought I have to say something. So I said 'Well, I'm going to make a record.' She laughed. She thought that was real funny. I thought right then I'm going to make a record. If it's just one record, I'm going to hand it to her and say 'Now laugh.' "

Rock & roll swept the country like a fire storm in 1956. It delivered its message to teenagers suffocating under the stifling cloak of the Eisenhower era. Underneath the primitive rhythms and clanging guitars, there was a hidden promise of deliverance. It offered freedom, excitement and even a raucous hint of sexuality in those drab times. Rick Nelson was not immune to its galvanizing force.

Igniting the blaze was a twenty-one-year-old former truck driver from Memphis with the unlikely name of Elvis Presley. He blossomed that year on the nation's television sets, working his way through appearances on the Dorsey brothers' show, Milton Berle, and Steve Allen, exploding out of the top-rated Ed Sullivan show in the first of three appearances that September. His first RCA Victor single, "Heartbreak Hotel," slowly climbed to number one, followed during the same year by "Don't Be Cruel" and "Love Me Tender," the title song of his motion picture debut that opened to blockbuster box-office sales in November.

But before Elvis, rock & roll smoldered like a thousand little grass fires around the country. Bill Haley and His Comets put rock & roll at the top of the charts for the first time in 1955 with "(We're Gonna) Rock Around the Clock." Alongside the Brown decision of the Supreme Court to order the desegregation of public schools in 1954, rhythm & blues records slowly began to desegregate the hit parade. Black musicians like Chuck Berry, Fats Domino, Little Richard, the Penguins, the Moonglows, and others all broke through the pop-music race barrier into the top ten. Slowly the sound of urban ghettos seeped into the world of white teenage America until young white Southerners transformed the black music into what came to be called rock & roll.

The first rock & roll record Ricky bought was "Blue Suede Shoes" by Carl Perkins. Born in Tiptonville, Tennessee, in 1932, Perkins grew up picking cotton and playing guitar. He was already a professional musician, earning as much as thirty dollars a week, when he heard the first Elvis record on the radio—a hyped-up, frantic version of the Bill Monroe bluegrass standard "Blue Moon of Kentucky"—and headed straight to Memphis to audition for the same label that re-

corded Elvis, Sam Phillips's Sun Records. Perkins's first records for Phillips were more hillbilly than rockabilly, although
one of the flip sides, "Gone, Gone, Gone," pointed the way to
the future.

In November 1955, after five regionally successful singles,
Phillips sold the Elvis contract to RCA Victor and turned his
attention to Perkins, who cut "Blue Suede Shoes" shortly
thereafter. In March 1956, when RCA was still having difficulty
launching "Heartbreak Hotel," "Blue Suede Shoes," a song
Perkins wrote on the back of an old paper bag, became the
first rockabilly record to hit the top ten.

"I thought, boy, this is great with that guitar break in it like
that," said Rick. "That's what I really tried to emulate, that
sound and that tone."

Like so many other people his age across the country, Ricky
caught rock & roll fever. David taught him a few chords on
their father's four-string guitar, an instrument modeled after
the ukulele, Ozzie's first instrument. The two would take to
the bathroom and warble the Johnny Cash hit "I Walk the
Line," another one of those Sun Records from Memphis. The
raw, Southern rock & roll stung Ricky. "Blue Suede Shoes"
changed his life.

Ozzie recognized the burgeoning music's power, hearing it
pound away upstairs in his son's bedroom and sensing a
similar impact outside his home. David did not share Ricky's
enthusiasm. At age twenty, he considered himself too old for
rock & roll, and his personal musical taste inclined toward
the Modern Jazz Quartet and Frank Sinatra. His father drew
the dichotomy in caricature on one episode where David
arrived at a costume party dressed as Yul Brynner from the
Rodgers and Hammerstein Broadway musical *The King and I*
and Ricky turned up masquerading as Elvis. Another episode,
"Musical Appreciation," pitted the two brothers on dueling
phonographs, Ricky blasting rhythm & blues upstairs, while
David tried to listen to symphonies in the living room.

But Ricky did not guilelessly start making rock & roll records merely to impress a girl. The ever-present hand of his father could be seen gently pulling the strings in the background.

Joe Byrne, a friend of David who worked on the show, overheard Ozzie bring up the subject with Ricky. "His dad approached him on it," said Byrne, "but the first time, he backed off: 'No, I'm not ready yet.' I remember. I was there. His dad said, 'If you want to sing, if you want to make records, there's a right way to go about it.' Ozzie was a very smart businessman."

David remembered Ricky making the record for the girl in a record your-own voice booth at Wallich's Music City, Hollywood's biggest record and music store. "Our nosy father found out about it," he said. Ozzie took matters over and began to arrange a professional recording debut for his son.

Los Angeles may have been the capital of the film and television industries, but it was a provincial backwater in the record business. Most major labels like Columbia or Decca were headquartered in New York. The only major one located in Los Angeles was Capitol Records, which specialized in mainstream artists like Frank Sinatra, Dean Martin, and Nat "King" Cole.

The best rock & roll records were being produced by small independent labels like Sun Records in Memphis, the Chess Records label in Chicago, or any number of independently distributed imprints run by George Goldner in New York. Without the vested interest in the status quo of popular music, these grass-roots labels were positioned closer to the ground, able to keep pace with the rapidly shifting currents in taste.

In Los Angeles, Art Rupe's Specialty Records, Lew Chudd's Imperial Records, and the Bihari brothers' Kent and Modern labels all experienced success in the booming rhythm & blues field. But Ozzie ignored all these companies, which almost exclusively featured black artists, and instead turned to jazz impresario Norman Granz, who made his name producing the famed Jazz at the Philharmonic concerts in Los Angeles during the 1940s.

Granz consolidated his jazz recordings onto his Verve Records label in early 1957 and hired guitarist Barney Kessel to oversee the development of a pop music program for the fledgling company. "I was looking for someone just like [Rick]," recalled Kessel, "someone young, well known, already popular, possibly could sing. . . . I had no idea whether he could sing or not."

Kessel, who had played briefly in Ozzie's band with the Red Skelton show, found it a heartening sign when a drummer friend who worked on the TV show told him that Ricky had a photo of Elvis on the wall and a drum set in his bungalow dressing room. He arranged some meetings with Ricky to discuss the possibilities of making a record. Various potential songs were considered.

"When the intervals were too involved," said Kessel, "when it required singing too much in one breath, when it required singing some words that I realized he didn't know what he was saying when he said the words, when the range was too wide, it was not the song.

"He was not a very accomplished singer or seasoned or experienced at all," said Kessel. "There wasn't even much voice."

Eventually, three songs were selected. "A Teenager's Romance" was a treacly commercial number submitted to Kessel by a publisher's representative. "You're My One and Only Love" was a tune Kessel and MGM staffer Frank Marshall wrote based on a bass figure Kessel lifted off Pat Boone records. "I'm Walkin' " was the latest Fats Domino hit. "It was the only song that I knew at the time," said Rick. "It had about three chords, so I could play it on guitar, and that's why I did the song. I really liked his version of it."

A session was booked for March 26, 1957, at Bunny Robyn's

Master Recorders on Fairfax Avenue. Robyn, a motion-picture sound mixer who recorded big bands for the air force during the war, ran a studio that virtually every rhythm & blues producer in Los Angeles used during the fifties. Rhythm & blues pioneers like Johnny Otis, Maxwell Davis, or Jerry Leiber and Mike Stoller cut historic sides in his small room, using what Robyn called "the Master's sound."

"It was a certain kind of sound for the rock and roll," Robyn explained. "Everything was powerful and exciting sounding. At the same time, you could listen and hear the guys. I always had that vocalist or trio, whoever was singing, so you could hear 'em. You could hear 'em on a seven-dollar box, and that was my test. I'd cut a test and put it on this junk piece, which had a little speaker and a crystal arm that couldn't take level, that would jump off the track. But if I could get it to track at high levels and I could listen to it, I'd say, 'That's it.' "

Among the musicians Kessel recruited for the session were country-music guitar great Merle Travis, author of "Sixteen Tons," and drummer Earl Palmer, who played on the original Fats Domino version of "I'm Walkin' " and had recently relocated to Los Angeles from New Orleans. Skip Young and David came by. "I was curious to see if Rick could pull this off," said David. And, of course, the ubiquitous Ozzie was there.

"It was scary," said Rick. "I remember all these people there, and I had gone straight from singing in the bathroom to the recording studio. There was nothing in between."

"That night, it was all very, very big for him to be there," said Young. "What the heck, he was only sixteen. He did it a few times and listened to it back and listened to it again. Barney would say, 'I think you can do that better.' Occasionally, Ozzie would go over and whisper something to Rick about it. Little by little, that night, Rick matured about that. Both David and I talked about it: 'If either of these get to be hits, I think Rick has found a real career for himself. He likes it.' "

"It really was an afterthought to do it on the television

show," said Rick, " 'cause I had just recorded the song and just that day my dad, he came up and said 'Why don't you do your new song on the show?' So I did and nobody realized at that time the exposure that television gives you."

Of course, nothing was really an afterthought with the always calculating Ozzie. With shows being filmed as much as six weeks in advance of their airdates, plenty of time remained to include the song in a show to coincide with the release of the record. The episode "Ricky the Drummer" took its story line from Ricky's Atlantic-crossing experience sitting in with the shipboard orchestra. At the end of the show, in the final two-minute segment after the last commercial break, Ozzie looked at the bandleader and made his immortal suggestion.

"How about Rick singing a rhythm and blues tune and the rest of us will give him a little moral support?" he said.

"Good deal," replied the bandleader. "What do you want to sing, Rick?"

"How about 'I'm Walkin' '?" said Ricky.

"Fine, I'll make the announcement," the bandleader said.

"Do you think it's alright for him to sing, too?" Harriet asked.

"Oh, sure," said Ozzie. "It's great experience for him."

Standing stock still, looking more than a little awkward, the camera focused on his face, Rick lip-synched the recording. Although the camera never showed it, he was wearing white socks with his black tuxedo. "His 'I'm Walkin' ' is a very embarrassed version," said David. "He did not know quite what to do with himself. He had listened to the record, and he could do it by himself. But I don't think he ever imagined standing up in front of people and doing it. He wasn't sure what his persona should be. So that's when he started his minor impersonation of Elvis."

Nobody could have been prepared for the response, once the show was broadcast on April 10. "When it hit, it was like an explosion," said Joe Byrne. "We thought it was OK. We didn't think it was anything special. What we weren't aware of as young kids—Ozzie was aware of it, but we weren't—was that twenty-five million people would see that. We did these shows, and they went on. We weren't aware of the impact.

"When that show aired, the response was immediate, absolutely the next day after it was aired. We had a department where all the mail came in and they'd get real good fan mail. But when Rick did the record, it did bags. It was overnight. We couldn't believe it. It like quad-tripled. We went back there and looked. The phones were ringing and mailbags were coming, just mailbags, full from that one appearance. We went, 'Whoa, look out.' And then the girls started coming to the stage five gate. And Rick, he'd smile. I said, 'Rick, you know what's going to happen?' He said, 'Yeah, all these girls we're going to meet, Joe.' "

When the record was finally released three weeks later, it sold an astonishing sixty thousand copies in the first three days. It crashed the charts the first week of release, stayed there for the next five months, and eventually sold more than 700,000 copies. "I'm Walkin' " took off first and made it into the top twenty. "A Teenager's Romance," the puerile other side, scooted all the way to the top ten. Some three hundred Ricky Nelson fan clubs sprung up virtually overnight. The San Fernando Valley chapter alone boasted two thousand members by the end of May. Rarely before had an amateur singer been more celebrated.

And what about the girl who started it all?

"About three weeks after all this happened," Rick said, "the record had already been played and was selling a lot of records. This friend of mine drove her up to the house and said 'Well, she would really like to see you.' And I said 'Oh really? Oh, sure.' So I remember walking out the front door and she was sitting in the car. I sat down and he got out and let us talk. She goes 'Why don't you ever call me or see me? Why don't we go out anymore?' And I said, 'You know, I've been real busy recording. I'll try and call you.' And that was another rush. It was one of those great moments, you know, those ego things. I got to walk out of the car and I said 'I'll call you sometime.' "

Suddenly Ricky Nelson was the country's hottest new rock & roll star. The combination of his already substantial appeal as a teenage television star coupled with the power of rock & roll vaulted him into regions his friends and family could only marvel about. In June, as he was mobbed by fans during an afternoon appearance on the radio show by local deejay Art Laboe, broadcast live from Scrivner's Drive-In, a few blocks away from Hollywood High, David wandered around the perimeter of the crowd, shaking his head in amazement. "Is this my brother," he muttered, "the one who leaves his underwear on the floor?"

Getting awkward Ricky to sing in front of a live audience was a different matter. "Rick's innate shyness made it difficult for him to think beyond standing in a recording studio and making records," said Bruce Belland of the Four Preps, "or sitting in the bungalow and performing with us. But getting out in front of real live people, that was a scary thing." His debut performance took place almost by accident, shortly after he cut his record but before it had been released.

The ambitious Preps, who scored a modest hit at the beginning of the year with a song called "Dreamy Eyes," spent a lot of time promoting their act around Southern California by appearing at high school assemblies. They also made occasional appearances on the "Ozzie and Harriet" show and knew Ricky and David from Hollywood High.

"The very first thing I ever did was with the Four Preps," said Rick. "They did auditorium shows at schools during lunch and they were doing one over at Hamilton High School. They talked me into coming along. We'd gone over 'Blue Moon of Kentucky' and I had my four-string guitar. That was my first taste and I was scared to death. I couldn't believe I even went out there.

"I started playing the guitar and going 'Blue moon of Kentucky keep on shining,' and all of a sudden these screams started happening. Oh my God, I thought, this is what I want to do. How do I tell somebody this. It was just a lunch hour. Who do you tell? They screamed. It was amazing."

The Preps were scheduled to both do an assembly and shoot an episode the same day, so Ozzie arranged for them to take the afternoon off to go to the high school show. "We're throwing stuff in the car," Belland said, "and we've been talking for two or three days with Rick about it. Finally, Glen Larson says, 'C'mon, Rick, c'mon with us.' So he takes his guitar and gets in the car. I'm watching as we're driving over there. He's kind of watching us 'cause he's out in the real world now, driving around to a high school.

"We were all, in a sense, street kids, strictly lower-, middle-income kids. To us, getting in Glen's Oldsmobile and driving over to Hamilton High to do an assembly and get seventy-five bucks and get some publicity made sense. But to Rick, you thought he was going to the twilight zone.

"So we get over there, get everything set up, test the microphones. They let the kids in. They introduce the Four Preps. We come out. We sing two or three songs and Glen, who is the spokesman of the group, said, 'We've got a little surprise for you. I think if you give him a hand, we can coax a pal of ours out here to sing a couple of songs. We got our pal Rick Nelson with us.'

"Well, you know the place exploded—*arghhh*—just at the mention of his name. Rick, I see him kind of looking around. He straps his guitar on, looks around, takes a deep breath, and walks out onstage. He hits the stage. Chaos. Fucking chaos. We're singing, and I'm looking at Rick. It's so loud we can hardly hear ourselves. Then, something I never saw before or since in any assembly in any high school, they left their seats and came rushing down to the front. It was forty or fifty deep up each aisle of girls, just screaming. I think we did one song and half of another. It was just chaos. So he kind of bowed and went offstage, and we finished the act with a couple of Preps numbers.

"We open the back of the auditorium to get to our car, and you can't even see the car, just people. Finally they rang the bell, and all the kids had to go back to class or get tardy slips. Some girls stayed anyway with their autograph books, and we managed to press through the few kids that were left and get in the car. We turn around and start driving back through the school. I look at Rick, and he's got this look on his face like, 'Holy shit, that was really exciting.'

" 'Wow,' he says, 'does that always happen that way?'

" 'No,' I said, 'it doesn't usually happen that way, Rick, 'cause usually it's just us. You understand, Rick Nelson was out there today.' "

Rick and the Preps took another dry run before taking the show out for real, making a surprise Saturday night appearance at the Birdcage Theater in Knott's Berry Farm. Skip Young still appeared there in melodramas and hosted the proceedings, and Ozzie arranged the impromptu performance with him. Even with the largely adult audience that attended the Knott's Berry theatricals, the young, timid Ricky scored. "He brought the house down," said Young. "They screamed, and everybody applauded. They thought it was great. It really gave him a lot of confidence. Afterward, there were people standing in the lobby waiting for him to come out so they could get his autograph."

From audiences in the hundreds, Rick immediately leaped to audiences in the tens of thousands, as soon as he left his amateur standing behind. He and the Preps headed out that summer to play state fairs in Ohio and Wisconsin. "I remember coming in on the airplane," said Rick, "and all these people were all over the airport. I didn't know who was coming in. I thought it was some politician or something. So we kind of walked off the plane and, all of a sudden, the whole fence caved in and they started running after us. I ended up under the plane somewhere."

The fairgrounds amphitheater held more than twenty thousand fans. "I was scared to death," said Rick. "I went out there and all these people were there. I think I knew about three and a half chords on guitar. I went out there and they said 'Oh yeah, we play rock and roll, we have a band, don't worry about it.' I just brought some friends of mine from Los Angeles, the Four Preps, and they were backing me up singing ba-da-ba-da. I remembered going out there and all of a sudden, all I heard was these drum marches being played for background music. It wasn't really my idea of rock and roll. I looked around and there was this old gentleman sitting at the snare drum playing marches on everything. I couldn't believe it. I made it through the show, but I thought, boy, if I'm going to do these types of things, I'm going to need a band."

"In Milwaukee," Bruce Belland said, "we got warned: when you get through the last number, come offstage, go immediately across the infield, down these stairs. There's a tunnel that goes back into the infield somewhere. You'll come out at the other end. You walk up the steps at the other end of this tunnel. There's a limousine. Get in the limousine. Do not loiter. Do not tarry. Get in and get the fuck out 'cause there's twenty-five thousand people over there and the only thing stopping them from coming down through that tunnel is a chain-link fence at the other end.

"We got through with the last number, and the crowd is screaming and yelling and hollering, which from twenty-five thousand people is an awesome sound. We went down the tunnel, and one or two of us tarried for pictures or to wave to somebody or something. We got down there, we could hear the crowd at the other end of the tunnel against the chain-link fence, and the chain-link fence is going ca-chunk, ca-chunk, ca-chunk. People are screaming and the guy at the other end of the tunnel is saying, 'C'mon, c'mon.'

"Rick was with me and we look back up the tunnel just as the chain-link fence popped open and slapped against the sides of the tunnel. About forty thousand teenage girls— *rrrah*—came screaming up that tunnel. So we run to the other end, up the stairs. We get up there, and there's twelve people trying to get in a stretch limo at the same time, so there's a traffic jam. I remember I had tassel loafers on. That was the big thing in those days, the tassels. I lost all four of the tassels on my shoes because some girl coming up the stairs reached up and pulled 'em off my foot as I was trying to escape up the stairs. It was like the French Revolution.

"We got in the limo and drove off, and there was Rick with that same expression on his face."

When Ricky got home, some things hadn't changed. "I kind of got used to being called Mr. Nelson," he said. "I remember it was kind of a depressing thing. I was living with my folks and I was watching TV. It was the first night we were back in the living room and my mom came to the top of the stairs and said 'Ricky, pick up your clothes. Get up here and pick up your clothes.' And I thought, wait a minute, doesn't she know who she's talking to? I'm Mr. Nelson."

Rick flew partway to Ohio with Marianne Gaba, a former Miss Illinois headed home for a brief stay in Chicago before returning to Los Angeles to enroll in USC. They met when she was cast as his girlfriend for an episode of the TV show, but the relationship was apparently casual, at least on Rick's part.

"Marianne Gaba, Miss Illinois, was going to come on the 'Ozzie and Harriet' show," said Bruce Belland, "and here's Rick, this famous, young, studsy-looking animal. Everybody kind of watched to see the sparks fly, but he was just painfully shy and said two or three words to her and then the scene started. I think he finally ended up taking her out, but I never sensed him to be an aggressive ladies' man."

According to Forrest Stewart, Gaba told him years later that she and Rick never had a sexual relationship. Daughter of a Chicago postman, she was a beautiful blonde, a year older than Ricky, so shy it took her three sessions just to get comfortable enough to shed her clothes to pose as a *Playboy* playmate several years later.

"He was really enamored with her," said Stewart. "That was a relationship he really liked. She was a very pretty girl. She showed she really liked him. She moved out here for him, and he liked that. Maybe because it didn't progress sexually; maybe he figured she didn't like him enough. I don't know. I don't know what his thoughts were on that one, but I know that was a big one."

By August Ozzie had negotiated a new, far more lucrative recording deal for Ricky with Imperial Records, more in keeping with his sudden standing in the industry. Lew Chudd, a university graduate who dabbled in electronics, founded the label in 1947. A gruff, hard-bitten man, Chudd once greeted a visitor about to take a seat by saying, "Don't sit down; you're not going to be here that long." But he made a fortune selling Fats Domino records and at the time was one of the few record-business independents with a reputation for paying his artists what he owed them. Although he and Ozzie did not like each other, they came to terms, and Chudd stayed out of Ozzie's way. "They were two uptight cats," said Bunny Robyn, "but Lew smelled money."

Verve cashed in immediately, rushing into the market with a single of the third song from the March session, the hideously trite "You're My One and Only Love," with a hastily recorded instrumental on the other side, "Honey Rock," which featured lots of drumming, slyly insinuating that Ricky himself was playing on the record. In September Ozzie filed suit against Verve, asking for more than $43,000 in back royalties, alleging the only money received from the label was a $150 advance.

"It was a minor detail," Rick said. "They didn't pay me."

Verve countered with a suit asking more than $2.2 million, charging that Ricky never signed the contract with the label that both he and Ozzie agreed he would. Attached to the filings is a five-page boilerplate artist's royalty agreement, with Ricky's name typed at the end in the space still awaiting his signature.

"We recorded without Ozzie having signed it," said Barney Kessel. "It was going to be delivered the next day and [then] the next day, [then] the next afternoon at four o'clock. Never was signed. Never was delivered. And, finally, Ozzie went elsewhere. On the strength of what had happened with that record it had built up a greater negotiating figure for Ozzie."

Four years later, the courts finally ordered Verve to pay more than $38,000 in royalties due Rick.

Imperial not only agreed to advance seventeen-year-old Ricky an astronomical $1,000 a week but also let him have final approval of all advertising, copy, and artwork associated with the records for the duration of the five-year contract. This staggering deal far outdistanced the record-breaking $40,000 that RCA Victor gave Sam Phillips for Elvis Presley. But Ozzie was already proving himself the equal of Colonel Parker, Presley's omnivorous manager, when it came to extorting maximum value for minimum talent. Ozzie knew to strike while the iron was hot, and this iron was scorching.

Since Chudd didn't want to cross paths with Ozzie any more than was absolutely necessary, he assigned the task of supervising Ricky's records to a green, twenty-two-year-old assistant. Jimmie Haskell was an accordionist who came to work for Imperial copying out lead sheets of Fats Domino records for copyright purposes. "My mother trained me that I wasn't good enough," said Haskell, "and that I had to work harder to get approval." This gave Haskell the perfect obsequious temperament to work with the demanding, abrasive Chudd, and he began to oversee Imperial sessions with little-known groups like the Spiders or the Scholars (whose members included a young Kenny Rogers).

Haskell met Ricky at Chudd's office and, at Chudd's request, drove him over to a local record distributor to pick up some Elvis Presley records. "The first thing he did was turn my car radio to the country station," said Haskell. "I didn't even know there was a country station."

"Have I Told You Lately That I Love You" was a country song by Scotty and Lulu Belle that dated from 1945 that Elvis had recorded on his latest album, *Lovin' You,* and Ricky wanted to do the song too. Chudd picked "Be-Bop Baby" for the A side of the single. Written by a professional songwriter, Pearl Lendhurst, the song reached Chudd through its publishers. "Lew liked it," said Jimmie Haskell. "Ozzie liked it. Ricky agreed to sing it. I don't know if he liked it, but he wasn't voicing his opinion very much in those days."

The first Imperial single featured a far more assured, confident Ricky than the Verve session. He tackled the simple "Be-Bop Baby" with some bite and drive and handled the other side with a trace of the Elvis swagger. The Jordanaires, background vocalists on all the Elvis sessions, were flown in for the session, and Haskell said Ozzie constantly hovered around in the booth. Haskell knew his job, as far as Chudd was concerned, was to make the demanding Ozzie happy.

"Ozzie had a lot to say about it," said Haskell. "We never thought about editing. Ozzie wanted it to be perfect."

With the second Verve single already on the charts, "Be-Bop Baby" swamped the insipid r&b–flavored ballad "You're My

One and Only Love," as it whooshed into the top five, leaving the Verve side in its wake. Recording sessions continued at Master Recorders all through September in preparation for the first album, *Ricky*, which was released in October and hit number one before the end of the year.

Song selection on the LP reflected a balance between Ricky's instincts and Ozzie's trite vision. Alongside covers of songs by Ricky's idol, Carl Perkins, like "Boppin' the Blues" and "Your True Love," he sang with little relish such obvious chestnuts as "Am I Blue" or Cole Porter's "True Love." Ozzie made sure that his son's repertoire, like that of his own big band, featured a little something for everybody.

Fan mail poured in at the rate of fifteen thousand letters a week; the Hollywood post office had to add extra staff to handle the avalanche. Connie Harper, granddaughter of Cecil B. DeMille, came to work at General Service to run the fan clubs and organize the mail. Publicist Maury Foladare, who had represented the family since the radio show, dropped his other clients to devote his time exclusively to Ricky. Only Elvis had managed to make anything resembling this kind of a splash with rock & roll; now Ricky just had to make records worthy of his chart-topping appeal, which owed little, so far, to the quality of his recordings.

Within the next couple of months, however, Ricky would make two associations that would help him move toward the realms of lasting contributions to the history of rock & roll. The first was guitarist James Burton.

"I was up in Lew Chudd's office," Rick remembered. "I just signed with Imperial. I was out really looking for a band. All of a sudden, I heard this music coming down the hall and it was Bob Luman and he'd just come up from the 'Louisiana Hayride' and he was auditioning for Imperial Records with James Burton and James Kirkland playing bass. And I said that's exactly what I want."

One year older than Ricky and raised in Shreveport, Louisiana, James Burton at age fifteen became the staff guitarist on "Louisiana Hayride," a weekly country music broadcast out of Shreveport, second only in popularity to the Grand Ole Opry. As a member of the backing band of vocalist Dale Hawkins, he first wrote his name into the vocabulary of rock guitar by designing and playing the guitar figure that anchored Hawkins's only major hit, "Suzie-Q."

Shortly after cutting "Suzie-Q," Burton left Hawkins for Bob Luman, a young Texas rockabilly singer. Luman, Burton, and the rest of his band came to California in 1957 to play a role in a cheapie, black-and-white rock & roll movie called *Carnival Rock*, produced and directed by Roger Corman, in one of his early efforts. While in California, they made three records for Imperial, including "Red Cadillac and a Black Moustache," which eventually became a cult favorite among rockabilly fanatics, and "Red Hot," a cover version of the Billy Lee Riley original on Sun Records that nearly smokes the Sun version off the map. Since Jimmie Haskell was also involved in making the Luman records, it seems more likely that Rick first encountered these singles—"Red Hot" roars right down his alley—rather than merely "happened" to hear the band down the hall at the Imperial offices. Ricky always had enough show business cunning to prefer a good story to the absolute truth.

"That particular day we were doing a rehearsal on a couple of songs for Bob's record," said James Burton, "and Ricky came in, stopped by. Jimmie Haskell and Lew Chudd brought him in to introduce him to us. So we talked, and he stayed there about three hours at least, just listening to the music.

"We had a house in Canoga Park, living together, Bob and I and James Kirkland, the bass player. So, in Canoga Park, the next morning, James Kirkland went out to get the newspaper and found a telegram on the front door. It was from Ricky, inviting us down to their studio, wanting us to come down and meet his dad, which we did. We took our instruments down and played some music. His dad liked what he heard and asked us to be on the television show as Rick's band. We did a couple of television shows, and it worked out real good."

Burton also sat in on a recording session for the second Imperial single, "Waitin' in School" and "Stood Up," although country musician Joe Maphis played lead guitar on those tracks. "Waitin' in School," a song that literally showed up on Ricky's doorstep one afternoon, was written by Dorsey and Johnny Burnette, two Memphis rockers who knew Elvis Presley before they were in high school and led a Memphis band Elvis occasionally sang with before he made his first record. If Ricky had admired the Southern rock & roll from afar, now he was beginning to surround himself with the real thing.

Johnny and Dorsey Burnette, born poor, were trouble boys, sent to Catholic school for the discipline, not the religion. As young boys, they used to throw rocks at the black kids who lived on the other side of the railroad tracks.

Johnny got married before he left high school, and the two brothers worked on the Mississippi River, Johnny as a deckhand, Dorsey in the boiler room. With guitarist Paul Burlison, they formed the Rock and Roll Trio and went to New York, where they won Ted Mack's "Original Amateur Hour" three times, signed with an unscrupulous manager, and made a classic album of hard-driving rockabilly for Coral Records.

These were tough, uninhibited young men, who drank hard and punched even harder. Both had been professional boxers. Johnny lasted only one fight and one knockout, but Dorsey worked for a while as a heavyweight. The Trio, in fact, broke up after a fistfight by the brothers interrupted a concert performance. Back in Memphis, they made up and decided to take their families—five children between them, along with their mother and father—and move to California to make it in the music business. All eleven of them moved into a two-bedroom house in Compton, on the outskirts of Los Angeles.

Johnny Burnette bought a map of stars' homes and located the Nelson residence. He and another hometown friend showed up and rang the bell one afternoon. He took his guitar; he didn't have a case for it. The maid answered the door and told them Ricky was at the studio. They asked if they could wait.

"He was happy-go-lucky," said his widow, Thurley Burnette. "He was the kind of person you'd let in to use your bathroom today if he was dancing a jig outside your front door. He had that look about him. She brought 'em out some cold water. Ricky drove up, and they introduced themselves and said they had some songs for him and would he like to hear them. And John said, 'What about this one?' and just played them for him. They sat down and talked a while. Ricky said, 'What's your number?' and took down their number. 'You'll hear from me— I love that song,' he said.

"The next day, Lew Chudd of Imperial Records called the house in Compton. He said, 'I hear you've got some songs for Ricky Nelson. When can you come in and play them for me?' They took their guitars and took off."

Ricky, with his tendency to embellish his autobiography, always remembered the meeting somewhat differently. "I was driving home from the studio from filming one night," he said in a BBC interview one month before his death, "and this car pulled up behind me as I was going in the driveway. They all got out of the car, and I thought, wait a minute, what is this? They ran back and opened up the trunk of their car and brought out their guitars and started playing. They had just driven out from Tennessee, Johnny and Dorsey, and they started playing 'Waitin' in School' and all these songs to me, and I thought, this is great. So they went down and cut a demo record, and, of course, needless to say, I got to know them real well."

With "Stood Up" and "Waitin' in School," Ricky Nelson, at last, began to step into his own as a rock & roll stylist. The chugging guitars of Joe Maphis and James Burton gave the rhythm tracks a bubbling, percolating undercurrent, and Ricky concisely captured the cadence of the lyric's interior rhythms. Bunny Robyn gave the record a dark, foreboding atmosphere that contrasted nicely with Ricky's unadorned vocals.

He was no longer a Hollywood imitation of rock & roll but was beginning to sound like the genuine article on his own. The record followed "Be-Bop Baby" into the top five, with both sides getting near equal acclaim. Double-sided hits had previously been the exclusive province of only Elvis himself. But shortly after the record's release, Burton and Kirkland went back South.

"Ozzie wanted to continue doing more shows every week," said Burton, "and this was during the holidays. We got homesick and wanted to go back to Louisiana. James and I packed up our stuff and went home. We didn't care about the money. We just wanted to go home and see our folks. I was home about a month, and I got a phone call from Ozzie inviting me to come out and be Rick's lead guitar player."

The money must have been irresistible. Ozzie offered to put them on a weekly retainer of $350, plus an additional $450 every time they did one of the TV shows.

Ricky met Burton at the airport in early 1958 and took him to Camino Palmero for dinner. Ozzie invited Burton to move into the Nelson home, and he and Ricky immersed themselves in music night and day. Rock & roll had become the trapdoor through which he finally could escape the old, rancid air of the TV show, a breath of relief from the inevitability of having to be, once a week, "the irrepressible Ricky."

Rick first met guitarist Joe Maphis through "Town Hall Party," a weekly country music telecast out of Compton, where he also met Lorrie Collins, the first real love in his life. Like the Burnettes and Burton, Collins represented the authentic side of the music. Cute as a doll, the petite, blue-eyed brunette boasted a big voice, even at age fifteen, and she and her brother Larry had been regular members of the "Town Hall Party" cast since 1953, billed as the Collins Kids. Even with all the breaks Ricky got, Lorrie Collins had the one thing he didn't: the certainty she had made it on her own talent.

"We were all going through the excitement of what's going on in the record business," said Bruce Belland, "Fats Domino and Elvis and everybody. We'd come to the show bringing records for each other to hear. He said, 'I found this guitar player named Joe Maphis; he's got two necks on his guitar.' So the next Saturday, we all went down to 'Town Hall Party,' where Joe played. It was a local TV show, hillbilly. We watched from the wings, and Rick said, 'You believe that, man?' So we were all discovering music together." (The Preps also used Maphis to back the group on their 1958 top-five smash "26 Miles [Santa Catalina].")

"Him and Lorrie got pretty serious there for a while," said James Burton.

Ricky, who used to watch the Saturday night show regularly, got Lorrie Collins's phone number from singer-actress Molly Bee, a classmate of Collins at Hollywood Professional High School. But he was too shy to call. Finally, Glen Larson of the Preps, no shrinking violet, called Collins up and introduced Ricky over the phone. "Of course, I didn't believe him," she said. "Rick Nelson was like the heartthrob of the world. Poor me. I just adored him."

Larson and Ricky went down to Compton the next weekend to watch the show being broadcast and, more importantly, to meet Lorrie Collins.

"We just kind of hit it off," she remembered. "He was real shy, and I think I was kind of shy. I don't think we said fifteen words to each other. But there were so many people around all the time that it didn't matter. We just had a lot in common because of our youth, the music business, country music, and he admired a lot of the people that were really good friends of mine. It was taking him out of 'Ozzie and Harriet' into the music business, and that's where I think he really wanted to be."

In distinct contrast with Ricky's comfortable, cushioned upbringing, Collins and her younger brother were raised on a dairy farm in Pretty Water, Oklahoma, and attended a one-room schoolhouse. Money to go to the movies came from cashing in pop bottles for deposits. At age eight, she won a talent contest at a Tulsa ballroom run by Leon McAuliffe, the famous steel-guitar player from Bob Wills and the Texas Playboys, who advised her parents to move to California. They picked up stakes, sold some livestock and headed west, where Lorrie and her brother landed on "Town Hall Party" and found themselves red-hot country & western sensations. Maphis took Larry Collins as a protégé, and soon young Larry sported the same kind of double-necked guitar that was Maphis's trademark.

If Rick's father frequently reminded him that the livelihood of the forty people who worked on the show depended on him, Lorrie and Larry Collins understood absolutely that their family's economic security was their responsibility. Ricky and Lorrie both knew the loneliness of the child star.

She also appreciated how important music was to him. "Nobody took him serious about his music," she said. "I don't feel that even his father took him very serious. It was like, OK, he's a good-looking guy and a popular TV artist and everybody cuts a record now and then and you never hear from them again. But he was dead serious about his music business, and he wanted to be a part of that. And I think that was one of the things that was appealing to him about me and my lifestyle because my life was music."

They spent evenings at her family's Woodland Hills home playing music together. They wrote a song together, "My Gal," Rick's first attempt at songwriting, and he wrote another, "Don't Leave Me This Way," inspired by their work at writing. She introduced him to Johnny Cash and Tex Ritter, who was impressed that the young Hollywood upstart would drive all the way to Bakersfield to pick Lorrie up after a show.

"We went steady," she said. "As young as we were, how do you know what you feel? But at that particular time, I guess we really loved each other a lot. We had a lot in common, and he gave me a beautiful ring."

They talked about marriage. She appeared on his parents' TV show as his girlfriend, and they sang "Just Because," one of the Collins Kids' records, together at the end of one show. Fan magazines played up the romance. But pressures around them interfered. Neither set of parents particularly encouraged the two teenagers to get too serious. Her overprotective parents often sent younger brother Larry along on dates to act as a kind of chaperon. People were always around. The most time they could steal alone was either up at David's new house in the Hollywood hills or just driving around aimlessly.

"There were times we would just ride around in the car and not even talk, just hold hands and be happy to be alone and be with each other," Lorrie said. "It was like being normal girlfriend and boyfriend. I think we both yearned for that. I know I did, and I think he did, too."

One night, Lorrie went to Covina to attend the opening of a shopping center with actor Nick Adams. Ricky, in a jealous pique, followed them home. Her mother was furious when he angrily rang the doorbell well after midnight, but he later apologized.

The relationship had cooled down considerably when it came to a sudden end a year later. "It was pretty awful, and it was my fault," she said, her voice shaky at the recollection even thirty years later. On the road with Johnny Cash, she came to know Cash's manager, Stu Carnall, nineteen years her senior. He belittled Rick to Lorrie, made fun of his shyness and his youth. "He won me over," she said. They flew to Las Vegas and were secretly married.

Rick found out about it the same way everybody else did: reading a gossip column in the *Los Angeles Herald-Examiner*. They spoke on the phone. "All he said to me was, 'I can't believe it. . . . I can't believe it,'" Lorrie said. They did not see each other again for almost twenty years.

In October 1957 the young prince of rock & roll finally met the king. Ricky was just one of many movie star celebrities who attended the Elvis concert on October 29 at the Pan Pacific Auditorium, along with the likes of Nick Adams, Carol Channing, Sammy Davis, Jr., Tommy Sands, and others. But he was the one who got mobbed sneaking out of the hall early. Many also attended the private party after the show, which Elvis hosted in a suite at the Beverly Wilshire Hotel. But of all the stars it was Ricky alone that Elvis wanted to meet.

"Excuse me, excuse me," said the burly voice, as Elvis pushed through the crowd, lifting Ricky off the floor in an enthusiastic bear hug. "Ricky, hey, it's Ricky Nelson," he shouted. "I never miss your shows except if I'm on the road. How's your mama and daddy? Did David come too?"

Rick stammered out some feeble compliment about Elvis's concert, but the shy seventeen-year-old was too shaken to have much composure. Marcia Borie, the *Photoplay* editor who brought Ricky to the concert and party, took Elvis aside and told him Ricky's first concert tour would be coming up shortly, and he could use some tips. With that, Elvis put his arm around Rick's shoulder and steered him off behind closed doors for a half-hour private audience. On the ride back to his car, Ricky bubbled. "You'll never know how much tonight has meant to me," he told Borie. "I'll never forget it as long as I live. Imagine Elvis Presley watching our show. He repeated episodes I'd even forgotten about. He remembered them word-for-word. And he gave me some great tips about things to do on my tour. I still can't believe it."

As he said good night to Borie when she dropped him at his car, Ricky leaned over and offered one final benediction. "Elvis will always be the king," he said.

A few days before, David celebrated his twenty-first birthday with the family, only to be, once again, upstaged by his brother. Before David had a chance to blow out the candles on his cake, Lew Chudd dropped by to present Ricky with his gold record award for selling a million copies of "Be-Bop Baby." Although David was hidden even further by the shadow of his younger brother, he was not exactly inactive. He, at least, still went to school, attending classes at Los Angeles City College. Ricky never graduated from Hollywood High, a fact conveniently glossed over in the publicity Ozzie so scrupulously controlled at the time. David flunked out of USC in the spring semester of 1956. Football, fraternity life, and the television show got the upper hand over his basic lack of interest in academics.

David picked up good notices for his part in the film *Peyton Place* and landed another role in *The Remarkable Mr. Pennypacker* the following year. He moved to a Japanese-style bachelor pad in the hills above his parents' house, a cantilevered A-frame with a view of Hollywood spread out in front of the deck. Joe Byrne shared the rent. His place became a favored hangout for a lot of his TV show sidekicks and their dates. Skip Young recalled that the sun would often rise with bodies strewn across the living room floor, asleep where they fell after all-night parties.

Ricky's rock & roll pumped new life into the show, as millions of teenage fans gave the family a whole new youth audience. Ozzie jealously guarded his new star, strictly limiting his television appearances to the family's show. They turned down major offers from Perry Como and Ed Sullivan. He and Elvis shared the distinction of being virtually the only rock & roll stars of the era to have never appeared on "American Bandstand" (although host Dick Clark once interviewed Ricky over the phone on the show). Maury Foladare told *TV Guide* they rejected more than $100,000 worth of appearances in 1957 alone.

Many of the season's episodes that year, not surprisingly, were built around the two boys—"Fixing Up the Fraternity House," "The Boys Land in Jail," "A Picture in Rick's Notebook," "Ricky's Big Night." David also suggested a show—"David Has a Date with Miss Universe"—and actually ended up taking out the lady in question, Carol Morse, for awhile. It wouldn't be the last time one of the boys used the show as a dating bureau. Rick told friends later that his father, too, enjoyed occasional escapades with starlets appearing on the show.

And, of course, any new release was trumpeted on the TV show, with Ricky giving a show-closing performance to the inevitable mass of girls smiling and swaying their heads. He lip-synched the "Be-Bop Baby" single without a band, strumming an acoustic guitar while leaning on a table. Several tracks from the first album were similarly featured. While Ricky sang "Your True Love," veteran character actor Edgar Buchanan commented to Ozzie, "By George, I like that rock and roll beat." Ozzie himself even got in the act, singing "Baby I'm Sorry," from the first album, right on the heels of Ricky's own performance of the song. The songs helped draw a new audience to the TV show, and the exposure helped sell the records. Ricky Nelson's star was ablaze.

When Will Thornbury came home that November from serving in the army in Japan, he found the neighborhood drastically changed. Girls in cars cruised the once-peaceful dead-end street night and day. Harriet had installed a forbidding fence around the Nelsons' house. "This heretofore had been a relatively quiet residential street," he said. "But it got to be really nuts."

In March 1958, with the release of his third single on Imperial, Ricky Nelson firmly planted himself in the forefront of contemporary rock & roll. The double-sided hit of "Believe What You Say" and "My Bucket's Got a Hole in It" easily equaled the best of the Southern rockabilly. Chudd rushed the record out so fast, he didn't take the time for the Jordanaires to add background vocals to the 45 r.p.m. version of "Believe What You Say." Their vocals, recorded later in Nashville, appeared only on the album version. The record hit the stores literally within a few days of being recorded.

Written by Dorsey and Johnny Burnette, "Believe What You Say" drove on furious, stinging guitar bursts played by James Burton, taking over solo guitar chores for the first time. This was also the first session where Burton introduced his famous "slinky" strings, attaching to his guitar lighter-gauge banjo strings that bend more easily than thicker guitar strings. Burton pealed off these bent notes in staccato clusters, sprayed out of the rhythm track like fire from a machine gun.

Ricky lifted "My Bucket's Got a Hole in It" directly from an obscure Sun Records single by Sonny Burgess, which was brand new when Ricky recorded his version. He used to haunt the record bins at Wallich's Music City in Hollywood for hours at a time, spinning sides in the listening booths and picking up virtually everything he could find on the yellow Sun label. Burton supplied a bristling, bluesy guitar break, and Bunny Robyn gave both tracks a taut, powerful feel.

Futhermore, Ricky came up with the strongest vocal performances of his career for the two songs. In less than a year, he moved from the tentative, whimpering vocal on "I'm Walkin'" to a full-blooded delivery where he had found his own natural and distinctive style. No longer did his brand of California rockabilly walk three paces behind its Memphis counterpart.

Both sides charged up the charts, and "Believe What You Say" gave him his fourth straight top-ten listing. Buckets of every shape and size began to arrive in the mail from fans, much as Graceland was swamped with stuffed toy bears after Elvis recorded his song "Teddy Bear."

Sharon Sheeley grew up in Newport Beach, and she and her younger sister, Mary Jo, were rock & roll–crazy teens. They finagled a meeting with Elvis himself when he stayed at the Knickerbocker Hotel during his Pan Pacific engagement. Next, sixteen-year-old Sharon set her sights on meeting Ricky Nelson. She knew where the Nelsons' weekend home was in nearby Laguna Beach, and she and her sister drove down there one afternoon.

"They lived in a cul-de-sac," said Sharon. "I pulled around the corner and stalled the car. All of a sudden the door opened. Ricky Nelson walked out tossing a football, just like on 'Ozzie and Harriet.' My sister dove under the seat. 'Don't even say I'm here,' she said. He said, 'Is there a problem?' 'Yeah, the car won't start,' I said. He fell for it just like that. Ricky Nelson was the same age I was. He was more famous, but he wasn't any smarter."

He invited the two girls inside. Glen Larson was visiting, and the four went upstairs to play records. Rick's two current favorites were "Great Balls of Fire" by Jerry Lee Lewis and "Bye Bye Love" by the Everly Brothers, and they played them over and over. Sharon and Ricky agreed that the two Everlys sang so high, they must really be sisters.

So, when the Everly Brothers arrived in Los Angeles on a package bill of various rock & roll stars a few weeks later, Sharon and her sister had to go. The show was sold out, so they couldn't get seats. But while they were hanging around the backstage entrance, rhythm & blues vocalist LaVern Baker beckoned to Sharon and pointed to the Everly Brothers. "The cute one wants to talk to you," she told Sharon, indicating Don Everly. "Tell him to come over here," said Sharon.

They didn't get a chance to do more than chat that night, but Don kept in touch in the coming weeks, calling long distance, and when the brothers headed to San Francisco for a concert, Sharon took a Greyhound bus for the ten-hour ride to the Bay Area, dressed up for a big date. Don greeted her backstage at the concert with a warm hug. "I don't believe you're here," he told her.

"Get your hands off her," shrieked his brother Phil. "Don't you know he's a married man?" he asked Sharon.

"Are you married?" she asked Don.

"Sort of," he mumbled.

With that, Don threw a minor fit and ordered everyone, including Paul Anka, out of the dressing room. Phil, Anka, and Sharon walked around the streets of San Francisco until it was time to board the next bus back to Los Angeles. As the Greyhound rumbled down the highway, she extracted an old air mail envelope from her purse and began to scribble: "I used to play around with hearts, hasten at their call . . ."

The next time she saw Ricky, she told him that a friend of her father's had written a song, that she didn't think it was all that good, but Elvis had heard it and was planning to record it. Of course, Ricky wanted to hear it too.

In rehearsal, Burton suggested slowing the tempo into a soft shuffle, and the pieces began to fall into place. It wasn't until after the song had been recorded that Sharon admitted to Ricky she really wrote it.

The number was recorded for his second album, *Ricky Nelson*, and when the LP was released in June, radio stations began giving the track a whirl. The only other rock & roll artist whose album cuts ever got radio airplay was Elvis, and Lew Chudd wanted to capitalize on the exposure and release the song as a single. Rick didn't like the idea—the song wasn't rock & roll enough to suit his taste—but Imperial went ahead and put it out. Rick did, however, exercise his contractual rights of approval of artwork, and a picture sleeve was never manufactured for the single.

"Poor Little Fool" finally earned Ricky Nelson his first number-one single.

5

Teenage Idol

RICK NELSON TURNED EIGHTEEN in Tucson, Arizona, on the set of *Rio Bravo*. For his birthday, costar John Wayne gave him a three-hundred-pound bag of steer manure. The contents were dumped unceremoniously on the ground, and Wayne and Dean Martin grabbed hold of the birthday boy and tossed him on top.

At an age when most young men were wondering what they would do with their lives, making plans to enter college or beginning to think about work, Ricky already had a career and was perched on the pinnacle of success. With "Poor Little Fool" his fifth consecutive top-ten hit and Elvis getting drafted earlier in 1958, Ricky Nelson stood alone as the leading teen idol in the country, and *Rio Bravo* director Howard Hawks later estimated that Ricky's presence alone meant an additional million dollars at the box office for his western. Hawks called working with Wayne and Martin the chance of a lifetime for a young actor like Ricky.

"That's why Ozzie and Harriet okayed his working in a film

at this time," he told gossip columnist Hedda Hopper. "Young singers come up so quickly that I was amazed to learn this boy earns $30,000 a performance over weekends and is moving up where Elvis Presley used to be." He also promised the film would feature Ricky singing, if only casually. "Cowboy songs," he said, "good news for his fans."

Hawks, of course, was already a Hollywood legend, the director responsible for such certified film classics as *The Big Sleep, Bringing Up Baby, To Have and Have Not,* and *Red River.* Hawks, however, was not the kind of director to sculpt a performance out of his actors. "He wanted you to be original, so if he showed you what to do it wouldn't be original. But yet he knew what he wanted," said actress Angie Dickinson, who got her first major movie role in *Rio Bravo.*

This big break didn't mean that Ricky took the assignment all that seriously. When David arrived on the set, after Ricky had been on location for a couple of weeks already but had not shot any of his part yet, he found Rick about ten pounds heavier from eating spaghetti at the motel's restaurant. Rick had been spending all his time riding horses and practicing his quick draw and hadn't even looked at the script. On the TV show, Ricky hated to learn his lines, leaving it for the last possible moment and often pasting bits of the script around the set for easy reference. David kept him up all night reading the film script aloud to him.

"I was on one bed and he was on the other," David said, "and I had my foot on his bed. Every time he would fall asleep, I would kick him. It was a big script. I know why he didn't read it. He figured he knew what scene was coming up the next day, and he was a real quick study. But I thought since this was his first big picture, it was important that he know what was going on. Howard Hawks and John Wayne were heavy duty."

"There weren't many lines," said Angie Dickinson. "Hawks

movies were very easy deliveries, which fit right into Rick's style. He was a Taurus and that's an easy, slow style, and he brought that to it. But it was not a lot of talk."

At last, Ricky did not have to be the cute younger brother. His character, a young wagon-train guard called Colorado, hardly qualified as a radical departure for the TV star, but any change was welcome. "The fellow I play in the picture kills six or eight people," he told a reporter on the set. "There's not much of that sort of thing in 'The Adventures of Ozzie and Harriet.' "

John Wayne took to Ricky, personally supervising the selection of a cowboy hat for Rick. He would fit one on Ricky's head, consider it, and reject it by simply sailing it behind his back. As a souvenir of their working together, after the filming finished, Wayne gave Ricky the hat he wore for one of his most famous roles in *Stagecoach*.

The film used old Tucson as a set, which drew large crowds as a tourist attraction even without Wayne, Martin, and Ricky, three sex symbols who spanned a lot of ages in appeal. Large crowds watched the filming, and it was difficult to keep the teenage girls quiet during Ricky's scenes.

His big scene came when three bad guys got the drop on John Wayne. Angie Dickinson threw a flowerpot through a window to distract them, while Ricky tossed Wayne a carbine and the two of them blasted away. With all the time Rick spent practicing his quick draw and his lightning-fast natural reflexes, he laid down a one-man fusillade before the rifle even made it into Wayne's hands. "Take it easy, will you Rick," he shouted. "There are only three guys there. Leave one of them for me."

With May temperatures as high as 130 degrees, the cast and crew retreated to air-conditioned trailers as often as possible, with Wayne and Martin spelling the inevitable waits between takes with long games of chess. Rick brought Joe Byrne down to Tucson for the month of location shooting. The two of them got invited to participate in a charity demolition derby run by a local radio station, exactly the sort of dangerous sport Rick couldn't resist. They kept the whole thing a secret from the movie company, in case anybody raised any objections, and Rick did his best to remain anonymous. "We looked a little strange before the race," said Byrne, "when everybody's sitting around their cars dressed casually and we're walking around with helmets and visors on."

They made a pact to concentrate on first wiping out the competition before taking on each other. "Of course, in my mind, the first guy I was going to hit was Rick," Byrne said, "and in his mind was the same thing." They took off after each other as soon as the bell rang. The crowd predictably went berserk when the announcer revealed that car number nine was being driven by Ricky Nelson. As soon as somebody else disabled Byrne's car, Ricky hammered down on him. "He knocked me around the track about six times," Byrne said.

Rick emerged the ultimate victor, only to have his car explode in flames as soon as he polished off the final competitor. He scrambled out of his window and hurried to safety. "I said, 'You showboat,' " Byrne said. "He said, 'Showboat? When that thing caught on fire, I was scared to death.' "

Once he returned home from location, Ricky found that David had embarked on an endeavor that upped the stakes in their continuous death-defying thrill seeking, one that would consume David for the next half-dozen years. During David's work on the film, *The Big Circus*, in which he had been cast against type as the psychotic killer, he fell in love with the trapeze. He played the part of a catcher in the movie's trapeze act but left the stunt work to Fay Alexander and Bob Yerkes, circus professionals. David was captivated, almost moonstruck, by the swinging bars. One day during a lunch break, he climbed up into the catch trap forty feet above the ground and immediately froze. Yerkes and Del Graham, technical advisor on the film, rescued him once they returned from lunch. But he kept climbing back up.

Del Graham and his wife, Babs, flyers with an act called the Flying Viennas, agreed to teach David to catch trapeze, and he drove daily out to their practice rigging in Agoura, at the far west end of the San Fernando Valley. Ricky could not be left out, so the Grahams taught him the fundamentals of flying too.

Ozzie, of course, immediately saw the possibilities of using the trapeze act on the show. A complete rigging was set up on a vacant soundstage at General Service, and the boys repaired to the bars on breaks between filming. The trapeze bug never bit Ricky as hard as it did David, but he developed a minor proficiency.

"He learned to do a somersault feet across," said David, "and he used to do what we called a pirouette back. Instead of just a half-turn, instead of leaving the catcher and looking over your shoulder and going for the bar, you do a revolution—like a spin—and then catch the bar. Ricky did that just naturally. That came from ice skating. He could always do an axel on speed skates, not figure skates, which wasn't too easy. So he had a real ability to turn, and it is an ability, believe me."

When the Flying Viennas lost their catcher, the Grahams invited David to join their act for real. Every summer for the next six years, he toured with the circus. He became fascinated with the history of the circus. "To me, show business began with the circus," he said. "I can't sing. I can't tap dance. . . . But I can do this, and I enjoy it."

At six-foot-one and 170 pounds, Ricky hardly made the ideal flyer. "Because we were brothers," said David, "we both took up the strain. But Rick would never have been able to do any real big tricks where you're really coming in hard, because I wouldn't have been able to hold him." Rick learned only two or three stunts, but it was enough for him to make special guest appearances with his brother's act and horn in on David's limelight.

They made several public performances on trapeze around southern California, including a halftime show at the Los Angeles Coliseum during a Rams game. Naturally, Ozzie turned his sons' act into a TV episode, "The Circus," where he went wild with a full-size circus tent, dozens of specialty acts, and hundreds of extras.

Rick went on a spree of indulging his capacity to quickly master the fundamentals of anything that demanded intense coordination and physical ability—bullfighting was next—but rock & roll was the only thing he remained devoted to more than long enough to be able to say he could do it.

He saw his first bullfight in Mexico with John Wayne on a break from shooting *Rio Bravo*. He went to a dude ranch where bullfighting was taught to greenhorns.

"Actually, it was two bull calves in this little ring," he said of his bullfighting experience. "Scared? I felt like my mouth was full of cotton. I didn't make a kill or anything, just a few passes. I don't know how good I was really, but one man there told me that I ought to fight more bulls. Only thing is, I think he was a music critic."

He mounted bull's horns on an old wheelbarrow and would inveigle David to push the wheelbarrow around the backyard, while he practiced with the cape. "I'm learning bullfighting from Luis McManus, an ex-bullfighter," he told the *Los Angeles Times*, "and I'm quite serious about entering the ring. I plan to go to Spain in the next few months, when we take our break on the show, and enter the ring there."

Such grand ambitions were never realized, but Ozzie, of course, managed to make a TV show out of Rick the bull-fighter. "He had a teacher," said Skip Young, "and he used to go to Griffith Park, where they had a very, very tame bull, and he would work with the thing. The guy was a former matador and taught him how to hold the sword and the cape. Most all of the cuts in the show are not Rick, of course. They are stock footage of a bullfighter. But they had the bull's head on the front of a camera truck, and they drove the camera truck right in through his cape."

Then there was the flamenco-guitar flirtation. Rick took lessons from Vincente Gomez, who appeared briefly with him on the bullfighting TV episode. "He would give him his lesson," said James Burton, "then he would give him all his paperwork and tell him, 'Go home and work on this, and the next lesson I want you to perform this for me.' Ricky would go home and mess with it a little bit and put it away. So, the night before the lesson, he would work hours. He would not really study the music part of it; he would get into doing it by ear. He would have it on tape, and he would practice it and get it down by ear. When he would go do the lesson for Vincente, he would say, 'Ahh, very good.' But he knew Ricky was fluffing it off, that he was not really taking care of business on that."

Ricky didn't want to grow his fingernails and throw away his guitar picks—"He wanted to do that for kicks, and he wanted to do the other thing for real," Burton said—and Gomez didn't want to waste his time on a dilettante. The association came to an end before long. "He took a lot of short cuts," allowed Burton. "He was good at that, short cuts."

His parents gave him a quarter horse for his eighteenth birthday, and on the *Rio Bravo* set he met a wrangler about his age named Zeke Budny. He invited him to Hollywood, where he got Budny a job on the TV series and put him in charge of handling his horse. For a while he went riding every day after work but then lost interest in horses. He pursued any interest that struck his fancy, but only rock & roll stayed with him.

Jam sessions would last into the night at Rick's bungalow on the studio grounds, long after Ozzie left for the night. He would poke his head in before going home. "Remember, you have an early call tomorrow, so don't stay up all night," he would remind his son. Rick could also be counted on to whip out his guitar and sing at the frequent parties at David's house. Burton worked with him on his guitar playing.

Rick learned music through on-the-job training. Few musicians have been more successful with fewer skills. But he plunged into his new craft with intense determination. "I think he knew three chords—E, A, and B," said Burton. "It got so ridiculous. It got to where every song he would want to sing in the key of E. He would say, 'If we do it in another key, I won't know what to do.' I said, 'Capo.' " (A capo is a metal bar that attaches to the neck of the guitar and adjusts the key mechanically.)

In addition to Burton and upright bassist Kirkland from the Luman band, Ricky's group included drummer Richie Frost, a jazz musician who had been playing rim shots behind comedian Lenny Bruce when his friend Don Nelson called him about working on the "Ozzie and Harriet" show. "I was a personable sort of a fellow," said Frost, "and I fit the whatever it was that Ozzie was looking for—Ozzie ran things at that stage—and I could play whatever they wanted." Although he was nearly twenty years older than Ricky and the rest of the band, Frost looked younger than his thirty-six years and jumped into the scene, jamming in the bungalow on lunch breaks and after shooting.

Ricky Nelson and Elvis Presley were the only two rock & roll stars of the time considered powerful enough attractions to tour on their own. Package shows featuring as many as a dozen acts on a single bill roamed the tour circuit, but Ricky never went out with supporting acts. Nor did he go out for long, grueling bus tours; everything was first-class on the short five- or six-week tours they did during summers or the quick weekend jaunts while the show was in production.

Traveling could be lonely for Rick. Special security arrangements were required to sneak him in and out of hotels, and he was virtually held prisoner in his hotel room, unable to leave until late in the night or he would be mobbed wherever he went. He always took a suite, shared by road manager Maury Foladare and bodyguards like Jack Ianerelli, from the TV show, or Paul Cameron and Jack Ellena, two former professional football players. He told people later that he was routinely supplied with prostitutes to fend off loneliness.

While James Burton claimed that Foladare served as a kind of chaperon on these tours, other people didn't quite agree. "Maury Foladare?" said Forrest Stewart. "I don't think he was there to keep girls away."

Although they weren't called groupies in those days, some older women could be found waiting around hotels, hoping to make themselves available. "It was nice to know you could just, like, take your pick," said Rick. "But you couldn't touch the real young ones who screamed and drooled on you."

Burton remembered sitting in their hotel rooms, strumming guitars and working on music for hours after the shows. "We'd party as much as we could," Burton said. "Being young kids, we didn't know that you'd have to go to bed to get up and work the show the next day 'cause we were pretty nuts. 'Course we had grown-up people working with us, pretty close to us, keeping an eye on us."

"We'd go out at one or two in the morning," said Joe Byrne, "drive around, stop and get some Cokes. That's about all we would do, drive around. It was not that happy-going."

Screaming fans at concerts posed a threat. As soon as he left the stage, Rick would slather his hair with grease to foil clutching, tearing fingers. Decoy limousines were employed. Joe Byrne remembered one time a zealous fan grabbed Rick right by the balls and didn't let go until Byrne performed a body block on her. Airports were also mob scenes, and as Rick came off the plane in Indianapolis once, somebody's jealous boyfriend scored a direct hit on Ricky with a ripe tomato.

During Labor Day weekend 1958, Ricky broke an attendance record at Atlantic City's Steel Pier, set the previous decade by Frank Sinatra. More than forty-three thousand people showed up for the six shows a day that the band churned out. Crowds were so thick a helicopter had to transport the band to the stage at the end of the pier.

Ricky excited the crowds with his mere presence. He did not speak to audiences, and he added nothing more physical to his performance than closing his eyes while he sang or occasionally bobbing his head to the beat. "His hit songs that were so popular everybody loved," said Burton. "But his performance was not quite as strong as, like, Gene Vincent, who was a crazy rock and roll man. Ricky still brought out enough excitement in huge crowds that they rushed the stage."

Burton remembered a show in San Diego that was stopped because of fans rushing the stage, while Ricky and the band retreated. "He was very shy and very nervous," said Burton. "I know a lot of entertainers feel uncomfortable before they get onstage and then, after they get onstage, they sort of relax. Ricky usually pretty well through the whole show was tense. Even on the television show I think he was insecure. . . . I can't really say he was personally insecure, even though he appeared to be insecure about a lot of things, musically or whatever. He would sing his songs but not show his emotions. It was hard to tell if he was even enjoying the song, the way it was coming off."

The shows raced by at a dizzying clip, one two-minute song after another with a mumbled "thank you" in between. To fill out the allotted half hour onstage, he would add material from Ray Charles or Elvis Presley to his own growing list of hits, occasionally singing "I Got a Woman" or "Loving You." Ear-shattering shrieks from teenage girls all but drowned out the music anyway. "They didn't come to hear him," said Richie Frost. "They came to show their adoration."

If the concerts were somewhat rote recitations without much animation, Ricky did not show strong feelings anywhere. Ozzie took charge of his career and, as with the TV show, closely supervised every detail. If his own schedule precluded Ozzie's joining the tours, he certainly showed up for virtually every recording session and ran them as if he were producing the records. Ricky never objected.

"He was always under control," said engineer Bunny Robyn. "He was very pleasant. I don't think I ever heard a mean word out of him or even a 'shit.' That was the extent of his expression."

His father felt Ricky lacked breath control as a vocalist and insisted that he never sing more than sixteen bars straight through. Rick would record vocals by singing alternate verses, then going back over and filling in the gaps. But Ozzie did not depend on raising his voice or intimidation tactics to get his point across. He needed to do nothing more than make a "suggestion."

"Any suggestions I made," he wrote, "were just that—suggestions."

Jimmie Haskell remembered one of Ozzie's suggestions. Ozzie wanted to use a banjo on one song being recorded, and Haskell went through an elaborate song and dance about how an electric guitar would work just as well. The next day, one of Ozzie's associates called Haskell.

"Jimmie, you have to understand that Ozzie knows a thing or two," he told Haskell. "He was a bandleader for a long time. So when he says something, it's not that he doesn't know what he's saying . . ."

"I understand," Haskell said. "From now on, when Ozzie makes any suggestions, I will understand that that's what he wants."

"That's good, Jimmie," the associate said.

"From that point on, no matter what suggestion Ozzie made, I made sure I followed through," said Haskell.

Buried in the voluminous files of papers pertaining to the 1957 Verve Records suit is a brief one-page document signed by Ozzie and Ricky assigning Ozzie the official role of manager to Ricky, for a fee of ten percent of the earnings. It seems doubtful that Ozzie was trying to chisel a few extra pennies from his son's income but more likely that he was chasing away any wolves who might be hanging around the door. But this document, whose very existence was, thirty years later, a surprise to David and others involved in Ricky's career at this stage, formalized an arrangement everybody understood to be fact anyway.

Ozzie set up publishing companies for Rick, Eric Music and Hilliard Music, that handled the songs he recorded. Songwriters like the Burnettes, Sharon Sheeley, or anyone supplying Rick directly with material were signed up to his publishing companies, allowing Rick to keep half the mechanical royalties. This was a common procedure for big stars like Ricky or Elvis, who also maintained his own publishing arm, even if they didn't write the songs themselves.

He was earning enormous amounts of money, which, of course, he didn't see. "Ricky will gross $150,000 in record royalties in 1957," Imperial owner Lew Chudd said, "and should become a millionaire from records alone." Ozzie bought apartment buildings for his son, made him a major investor in a year-round amusement park called Santa's Village outside Santa Cruz, and continued to salt away the earnings in two separate trust funds, one scheduled to mature at age twenty-one and the other when he turned thirty.

"I never see any of the money," Rick told a reporter. "It all goes in the bank. If I ever need any money, I just ask my parents for some. I have no idea how much I'm making. All I know is that I'm in a 93 percent income bracket."

Recording sessions started early in the evening and could last until near dawn. Pianist Gene Garf, an older man who

worked for many years as musical accompanist to hoofer Ray
Bolger, usually joined the band for record dates. Tunes were
rehearsed in the studio. "They were not arranged at all," said
Garf. "Jimmie would scratch out a part for me, chords. It was
the only time I ever worked that way."

Since the other band members did not read music, Haskell
developed a system of hand signals and flash cards to cue
them to the chord changes. Ozzie used to demonstrate musical ideas for the band on his ukulele.

During the sessions for the second album, Ozzie and Ricky
decided to recut an instrumental track for a country ballad
after the musicians had already dispersed. Burton and Kirkland were found in the parking lot, but Frost and Garf were
already gone. Ricky knew he could handle the drum part, and
nobody had to twist Ozzie's arm to get him to play the piano.

The album mixed Ricky's penchant for Sun Records rockabilly with Ozzie's idea of updated pop. Selections veered
madly from a fiery cover of the Bobby Lee Trammell rocker
"Shirley Lee" and a tough version of the jumping Little Walter
blues song "My Babe" to Ricky weakly warbling "Unchained
Melody." "I don't recall Ricky ever objecting to singing any
song," said Haskell.

However, Ozzie did object to him singing certain songs. Rick
took a liking to the dark Billie Holiday blues tune "Gloomy
Sunday" and actually recorded a version of this unlikely song.
But Ozzie convinced him the song was too downbeat to ever
release, repeating the apocryphal stories about people com-
mitting suicide after hearing it.

If rock & roll once promised him freedom, now it was
beginning to ensnare him. His father moved to control this
end of his life too, almost as soon as Rick stepped out of
singing in the bathroom. If he didn't outwardly resent the
results the always competent Ozzie created, he must have at
least recoiled inwardly at the intrusion. Rock & roll was meant

to be the exclusive province of the young, and not only was Ozzie making public pronouncements about how the music was OK, really just western music with a beat, he had also made Rick's rock & roll into a crucial part of the family TV show. Rick was more locked in than ever, but whatever feelings he may have had, he never showed them.

Friends noticed a distinct change in Rick. No longer the "miniature Jerry Lewis," the brash, skinny kid with the smart lip, he had turned quiet, shy, virtually sullen. He became almost pathologically noncommunicative with strangers. Newspaper interviews tended toward the monosyllabic. Among intimates he retained his dry, quick wit and barbed tongue, but as soon as one person he didn't know entered the scene, he retreated tortoiselike into his shell.

He escaped the pressures by taking long, nocturnal baths, turning on the hot water with his toe when the bath got cold and falling asleep with his guitar lying beside him on the bathroom floor, his skin wrinkled like a prune. He stayed up as late as he could, often falling asleep an hour or two before he was due at the studio, then waking in a rush, cramming a handful of M&M's into his mouth, and learning his lines on the way to the shooting. Often he didn't even bother to learn them but posted crib sheets torn from the script on the backs of doors, in cookie jars, or inside drawers. He would wander into a scene and innocently swing a door open, pull out a drawer, or lift a cookie jar lid and then deliver the lines.

"He was such a good study," said Skip Young, "that he could learn his lines standing there asleep on the set."

Although Ozzie would never embarrass an actor on the show by dressing him down in front of the company—he would generally take people aside and whisper in their ears—this was not a consideration that extended to his sons. He was an exacting director who wanted to hear the dialogue he wrote read back to him precisely as he originally envisioned it.

"He's the only director I've ever seen give a direct line reading," said Bruce Belland.

"It was a kind of repeat-after-me thing," said David.

As affable and easygoing as the character Ozzie created for himself was, the real Ozzie held the reins tightly. Glen Larson of the Four Preps, who later became one of Hollywood's top TV producers, offered some unsolicited advice on a shot once, only to have Ozzie firmly put him down. "I don't need any associate producers here, Glen," he said grimly. Off-camera, Ozzie suffered from facial tics, and Rick would crack up other cast members by contorting his face and mimicking his father as soon as Ozzie turned his back and walked away.

In October 1958 Ricky recorded "Lonesome Town" and "I Got a Feeling," two songs that introduced songwriter Baker Knight. A native of Birmingham, Alabama, Knight would write almost two dozen songs recorded by Rick.

After earning a regional hit back home with his 1957 record "Bring My Cadillac Back," Knight abandoned the music business for Hollywood and a movie career. An agent sent him a plane ticket and, with sixty dollars in his pocket, he headed west. "I got there April 1, 1958—April Fool's Day," said Knight. "That should have told me something right there."

He lost a role in *Please Don't Eat the Daisies*, and no further parts were forthcoming. He was living in an apartment building called the Park Sunset in Hollywood, where Eddie Cochran's manager, Jerry Capehart, also lived. Cochran was a tough Los Angeles rock & roller who made a brief appearance in *The Girl Can't Help It* and was beginning to make some noise with minor hits. He and Knight became friends. Knight, in fact, took a nap rather than help Cochran and Capehart write "Summertime Blues," which turned into Cochran's only top-ten hit later that year. Sharon Sheeley was Eddie Cochran's girlfriend.

"Sharon brought Rick over to the place one day," Knight

recalled, "and it was a funny thing because he was so shy and I was too. I think I had about thirty-six cents left, pennies in a jar. It was like 'Hi. . . . Hi.' Here was this man I'd seen on TV, and I was so star struck I could hardly talk myself. 'You wanna sit down?' 'Yeah.' 'You want a beer?' 'No. Got any songs?' 'Yeah. You want me to play some?' 'Yeah.' "

He had written "Lonesome Town" a couple of weeks earlier while sitting by the pool, thinking of the Everly Brothers. Eddie Cochran sang the demo version for Knight. He played Rick both "Lonesome Town" and "I Got a Feeling" and a few others, and Rick left. Two days later, the record company called Knight and asked him if he would accept a $2,000 advance for the two songs. "I had no problem with that," he said.

Baker Knight was a tragic figure. He didn't know it at the time, but he suffered from agoraphobia, a crippling fear of going outside that doctors knew nothing about at the time. Knight medicated himself with abundant amounts of alcohol, and he developed ulcers. Doctors treated him with drugs. People shunned him as strange and weird, and Knight thought himself mad. He tried suicide. One incident that may have been a suicide attempt by gas ended when Knight lit a cigarette. The explosion nearly blew him up, but he survived. "I was sort of in a daze," he said. "I didn't know what was going on."

"Lonesome Town," a song that Bob Dylan would later perform in concerts as a tribute to Rick, came out of Knight's depression. "It was Hollywood," he said. "I was sitting in the middle of this whole thing. I was broke, didn't know what I was going to do. My manager was giving me a few bucks, keeping me going, paying my rent."

Both "Lonesome Town" and "I Got a Feeling" headed straight into the top ten, but that didn't help. "The ball started rolling for me," he said, "and I got the anxiety. More and more songs. More and more pressure. A lot of shattering things happened. I had no idea what was going on. When. I was crocked, I could get by."

With its stark lyrical imagery and the spare instrumentation of a sole acoustic guitar, "Lonesome Town" sounded like nothing to ever come from Ricky before. He sang the song in the bottom end of his range, his dark vocal wrapped in the billowing harmonies of the Jordanaires. Originally, the song was recorded with a full instrumental track, but Ray Walker of the Jordanaires suggested it might sound better with just an acoustic guitar and it was rerecorded that way.

For some unknown reason, about this time Ozzie decided to go in the studio with his wife and make an Ozzie and Harriet album for Imperial. Using some of the musicians from the TV show and some of Ricky's band, Ozzie and Jimmie Haskell assembled an album of old standards set to a watered-down rock & roll sound. Ozzie wrote "Baby Keep Cuddlin' Me," a ridiculous effort at a rock & roll hit, and Harriet tried "Goody Goody." The very idea was preposterous, and the results were no better. Lew Chudd couldn't have cared—anything to keep Ozzie happy. The album disappeared without a trace after its release, and Ozzie didn't even mention it in his autobiography. Haskell remembered asking Harriet how she liked making the record.

"Jimmie, I have an appointment with the dentist tomorrow," she said. "I'm looking forward to that with more pleasure than I've had doing this entire album."

Ozzie watched his youngest son ascend into the show-business stratosphere. By the end of the year, Rick was unrivaled as the top-selling rock & roll artist of 1958. His popularity built the TV show the biggest audience since its inception. Mobs of frenzied fans swarmed Ricky wherever he went. The money poured into the trust funds. In December he appeared on the cover of *Life* magazine, a media triumph his father never managed despite decades of success in show business.

In March 1959 *Rio Bravo* opened. While Ricky didn't exactly send reviewers scrambling for the thesaurus, he received reasonable notices for his part. According to the *Los Angeles Times*, "Nelson impresses as quiet but efficient." He came by his wooden acting style naturally. Director Hawks, in letting his actors be themselves, allowed Ricky to come across as a slightly withdrawn, somewhat uncomfortable presence, all the more so in contrast to relaxed old hands like John Wayne, Dean Martin, and Walter Brennan.

Hawks kept Ricky in the background and corners of scenes, keeping what could have been a major role to a minimum. Ricky entered the movie as a wagon-train guard who, at first, refused to join the sheriff in his looming battle against an outlaw gang. His defiant independence came off a little weak, but he grew in the part, effectively holding his own in the scenes with Wayne, if not exactly burning up the screen with a smoldering presence.

He and Dean Martin traded lines on "My Rifle, My Pony and Me," a dumb cowboy song, and Ricky sang a brief snatch of an old folk tune, "Cindy," in a jailhouse scene that was obviously imposed on the script as a sop to the real-life stature of the two singing idols. Both those songs were recorded separately by Ricky for a single on Imperial but never released. Ricky convinced Johnny Cash to write a song for him to sing in the movie, but soundtrack composer Dimitri Tiomkin kept strict control of the score and the song never made the final cut.

"I knew Johnny Cash real well back then," said Rick. "I had just made *Rio Bravo* and I was talking to him about the story. I told him that my name was Colorado and I was a gunfighter. He said 'I'll write a song about it' and that is where 'Restless Kid' came in. He wrote it that night and the next morning it was in the mailbox. They didn't use it in the film unfortunately."

"Restless Kid," however, was included on *Ricky Sings Again*, his third Imperial album, also released in March. Fifties rock & roll albums tended to be afterthoughts to hit singles. Only a few ever realized the potential of rock & roll in the long-playing format—the first Elvis Presley album and Buddy Holly's *The Chirpin' Crickets* come to mind—but *Ricky Sings Again* was as good as 1950s rock albums got.

This artistic apex revolved around hit singles like "Lonesome Town," "Believe What You Say" (with the Jordanaires background vocals finally appended), and both songs from a brand-new double-sided hit, "It's Late," a Dorsey Burnette number, and "Never Be Anyone Else But You," another Baker Knight composition. "I almost threw 'Never Be Anyone Else But You' in the wastebasket," said the always self-deprecating Knight.

In addition, Ricky reprised an Elvis Presley number from his Sun Records days, "Trying to Get to You"; an old Hank Williams country tune, "I Can't Help It"; and a fiery Baker Knight rockabilly piece, "You Tear Me Up." The only evidence of Ozzie's hand was the old war-horse "It's All in the Game," a song originally written by Calvin Coolidge's vice president, Charles Dawes, and recorded in 1951 by Tommy Edwards. That 1951 recording had mysteriously reappeared in 1958, when it made it all the way to number one on the charts. Country singer Nat Stuckey and bassist James Kirkland supplied "Be True to Me," and Merle Kilgore's "Old Enough to Love" and "One of These Mornings," another Dorsey Burnette selection, rounded out the album.

Not only did the album smoothly integrate Ricky's rocking predilections with the silkier, ballad-type numbers, but he had clearly finally found his own style. This was not an album of compromises between Ozzie's direction and Ricky's rock & roll. The shifts of mood didn't sound abrupt and unconnected but rather, gave the album color and shading. Each song was suited to his delivery, and he sounded at ease with every one. The accompaniment pulled together behind Ricky almost intuitively after nearly a year and a half of backing him up. Burton sounded especially inspired, establishing the rules for rock guitarists of the future with every bent note and sputtering solo.

Ricky's remarkable transformation from worshipful imitator to worthy member of the elite of rock & roll was complete.

After playing on the single of "It's Late" and "Never Be Anyone Else But You," bassist James Kirkland left the band to work with country star Jim Reeves ("He'll Have to Go"). "He wanted to play country music," said James Burton. "He didn't want to play any more rock and roll. He didn't want to slap that bass anymore. He wanted to play some nice, soft country music." Kirkland was replaced on electric bass by Joe Osborn, who had been an acquaintance of Burton back in Shreveport. Ricky performed "Never Be Anyone Else But You" without the band on the TV show, strumming an acoustic guitar and crooning the sweet love song to a young Tuesday Weld, a girl with a raunchy reputation who also used to show up at parties at David's house.

With the royalties from "Poor Little Fool," Sharon Sheeley moved to her own apartment, a second-floor corner unit in a gabled apartment building on Fountain Avenue in Hollywood, not far from the Nelsons' Camino Palmero place. She shared the three-bedroom place with her sister and Dottie Harmony, a one-time Las Vegas dancer who used to date Elvis. The apartment became a central headquarters for Ricky's rock & roll gang, where he would drink Cokes and strum guitar with people like Sheeley's boyfriend, Eddie Cochran, the Burnettes, Baker Knight, and other less regular members of the crowd, an alternative to hanging out at David's Hollywood hills bachelor pad.

Red West, Elvis's sidekick since their days together in Mem-

Harriet Hilliard and Ozzie Nelson: Stars of the NBC radio
program, which also featured columnist Feg Murray, in a
1938 publicity photo. (NBC)

The Nelson family: Dining out at Hollywood's Brown Derby restaurant with Ricky, seven, and David, eleven, in 1948, before the boys joined their parents' radio show.

The Young Radio Stars: David and Ricky take the mike in 1948, at ages eleven and eight, respectively.

Here Come the Nelsons: After two years of appearing together on radio, the entire family made a movie that translated the show to the big screen in 1951. They're pictured here studying the script on the film set. *(Wide World Photos)*

"The Adventures of Ozzie and Harriet": The caption accompanying
this publicity shot read: "Harriet Hilliard Nelson, David (right), and
Ricky will make their television debut with Ozzie Nelson Friday,
October 3, at 8:00 P.M. EST in 'The Adventures of Ozzie and Harriet'
on ABC-TV."

America's Favorite Family: Gathered around the piano in this 1953 publicity photo are David, Ozzie, Ricky, and Harriet.

The Nelson Boys: Already show-business veterans, David, seventeen, and Ricky, fourteen, began their third year on television in 1954.

Teenage star: A pensive-looking Ricky at age sixteen, before he became a rock & roll sensation.

His first girlfriend: With country & western vocalist Lorrie Collins before a date in 1957. *(Courtesy of Lorrie Carnall)*

"I'm Walkin' ": A month after the release of his first record, Ricky and deejay Art Laboe are surrounded by fans in June 1957 at Scrivener's Drive-In, a couple of blocks from Hollywood High School. *(Courtesy of Art Laboe)*

On tour: With the Four Preps, Ricky poses on his way to his first public performance, at the Ohio State Fair in 1957. *(Courtesy of Bruce Belland)*

Screaming fans greet Ricky and his band during Labor Day 1958 at Atlantic City's Steel Pier, where he broke the attendance record previously held by Frank Sinatra. *(Courtesy of Malcolm Leo Productions)*

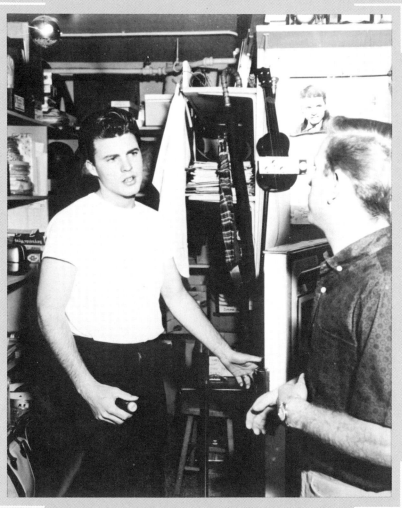

Backstage at General Services: Ricky and his stand-in and friend, Joe Byrne, 1958.

Rio Bravo: On the film set with John Wayne, Dean Martin, and director Howard Hawks in May 1958. *(Warner Brothers)*

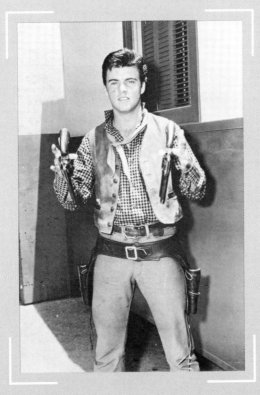

The Colorado Kid: Practicing his fast draw, 1958. *(Warner Brothers)*

The flamenco fling: Ricky practices the nylon-string guitar during a break from shooting the TV show, 1958.

Bullfighter: In costume for the episode "Ricky the Matador," 1958.

The trapeze act: Ricky and David ready to film their part in the episode "The Circus," 1958.

As minstrels, Zeke Budny, Rick, and Skip Young, 1959.

With songwriter Sharon Sheeley, the day after Zeke Budny died and the first time he saw Sharon since she was in the car crash that killed her fiancé, Eddie Cochran, in England, 1960. Cochran's ring is still around her neck. *(Courtesy of Sharon Sheeley)*

As ensign Thomas Hansen in *The Wackiest Ship in the Army*, 1960. *(Columbia Pictures)*

With costar Jack Lemmon in *The Wackiest Ship in the Army*, 1960. *(Columbia Pictures)*

Rick's twenty-first birthday: Celebrating with starlets
Roberta Shore, Sharyn Hillyer, and Judy Crowder,
1961. *(UPI)*

Engaged to Kristin Harmon, daughter of
sportscaster Tom Harmon, December 26,
1962. *(AP)*

phis, dropped over one night and invited Ricky and Joe Byrne
to join Elvis at a party. They found Elvis in the kitchen and
talked about music, movies, and the TV show. Elvis told Rick
how much he liked the episode where Harriet ended up
taking off on a motorcycle and was surprised and delighted to
learn that Byrne had doubled Harriet for that shot.

As a bona fide member of rock & roll's royalty, Ricky was a
welcome visitor to any traveling musician. He met Buddy
Holly. Sheeley took him to the Hollywood Hawaiian, where the
Everly Brothers were staying, and they struck up a friendship.
When they went to a party at the Knickerbocker suite occu-
pied by Jerry Lee Lewis and saw the crazed pianist taking a
piss in the corner of the room, Rick got turned off and left
before introductions were made.

Rick greatly admired Eddie Cochran. Cochran was a skilled
guitarist, a sensational performer, a songwriter, and a confident, rough-and-tumble rocker—all things Rick wasn't. Eddie
liked Rick, without admiring his music all that much, and was
somewhat jealous of Rick's easy success. "There may have
been a little envy on both sides," suggested Baker Knight.

James Burton remembered picking up Cochran and his
buddy Gene Vincent, another wild rocker, at the Knickerbocker Hotel on motorcycles owned by Byrne and David and
cruising in the Hollywood hills. Cochran kept taking slugs out
of a flask of liquor he carried in his sport-coat pocket.

Sheeley went with Ricky once to visit Cochran's manager,
Jerry Capehart, and they parked in back of the apartment
building in spaces reserved for tenant parking only. When
they came back, a police car had pulled up, and a cop was
looking over Rick's Plymouth Fury. "Is this your car?" he
asked. Rick told Sharon, "When I say jump, jump." He hauled
off and slugged the cop in the stomach, doubling him over,
jumped in his car, and raced back to his home—"as if the cop
wouldn't know who he was," said Sheeley. They dashed in the

back door and hid behind a refrigerator when they heard the front doorbell ring. "I heard that immortal voice," said Sheeley. " 'Son, can I speak with you for a moment?' "

But Ricky rarely displayed even a trace of anger, let alone engaged in violent incidents like that. He maintained a placid, calm demeanor with an eerie consistency. His friends strained their memories to recall him so much as raising his voice. Certainly, he never displayed the kind of volatile tempers the Burnettes did.

Rick was present at Sheeley's apartment for an incident whose exact details have disappeared into the fog of memories thirty years later, but the basic story remains the same from all the people who were there. It was a hot afternoon in the late summer, and the apartment's downstairs door was open. Visiting Sheeley and her roommates along with Rick were the Burnettes, Eddie Cochran, Baker Knight, an aspiring record producer named Nik Venet, and his brother, Ted.

Off the street walked a man with a knife. He may have been an escaped mental patient. Nobody's memory is too clear on the man's identity, and police reports were never filed on the matter. "I'm here to stab someone," the man said, stepping toward Rick. He got no closer, as both Burnettes tackled him and all three tumbled down the stairs in a tangle. In the fall, the man cut his own arm with the penknife he had been brandishing, and there was blood all over the steps.

Downstairs, another young hustler who was living with Ted Venet at the time, Kim Fowley, was on the scene. Fowley would later become a notorious record producer and Hollywood music-business gadfly, but at this stage he was a starving young musician whose father had played Doc Holliday on the TV series "The Life and Legend of Wyatt Earp." Hoping to pick up a few bucks, Fowley alerted the newspapers, which caused a scramble upstairs. None of the ascendant rock & roll stars needed this kind of publicity, and Sheeley and her roommates frantically hid people around the apartment, pushing Ricky out the back door and urging him to beat it home. He stuck his head back in the door for one parting shot.

"At times like this," he said, "I wish my name was Pete Smith."

Tiny Dottie Harmony, one of Sheeley's roommates, remembered being so incensed at Fowley's precipitous action that she later marched down to the apartment he shared with Ted Venet, stood on a carton so she could reach, and punched him in the nose. Fowley himself denied anybody ever hit him.

"Ricky, because of the pressure put upon him by his dad, drifted to the dark side of life," said Forrest Stewart. "Not that Ricky Nelson was a person of excesses, because the drugs and the alcohol that he did when I was around were very light. He introduced me to marijuana. I was terrified. I tried it only because it was him.

"It was at his house. When he was doing things like that, it wasn't something that he looked forward to regularly. It was once a month or whenever it happened to be there. He didn't go out and buy it.

"We went to see some musicians. There was a black bass player in this jazz band. Ricky was talking to these guys in street hep-talk. I couldn't even follow the conversation. 'Wanna go back for a touch?' These guys were talking like that. Musicians like these were smoking that stuff all the time.

"There was no cocaine when I was around. That was not a deal. Although I didn't know them, there were words around about drug use and so forth. I could never picture him as a heavy drug user. He was not really a compulsive type of personality. But he did drift toward what I call the dark side of life."

Joe Byrne confirmed that Ricky experimented with smoking pot. "We all did," he said. On the other hand, Byrne said, Ricky didn't touch anything harder. "He knew that stuff was deadly.

He never messed around with that shit. It was scary, and he had too much to lose. We'd see all these guys coming to our houses and they'd be all fucked up. I threw 'em out."

David gave up his Hollywood hills house when he entered the national guard for eight weeks of basic training. "When I came home," he said, "Mom had moved me out of my leased house, and she had found another house, leased it for me, and actually moved Rick into the house with me. She moved Rick in much to my chagrin because we were still in different groups. I had my friends, and Rick had his friends. That's when we started to become close friends."

At first, it was far from a match. David liked things neat, and Rick couldn't care less. He moved in with a massive wardrobe and a beagle, and David couldn't help but be dismayed by Rick's habits. Rick nicknamed him "mother." "He would take off his clothes," said David, "and they'd stay in one lump. I'd ask him to go out and get something for dinner, and he'd come back with bonbons and a case of Coke. He lived on cherry cough drops for years."

It was at David's that Rick first met Leslie Petit. He dated an enormous number of pretty girls after Lorrie Collins but shied away from anything steady. He liked wholesome, clean-cut women and could be seen around town on occasion with freshly scrubbed starlets like Yvonne Lime or what David called "the actress of the month." The TV show always provided a fresh pool of talent. For a while he saw actress Venetia Stevenson, who went out with David first and, after seeing Rick some, went back to dating David. "He was never real serious about girls," said James Burton. "Just Lorrie Collins and Leslie Petit."

"She was the love of his life," said Sharon Sheeley, who became quite close to Petit. "A wonderful girl," said Joe Byrne. "Really the first free-form kind of spirit-waif-gal I ever met and I think Rick too. I think she pushed a button in Rick that I don't think any other girl did. He was very joyous around her.

She was not threatening. She didn't want anything. She wanted to be with him. She really treated him nice. She was very sexy and very funny. They could just go and do nothing, and that was absolutely fine. Rick loved that."

As Sheeley related it, the Leslie Petit story could have come out of the pages of a sordid magazine of the era. Her parents abandoned her in Greenwich Village when she was a young teenager. She hooked up with an older lesbian, who initiated her into the pleasures of same-sex relationships, as well as allegedly introduced her to heroin and prostitution. Actor Dennis Hopper was apparently the person who met her in New York and brought her to Hollywood, according to Sheeley.

"She was kind of a beatnik," said Forrest Stewart, "offbeat, way off-center type of a girl. But she was not what I would call a wholesome type of a girl. I'm not trying to say she was a terrible person. There were rumors about her being involved with girls. You can't substantiate any of that stuff, but Ricky told me that. I don't know, maybe that kind of stuff turned him on. I really don't know. He had a relationship with her, but it wasn't the kind where she was showing up for dinner at Ozzie's house. Whenever I saw her, she was always dressed in black. But she had this white hair, this short blonde hair. She was a cute, cute, attractive girl. She was what I mean by the dark side of life. She was definitely from that side of it, the seedy side of life."

But it was David Nelson who first met Leslie. "She was an urchin-about-town that was a strange little girl," said David, "really pretty, like a pixie. She was kind of wacko, to be honest. But really pretty, extraordinarily pretty. It was just a shame she didn't have parents who cared. She was on the street by herself. She had street friends, but she didn't have a place to sleep. She would come over to the house to sleep."

The Sea Witch, favored by Rick and David's crowd, was a restaurant on Sunset Boulevard next to Dino's, the genuine site of TV's fictional "77 Sunset Strip." Baker Knight met his future wife, Dorothy Petty, when she was working as a waitress at the Sea Witch. David spotted Leslie there one night and bought her a drink. "From that she came over to the house," he said. "We invited her to a couple of parties with her girlfriend."

"Only bad rub of that," said Joe Byrne, "that was David's girl. I knew that was a tough one between David and Rick. Rick came to me and said, 'Leslie is really coming on.' And Leslie did. And David was nuts about her. She was fine. She was cute and sexy and just this free spirit, just this great, great girl. He said, 'I really like her, and we really have fun.' It became really obvious. I told David, 'You see what's happening?' and he said, 'Yeah, he wins again.' "

The first time Sheeley laid eyes on Leslie she answered David's door wearing nothing more than bikini underwear. Sheeley took Leslie to live with her after Rick entered the picture. She was still using heroin, although Rick didn't know it. "The heroin I knew about," said Joe Byrne. "Rick never did. I damn near told her I'd take her head off if she exposed herself in that respect."

Leslie was a wild doe, a sprightly, unsophisticated young lady whom Sheeley had to show how to walk in high-heeled shoes. She was not someone Rick took on his arm to a movie premiere with his family. She was someone he went to in the dark of the night. "He sort of hid her," said Baker Knight. "You never saw her."

He never knew what happened to her. She just disappeared. Byrne said Rick talked about hiring detectives to find her but never did. Sheeley said she became pregnant with Rick's child and had an abortion without telling him. Sheeley nursed her through the bloody aftermath of the illegal operation. The last Sheeley heard she got married and went off to live in Mexico. Rick spent the rest of his life wondering what became of Leslie Petit.

6
Travelin' Man

SO MANY LIMOUSINES PULLED UP at the public park on Beverly Glen Boulevard above Sunset Boulevard that, according to one of the participants, "It looked like a meeting of the Mafia." In April 1960, after leaving the army a month earlier, Elvis took nine of his Memphis buddies and moved to Los Angeles, where he rented a Bel-Air mansion and began filming *G.I. Blues*.

They formed a football team and began trouncing all comers at Sunday afternoon games in that park. Some brutal physical specimens—like Lamar Fike, Red West, and Sonny West—belonged to the entourage, and although the games were nominally touch football, Elvis's crew played to win. Eventually they challenged Ricky. What occurred must be one of the great heretofore unrecorded clashes in rock & roll history.

Of course, football players could always be found around the TV show and Forrest Stewart went to UCLA on an athletic scholarship, so raising a competitive team proved no problem for Rick. Future all-pro Mike Haffner was a fraternity brother

117

of Stewart, and he recruited a USC player named Kent McWhirter. Jim Stacy, who had worked on the TV show for a couple of years, played ball. Dick Allen, Mitch Dimkitch, and Frank McCari from UCLA signed up, and the game was set for the following week.

A crowd of several hundred, mostly female, onlookers gathered. Skip Young showed up, and Pat Boone, whose team had been previously thrashed by the Elvis squad, watched from the sidelines. Ricky's team all wore blue jeans and T-shirts, but Elvis's guys had jerseys with numbers. Only Elvis wore a helmet. His face was too important to risk injury. The opening kickoff set the tone of the game.

"Kent McWhirter was an eighteen-year-old kid who weighed 240 pounds," said Forrest Stewart. "He was solid muscle, just a big, raw kid." He would become one of Rick's closest lifelong friends and, after changing his name to Kent McCord, would move from bit parts on the "Ozzie and Harriet" show to costarring for seven years with Martin Milner on TV's "Adam 12."

"I hear this tremendous noise on the kickoff," said Stewart, "and I look around. Kent McCord had hit Red West and knocked him cold. He was out. He hit him so hard, he was just lying on the ground. All the guys on their team looked over. This indestructible Red West was lying on the ground, and we immediately had a big advantage."

The game lasted five hours. Stewart racked himself up against a tree catching a pass, skinning the whole right side of his body. Elvis got a bloody nose, helmet or not. "It turned into a bloodbath," said one of the players. The Presley team never caught up after the first touchdown; the Southern boys were humbled by the Hollywood upstarts. But everyone made peace at the party at Elvis's mansion that night, and the football games continued sporadically. Ricky even enlisted the McKeever twins, gruesome USC linemen, for one of the matches.

These were high times for Ricky. He was a famous bachelor living with his brother in the Hollywood hills, surrounded by beautiful women, friends who worked on the TV show, and good times. For the 1960 season, David managed on television what he never could in real life and graduated from college. On the show he went to work as a clerk for a law firm while Rick took over as the show's resident college student, living in the fraternity house vacated by David and populated by a group of good-looking guys who were his friends, on-camera and off. "It was kind of a fraternity away from college," said David.

Taking a couple of the fraternity brothers along, the young star took two trips to Hawaii during the first half of 1960 to film *The Wackiest Ship in the Army*. Because he had already signed for that part, he had to turn down an offer by John Wayne to appear in *The Alamo*, a role that eventually went to Frankie Avalon. Rick had gone to Hawaii the year before with his family to shoot some commercials for the show's sponsor, Eastman Kodak, and to appear with the band at the Waikiki Shell as part of the statehood celebration. (Hawaii became the fiftieth state that year.)

Harriet hated to fly, so Rick and David tossed a coin and David went to Hawaii with their mother by boat. Rick and Ozzie flew over later, and huge crowds flocked to the airport to greet Ricky. In 1959 the tidal wave of tourism had not yet swept Hawaii, and Waikiki was still Waikiki, where they stayed at the Royal Hawaiian. The two weeks on the beach were the family's first trip together since Europe. Dave and Rick, of course, sampled the native sport of surfing, still largely untried on California shores. The boards were huge pieces of lumber, and the Waikiki waves broke steadily and evenly. "It was almost impossible not to be able to surf," said David.

The commercials featured the boys surfing, as Ozzie and Harriet photographed the action from a catamaran, a tricky shot that took several hours to complete. The four shows at the Waikiki Shell gave his parents their first opportunity to see Rick perform his songs in concert. They stood backstage and watched in amazement as the teenage girls screamed and squealed; it was a spectacle that no amount of warning could have prepared them for.

Without his parents in February the following year, Rick could be a little more uninhibited. Joe Byrne, Skip Young, and, of course, Maury Foladare came along, and again several hundred teens mobbed him at the airport. His costar Jack Lemmon threw a party in his suite with a handful of strippers and plenty of loud music that got them thrown out of the hotel. Lemmon may have been one of the hottest young movie stars in Hollywood at that point, following starring roles in *Some Like It Hot* and *The Apartment*, but it was Ricky's autograph everyone wanted.

Director Richard Murphy started out as a screenwriter of B movies and wrote the remarkable *Panic in the Streets* in 1950. He directed his first feature, *Three Stripes in the Sun*, in 1955 and drew much of the material for his second directorial assignment, *The Wackiest Ship in the Army*, a lightweight adventure-comedy, from his own wartime experience in New Guinea. Rick played Ensign Thomas Hansen, and Ozzie insisted on two things: that Ricky would get to sing (a song was shoehorned into the script) and that there would be "no physical endangerment."

"I had planned a sequence where we picked him up from the boat," said Murphy, "and took him over the navy ship on a hoist. But that just meant we put a stuntman on it and not get close."

Murphy soon found out that Rick had a different idea about physical endangerment from his father. David was passing through the islands at the same time with the trapeze act, and Rick took the company to watch his brother perform.

"They announce the Nelsons," said Murphy, "and I said,

'Jesus, did I hear right?' Three guys come out, Rick, David, and the other guy with the act. I said, 'Holy Christ, the kid is going to do an acrobatic act, and I've got a big day with him tomorrow.' I'm trying to catch his eye and say don't go up there, for Chrissake. He goes up there. The spot goes on Rick, and I'm dying. He swings out and does a flip. David catches him, but it wasn't one of those real professional catches where it looks easy. He slipped a little.

"Rick swings back, flips over, and gets the bar cockeyed and hangs with one hand. He misses with his right hand. It ain't easy to hang with one hand, particularly when you're swinging on a bar, and virtually impossible to chin yourself. The son of a bitch pulls himself up and grabbed with the other hand. He looks down at me and waves. I could have shot him. And we had to double him on the other shot. God."

"He must have passed out," laughed Skip Young, remembering Murphy leaping over the rail and shaking Rick's hand as soon as he touched ground. Joe Byrne captured Murphy's agony on a home-movie camera.

An actor's strike interrupted filming, and the crew and company returned in May to finish the film. There was a sequence planned where Rick would shoot a fifty-caliber gun from the back of the boat at Japanese planes overhead.

"There's no bullets in the gun," complained Rick.

"What the hell did you think we were going to do, fire a fifty-caliber out here?" Murphy said. "You've got to shake the thing, and afterward we'll put in the tracers, special effects."

"You could have got some real bullets to put in this thing," said Rick.

"Tell you what, kid," said Murphy. "You behave yourself, we've got another sequence with the fifty-caliber, and I'll get some real slugs to put in it and you can fire the thing."

Murphy dubbed Rick "Gunner," and when the time came for the second scene with the gun, Murphy got live ammo from the marines and let Rick shoot it off in the Kauai harbor where they were filming. Murphy and Rick shared the same birthday, which they celebrated on the set, and Rick presented the director with a cigarette lighter inscribed "From the Gunner."

Entertainment was a little difficult to come by on the quiet, remote island of Kauai, where the stars stayed at the Cocoa Palms. The hotel featured a daily evening ritual of a runner dashing through the grounds lighting torches as he went, an event always begun with a blast on a conch shell. As soon as the conch shell sounded, the hotel bar stopped serving drinks until the torch lighting was complete. The movie company always hurried to the bar after shooting, trying to get their orders made before the tap was turned off. One night, as the crew crowded into the bar, Rick sneaked out to the conch shell and blasted it himself, much to the displeasure of the thirsty moviemakers and causing considerable confusion for the hotel staff.

"He was not a helluva actor," said Murphy. "But he was so honest that you pretty much believed what he was doing. And likable. Everybody loved him. Jack carried him through a lot of the scenes. I'd see Jack take him aside and tell him this and that. I didn't interfere. I told him he could shoot the god-damned gun if he knew his lines. Jack was so professional. I think a few times he said to Rick, 'Don't fuck around; know your lines when you get here.' "

When the movie was released in February 1961, critics barely noticed Rick, in the face of an expert performance by Jack Lemmon. While Rick did not get tucked away in the corners, as he did in *Rio Bravo*, he supplied little more than a cardboard foil for Lemmon's energetic portrayal of a frustrated skipper given an inexperienced crew and a decrepit boat. The plot revolved around Lemmon transforming the green troops into a crack unit and carrying off a dangerous mission, dropping off an Australian coast watcher behind enemy lines. Rick played an earnest and proper young ensign whose novice status was just another obstacle for Lemmon to overcome.

"Ricky Nelson plays the young ensign interestingly and also sings a tune," noted the *Los Angeles Times*. If he gave the role a somewhat flat and colorless performance, Nelson also did not get the kind of punch lines and comic turns he used to such great effect on his father's TV show. But, again, his mere presence in the cast added substantially to the coffers at the box office, as the film scooped up a cool $6 million in receipts.

During the last year of the decade, the music scene turned a corner and headed away from fundamental rock & roll. "Mack the Knife," by Bobby Darin in his Sinatra suit, took the honors as record of the year, and "American Bandstand" boosted into popularity a succession of clean-scrubbed, smiling faces like Bobby Rydell, Frankie Avalon, Jimmy Clanton, and Fabian, more noteworthy for teen appeal than musical substance. Ironically, it was a wave initiated in no small part by Ricky himself.

But Rick found it increasingly difficult to carve himself a niche in the changing world of rock & roll. His last single of 1959 became the first record he ever released that did not make the top ten. "I Wanna Be Loved" clipped the exact bottom of the top twenty without rising any higher, after nine consecutive top-ten hits. The strutting, finger-snapping Baker Knight blues did not really suit Ricky. The vocal called for a more commanding presence than he could muster, and the stark arrangement posed a severe contrast to the kind of heavily orchestrated rock & roll that was dominating the charts.

In 1960 Rick turned to softer, more syrupy songs like "Young

Emotions," "I'm Not Afraid," and "You Are the Only One" for single releases, which all proved modestly successful. But clearly his impact was diminishing. He also was abandoning the kind of gritty, spunky rockabilly he personally favored for sappy commercial songs with no guts and of dubious artistic value.

"When he was asked to do 'Young Emotions,' " said Jimmie Haskell, "he felt that it was not his style. But Ozzie talked him into it. I put strings on it, which was not his style. If it wasn't rock and roll, he wasn't crazy about it."

Still, on the B side of "You Are the Only One," an inane piece of Baker Knight bubblegum, was a fired-up "Milk Cow Blues," a tough, biting take on one of Elvis's earliest Sun Records sides, Osborn's bass rumbling ominously, Burton squealing licks into the track, and Rick driving the side with an idiomatically perfect vocal. His intuitive feeling for raw, basic rock & roll remained intact, regardless of how out of step the sound was with the commercial conventions of the day.

Songs by Ricky, his last album of the 1950s, largely featured songs from the Burnettes and Baker Knight, although nothing as distinctive as the material on *Ricky Sings Again*. His uncle, Don Nelson, provided an offbeat, late-night blues number, "So Long," that found Rick appropriately wistful and detached. But *More Songs by Ricky*, his only 1960 LP release, foundered under the weight of its brassy orchestrations. There were chirpy girl group background vocals (former Miss America runner-up and future homophobe Anita Bryant was one of the singers) and other such heavy-handed efforts to update his sound. Without his liking it, he moved away from the California rockabilly he had honed to perfection only the year before. A full-color, fold-out poster pandered further to the booming trade in teen idols.

Also that year, Rick released the strangest record of his career, a four-song extra-play 45 called *Ricky Sings Spirituals*. It may have been inspired by Elvis's devotion to gospel music, but it certainly didn't come from his own religious upbringing, which was nonexistent. It may have been one of Ozzie's ideas—Ozzie wrote one of the songs—although Ozzie didn't practice any organized religion. It did include a driving, fervent Baker Knight tune, "Glory Train," that Rick performed convincingly on the TV show, but it was an utter commercial failure and a bizarre, out-of-character footnote to his fifties rock & roll.

Despite an almost two-year absence from the top ten, however, Rick was only one record away from the biggest and best record of his career.

Jerry Fuller left Fort Worth, Texas, in 1959 to find success in the music business in Hollywood. He signed with Challenge Records and managed to get a few singles on local radio stations, but he was not getting rich. He played record hops for gas money and lived on tostadas and beans. He changed apartments every month rather than pay rent he couldn't afford.

"I used to sit at this little park in Hollywood while my wife was at work," he said. "I'd go there about two hours before she was supposed to get off. We had one car, which is a sin in Los Angeles. I was writing—just a pencil and paper, I didn't play guitar then, I'd just hum the melody—a couple of hours before I picked her up."

He would make demo versions of the songs with Dave Burgess, who led a successful instrumental group that also recorded for Challenge, the Champs, named after Gene Autry's horse since Autry owned the record label. Another friend whom Fuller convinced to move to Los Angeles, Glen Campbell, usually helped out. Burgess worked for a publishing company too, and he would show Fuller's songs around town to little or no avail.

Sitting in DeLongpre Park one afternoon, he wrote "Travelin'

Man," with the help of a world atlas, in about twenty minutes.

"I wrote it for Sam Cooke," Fuller said. "I wanted a Sam Cooke record so bad because he was my second favorite singer, the favorite being Nat Cole. We went into the studio the next morning, and I sang it like Sam Cooke. The original demo was just guitar and me pattin' on the back of a guitar. I even put the 'whoa-oh' things in.

"I took it to J. W. Alexander, who was Sam Cooke's manager. Glen was with me. J.W. said, 'I'll listen to it when I get a chance, Jerry, jes' leave it right there.' It was one of those little disc demos, and I left it on his table. Normally, if people didn't like something, after they would listen to it, or whether they heard it or not, they would bend those demos before they tossed them in the garbage can, so they would fit.

"J.W. obviously didn't bend it, but he did hear it because Joe Osborn, who was Rick's bass player, was next door at Imperial Records in Lew Chudd's office picking up his retainer check, and he heard it through the wall. He went next door and said, 'Can I hear that song you just played, the traveling one?' J.W. said 'Yeah, you can have it' and pulled it out of his garbage can and gave it to Joe."

Not knowing what happened to his demo for Sam Cooke, Fuller fielded a phone call a few days after Osborn found the song.

"Is this Jerry Fuller?" a voice asked. "Rick wants to know if you have some more songs."

"Rick who?" asked Fuller.

"Rick Nelson—this is Joe Osborn. Rick Nelson cut your song," he said.

"Which one?" said Fuller.

" 'Travelin','" he said and explained how he got the song.

"Yeah, I got some more songs," answered Fuller.

Rick also liked the background vocals on the demo, and Fuller, Burgess, Campbell, and Rick himself singing the low parts replaced the Jordanaires as his harmony vocal group on future sessions. They even put out a couple of records as a quartet, released pseudonymously as the Fleas and the Trophies.

The other side of the single came from a New York–based songwriter just starting his own recording career named Gene Pitney. Pitney's demo version of "Hello Mary Lou" didn't sport the sleek sound of Rick's master, but it did feature the cowbell part that figured so prominently in Rick's arrangement. Pitney's publisher, Aaron Schroeder, nominally a New Yorker with an office in the old Irving Berlin building on Broadway, also kept a West Coast office on Sunset Boulevard and got to know both Ozzie and Rick on the tennis courts. Schroeder got Pitney's demo to Rick. "I thought for sure," said Schroeder, "it would be a perfect marriage of song and artist. Casting a performer for a song is like casting an actor for a part in a movie."

Ozzie was concerned that because Pitney was already signed for publishing, they wouldn't be able to get the publishing for Rick—Fuller was already committed to another publisher too, although Ozzie negotiated for a percentage of the publishing to that song—but Rick insisted on doing the song anyway.

"Hello Mary Lou" proved to be a relatively complex recording for the period. Jimmie Haskell linked two separate two-track machines to facilitate overdubbing, and the final master ended up with seven generations of recording on the tape, somewhat muting the bubbling percussive undercurrent of the track. Rick sang a flawless high harmony against his own lead vocal on the choruses. Ozzie drove home at three o'clock in the morning to get his four-string guitar and return to the studio, so he could overdub a tenor guitar part to brighten the top end. The production brilliantly captured Rick in a rhythmic setting that gave the record an irresistible, incandescent appeal from the first note to the cold ending.

It turned out to be probably the finest single record of his

career and sold more than six million copies. Both sides—
"Hello Mary Lou" and "Travelin' Man," which went all the way
to number one—made it into the top ten within weeks of the
April 1961 release.

Ozzie unconsciously invented the conceptual music video
in the process. Instead of having Rick and the band simply
stand up and sing the song on the TV program, Ozzie went to
work in the editing room and superimposed some stock trav-
elogue footage over Rick's face as he sang "Travelin' Man," a
rudimentary model of music videos twenty years before they
exploded on the music scene.

"Somebody from Rick's office had called me and told me it
was going to be on," said Jerry Fuller. "I was visiting back
home, and I said, 'We gotta watch "Ozzie and Harriet." ' We
turned it on, and, at the end of the show, there it was. It had
nothing to do with the show. It just went into that. It was the
greatest thing that ever happened to me at that time. I was
really excited. They kept playing it and playing it. What a tool.
I guess they found out. Rick Nelson must have been the first
one to show what a tool TV can be to sell records."

And what a tool hit records can be to sell a TV show. The
ten-year contract with ABC expired in 1959, and, thanks to
rock & roll and Ricky, the show was renewed for another five
years. David was responsible for finding Joe Flynn, the actor
who was cast as his boss at the law firm. Flynn later played the
beleaguered Captain Binghamton in "McHale's Navy." His
character on "Ozzie and Harriet" was named Don Kelley, after
Ozzie's real-life lawyer, and his secretary was played by Connie Harper, Ozzie's real-life secretary, who would do her off-
camera typing on-camera. Originally hired to supervise Rick's
fan mail and fan-club activities, Harper, who later became Don
Nelson's second wife, also ended up serving as a screen between Rick and the outside world.

"She was a real bitch," said Baker Knight, who also remembered that his strange behavior kept him excluded from the Nelsons' inner circle, no matter how many of his songs Rick recorded. "They held me at arm's length," he said.

Rick's fraternity brothers were played by his friends. Either they were friends who got jobs on the show or became friends after joining the cast, but people like Joe Byrne, Zeke Budny, Karl Kindberg, Jim Stacy, Jimmy Hawkins, Skip Young, and others could be commonly found off the set at Rick and David's house. Young even moved in with them for a while.

Budny died in a tragic boating accident with Skip Young in November 1960. The two actors and their dates took a day trip to Catalina Island on Young's beloved twenty-two-foot cabin cruiser. The ship ran aground and sank in rough weather on the return trip in the afternoon. Young alerted the Coast Guard and had everybody strap on life jackets. He and his girlfriend made it safely to a nearby jetty. They saw Budny's date clinging to the mast of the sinking ship, but Budny was nowhere to be seen. After drying off and getting some coffee, they returned to the dock, where the Coast Guard was.

"It was the most horrible experience of my life," said Young, "to see them carrying Zeke's body off the Coast Guard boat onto the dock. They called an ambulance, but it was too late. He was a good swimmer, but he had evidently gotten tangled in kelp or panicked or something. I don't know what it was. It was just a freak."

Budny was an orphan who became Rick's friend during the location shooting of *Rio Bravo* and came to be a favorite of the whole TV show cast, as well as an especially close friend of Rick. Bruce Belland took over Budny's role in the TV fraternity house. Another friend, Eddie Cochran, had also recently died when his head went through a windshield in a car crash in England. Sharon Sheeley survived that crash but could barely walk when she finally made it home and visited Rick shortly after Budny's death. He was disconsolate, as depressed as she had ever seen him. They talked sadly, Eddie's ring still dangling from a chain around her neck. Eddie and Sharon had plans to be married. It was a sobering encounter with real life for Rick.

In many ways, Rick lived in a bubble. He accepted his enormous celebrity and the privileges that went with it as a birthright. He never developed a star's temperament, but he had no idea what it meant to struggle, to do battle with life's vagaries. Whatever he wanted came to him with deceptive ease. He led a charmed existence and apparently never questioned it or even found anything unusual about how things went for him.

"Rick was simplistic in some ways," said Belland. "He said wonderfully spontaneous, ingenuous things. He came in one morning to the set, and we were getting ready to shoot. He'd been out the night before with a girl that he'd taken out for the first time. Her father said her curfew was one o'clock and something happened, a flat tire or whatever the heck it was, and he didn't get her back until, like, 2:15. The father was furious and chewed his ass out when he brought the girl home. He was waiting at the front door and really let Rick have it.

"The next day, Rick said, 'Can you believe that? We're one hour and fifteen minutes late and he's going crazy on me.'—This is probably a seventeen-year-old girl, right?—'You'd think he'd be honored that I even took her out.'

"He didn't stop and think how that was going to sound. That was a totally ingenuous thing for him to say. 'I'm Rick Nelson.' He didn't mean it bragging at all. It was just a statement of fact."

Joe Byrne remembered cruising around one night with Rick, a couple of girls, and a six-pack of beer, looking for a place to do what teenage boys do with girls and beer. "I own an apartment house around here somewhere," volunteered Rick.

"You do?" said Byrne, and they drove to it. "You got a key?" he asked Rick.

"No," he said, "but I'm sure there are eight or nine of them empty."

"What good is it, Rick?" said Byrne. "We can't bust in there."

"But if we crawled through the window," said Rick, "and we got caught, I could say I owned it."

Ozzie kept strict control over any publicity surrounding his sons. Although fan magazines blared headlines like "Why We're Worried About Ricky Nelson" or "Trouble Among the Nelsons: Ricky Is Leaving Home," the stories were invariably harmless. Any magazine desiring an interview with the Nelsons was forced to select from a short list of approved writers in advance of any cooperation being granted, effectively squelching any untoward journalistic portraits that might besmirch the rosy public image of the family before they started.

"I remember one time Ricky was unhappy," said Jimmie Haskell. "I said, 'That was a beautiful girl I saw you with.' He said, 'I can't see her anymore. She went ahead and talked about me in an article.' I don't remember whether he said damn or not, but I think he did, which was unusual for him. 'I'm not going to be able to see her anymore.' He wasn't as upset about the fact that she had talked about him in the trades as the fact that having done so did not allow him to see her anymore. He just knew that he was in that kind of situation.

"He had been raised to know that there were certain rules that applied to his family. They were on television. They represented the wonderful, sweet, kind, good American family that lived next door and that Ricky could not do anything that would upset that image. He knew those were the rules."

If his family posed something of a repressive influence, Rick no longer engaged in open confrontations with his father, as he did when he was younger. He faced the exceptional burdens of his family with resigned acceptance and did as he was told.

"He'd been on the show for a long time, and it was not his favorite thing to do," said Forrest Stewart. "There was always a bit of friction. But whenever he wanted a new car, Ozzie said OK. When he wanted his Cadillac, he got to buy the Cadillac. If he wanted to go to the beach, he got to go to the beach house. Ozzie gave him a lot of privileges for the one thing he wanted from him. Ozzie tried to be fair about everything. He tried to be real decent. He made a living a certain way, and he wanted to run his television show the way he wanted it to be run. He had to be disciplined about it. So there was a son who didn't want to do it; he had to deal with that the best he could. Ricky had a lot of privileges a lot of young kids didn't have for doing that show. But Rick didn't see it that way."

Quitting the show was out of the question. That would be the same thing as resigning from the family, and Rick had a tremendous bond of loyalty with his family. The TV show also served as the fountainhead of his life, and everything that mattered—his friends, his music, his dates, his fame—poured forth from that source. His enormous popularity made him even more crucial to the show's standing.

In fact, he was once offered a role in a major motion picture that would have required that he miss most of the season's TV filming. ABC informed Ozzie that without Ricky there wouldn't be a show. But Ozzie left the decision in his son's hands, anxiously awaiting word whether his TV show would continue or whether Rick would go off to pursue a more serious acting career of his own. Of course, Ricky stayed with the family show, but not without some agonizing.

Almost two years after moving out of his parents' home, they still controlled the purse. So when Rick turned twenty-one on May 8, 1961, a signal event in any young man's life, the

occasion held more meaning for him than it did for most. Far
from just being able to vote or buy a legal drink (he still liked
Coca-Cola better than any kind of booze), Rick now came into
possession of the first half of the trust fund his parents had
started when he went to work in radio thirteen years earlier.
While newspaper reports at the time estimated the amount
between $250,000 and $500,000, David thought the sum must
have been closer to three or four times that much, given Rick's
record sales and concert dates.

David had become romantically involved with a voluptuous,
red-haired actress named June Blair, and when they got married on May 20 in the chapel at Forest Lawn Memorial Park in
Glendale, Rick was the best man. David first saw June in a
movie called *The Rabbit Trap* and asked his father to give her
a role on their TV show. They dated on and off for more than
a year. Some people felt that Ozzie was not strictly in favor of
the union; nonetheless, the wedding took place, and she
joined the cast of the TV show the next season as Mrs. David
Nelson.

For a honeymoon, David and June took off to northern
California, where David was playing a county fair in Santa
Clara with his trapeze act. Skip Young and his girlfriend came
along, and five days later they too got married in Santa Rosa,
with David and June as witnesses. The two newlywed couples
went to see Andy Williams that night at the Fairmont Hotel in
San Francisco. The trapeze tour continued, with Young serving as ringmaster at these small circuses, culminating with a
week in Anchorage, Alaska.

June Blair was an orphan raised by several foster families,
and the adjustment as a member of the country's most televised family was not an easy one for her. "I felt overwhelmed
coming into such a huge and famous family," she said, "and
then being on public display as the new bride and daughter-
in-law."

Hesitant to work on the TV show, she nevertheless didn't feel comfortable refusing Ozzie's offer. David left the decision up to her. "It proved devastating," she said. "Everything was too fast. I didn't even know David that well. I had to get used to him, used to marriage, used to the family, while being directed by a man I was told to call 'Dad' and working with my new 'mom.' David said I was the only girl who could make the words *mom* and *dad* sound like foreign phrases."

The day David moved out of the house he shared with Rick, Charley Britt moved in. A defensive back who had just finished his rookie season with the L.A. Rams, Britt was an All-American from the University of Georgia. He met Rick the previous year when a mutual date brought him to a party at Rick and David's. Rick invited him to the studio the next day to meet his father. Ozzie knew that a couple of studios had already been sniffing around the handsome All-American and, with his predisposition for football players, offered him a role on the TV series as one of the fraternity brothers.

Life seemed mighty fine to Charley Britt. "I was twenty-one years old," he said, "living in a house on top of the Hollywood hills. I'm rookie of the year for the Rams. He's hanging a gold record on the wall every week, and there's an awful lot of traffic going on."

Charley Britt was a devoted ladies' man. "He used to show up with a bevy of beauties at the house; where they came from I have no idea," said Skip Young. "Where the extras were sitting, he was always over there, trying to cut a few out from the herd."

"It didn't make any difference to me whether they were in the leads or extras," Britt said.

"Charley Britt was great at cocksman's stories," said Bruce Belland, who also now belonged to the TV show fraternity. "He was a great-looking, studsy guy with a suntan and sun-streaked blond hair. An animal. Charley would tell us about some of his adventures between shots on the set."

"Charley had really strong religious views," said Forrest Stewart. "Rick told me this. But then he had all these girls. He had more girlfriends. Charley came into the picture and became real close friends with Ricky and ingratiated himself into the family. Outwardly Charley had everything going for him, but he was just a disaster as far as relationships with women. He couldn't hold a relationship. He was basically a very immature guy but very charming."

"I've been spoiled by girls," said Britt. "When you come up playing football at a major university, you date all the Orange Bowl queens and the homecoming queens. Those were the kind of girls I was used to. When I first moved in with Rick, I told him, 'The quality of the women around the house definitely has to be upgraded.' We immediately took care of that situation, trust me."

Britt found Rick's taste in women ran "heavy on car hops." He devised a plan where the two roommates would scan the *Players' Directory*, a pictorial guide to available actors and actresses, locate promising-looking candidates, and ask Ozzie to invite them in for interviews. "We would just happen to show up when they were coming out of the interview with Ozzie," said Britt. "Ozzie was just great about doing that, plus it was great for the girls because he hired most of them.

"It was a great situation to be in," he said. "I don't think we ever asked anybody out who didn't say yes, unless they were engaged or married or something like that."

But Rick's bachelor days were drawing to an end. Within six months, he began dating Kristin Harmon.

7

Hello Mary Lou

THE LIFE STORY OF TOM HARMON could have come from one of those fictional boy's tales he undoubtedly read as a child, like *Jack Armstrong, All-American Hero*. But in Harmon's case, it actually happened. Football star, war hero, he lived the life young men of his generation dreamed about.

Born in 1919, he was the youngest of six children in a devout Irish-Catholic family in Rensselaer, Indiana. When Tom was five years old, his family moved sixty miles north to the steel town of Gary, where his father got a job as a night watchman in a steel mill. His mother attended mass daily, and his oldest sister, Sally, seventeen years his senior, watched the youngest child.

A top high school football player, he entered the University of Michigan in 1937 and made All-American lists in his junior year. In his senior year, Tom Harmon wrote his name into college-football record books.

He opened the 1940 season against the University of California at Berkeley. He scored twenty-eight points, four touchdowns and four conversions. He ran the opening kickoff back ninety-four yards for a touchdown. He ran a punt back seventy-two yards for another and ran another eighty-six yards from scrimmage for a score. That run so frustrated one Cal Bears fan that he dashed out of the stands and onto the field to try to stop Harmon himself. Harmon even passed for another touchdown. He handled the ball nine times in the first half and gained a total of 274 yards. Michigan won, 41–0. It was his twenty-first birthday.

By the end of the season, he had broken Red Grange's Western Conference record for scoring; won the Heisman, Walter Camp, Maxwell, and Knute Rockne trophies; and been named All-American again and Athlete of the Year by an Associated Press poll. Even before he graduated, Harmon was feted and celebrated, appearing on the Eddie Cantor radio show and lunching at the White House with President Roosevelt.

He went to Hollywood and made a movie, *Harmon of Michigan*, where he met actress Elyse Knox, whom he nicknamed "Butch." The daughter of Frank Knox, the Chicago newspaper publisher who ran for vice president with Republican candidate Alf Landon in 1936, the blonde beauty was trained as an artist and started her professional career as a designer for *Vogue* magazine. Nobody could miss her good looks, however, and she soon found herself working as a prominent Powers fashion model. She made her film debut in 1940 with a movie called *Free, Blonde and Twenty-One*. She went to Chicago with Harmon to watch him play in the Chicago All-Star game.

Harmon began work as a sports announcer for radio station WJR in Detroit. He was drafted by the Chicago Bears for professional football, but before he could actually play, another draft interfered. His local board turned down his plea to be classified 3-A as the sole support of his parents, and one month after being reclassified 1-A, Harmon enlisted in the army air force in November 1941.

In April 1943, Lieutenant Harmon bailed out of his plane—
which he dubbed *Little Butch*—over Brazil, after one wing
broke off during a thunderstorm. He parachuted into a tree
and spent five days tramping through rain forests, swamps,
and jungle. He finally found a French-speaking native who
returned him to civilization in a canoe, and stateside newspapers trumpeted the news of his miraculous rescue. The other
five members of his crew did not survive.

He graduated from fighter-pilot training in Casablanca and
was assigned to China, where he was attached to the notorious Flying Tigers under General Claire L. Chennault. He saw
plenty of action. In November, in a dive-bombing attack on
shipping and river docks over Kiukiang, Harmon's plane—
Little Butch II—was shot down by Japanese Zero fighter
planes. As he, once again, parachuted to safety, he played
dead in his harness as Japanese machine-gun fire burst
around him. Japanese forces destroyed four American planes
that day. Only Harmon survived.

He suffered severe burns on his face and legs, which the
Chinese guerrillas who hid Harmon from the Japanese could
only treat with cold tea, medical supplies being virtually
nonexistent. He lived on a diet of rice for thirty-two days, until
he was able to make his way back to base; once again, news of
his return made headlines across the country. He was
awarded both the Purple Heart and the Silver Star.

Elyse broke their first engagement shortly before she married photographer Paul Hesse, whom she divorced after a brief
marriage in 1943. On Easter 1944, they announced their second engagement and were married on August 26 in St. Mary's
Chapel on the University of Michigan campus, Elyse wearing
a wedding gown made from his parachute. "I think the white
silk will make a beautiful gown," she said, "if we can just
embroider around the bullet holes."

They returned immediately to California, where he served

out the rest of the war and Elyse continued her career in films. Although mostly confined to B movies, she did play the prize-fighter's girlfriend in *Joe Palooka—Champ* and the title role in *The Sweetheart of Sigma Chi*. Around Christmas they announced they were expecting their first child. Sharon Kristin Harmon was born on June 25, 1945.

Three-year-old Sharon appeared on the cover of *Life* magazine, illustrating an article on Hollywood children. "Sharon's pet pastimes," said *Life*, "are her ballet class and hearing any fairy tale into which the character of Hopalong Cassidy can be wangled. Whenever Sharon has a hard job to do, her mother helps out by intoning the magic phrase 'Hocus-pocus shina-kokis stokis,' which seems to work wonders." Inside she was pictured crouched, entranced, next to her mother in front of the window of Uncle Bernie's Menagerie, a Beverly Hills toy store.

By the time she entered Marymount School for Girls, an elite enclave across Sunset Boulevard from the UCLA campus, she was called Kris. She was not academically inclined. "In school, I was a daydreamer," she said. What she had day-dreamed about since age eleven was rock & roll star Ricky Nelson. She once waited in line to get his autograph, only to find he spelled her name "Chris."

The nuns at Marymount ran a strict school. The girls all wore navy blazers and jumpers with a white blouse and blue-and-white saddle shoes. There were mandatory religious classes, and each month, students were required to attend a mass in a white uniform, gloves, and veil. It was a school for the model children of the wealthy and privileged.

Kris's austere father made his children toe the line, while her mother was warm and sweet, loving in an open way Tom Harmon never managed. "In my parents' house," Kris said, "everything was very traditional. My father worked, my mother took care of the children, and she had no identity of her own. It was OK for the rest of us to have opinions, but it was my father's opinions that really counted."

As the oldest child, Kris shouldered a lot of expectations from her rigorously Catholic parents. Like Rick, her instincts told her to rebel, even if the circumstances didn't allow it. "I had a hard time with my mom," she said. "I never cared much about being on the covers of magazines. She did. And cared about her children being there, too. More than once, I was told to pinch my nose so the nostrils wouldn't flare. Her values are different."

At school Kris acted the part, even if she loathed the starchy atmosphere. She was very popular, active in afterschool events and the host of occasional swimming or birthday parties. Her classmates included Mia Farrow and Tisha Sterling, daughter of actor Robert Sterling and actress Ann Sothern. Kris and Tisha were junior cheerleaders together and became lifelong friends. "Kris and I never set foot on that campus again after we graduated," said Sterling.

Football fan Ozzie, of course, knew Kris's father, the famous "Ole 98." Tom Harmon was a successful sportscaster who had worked for CBS since 1950, and he and his wife were members in good standing of the Brentwood rich and famous. The Harmons and Nelsons were friends long before the 1959 basketball game where Kris and Rick were first introduced.

Stage Five Productions won the Studio Basketball League championship that year, and one of their nonleague games was a charity event against the Phi Deltas of USC, who brought along an older ringer, a Phi Delta from Michigan, Tom Harmon. His three children, Mark, Kelly, and Kris, came with him, and Kris was dying to meet her own teen idol, Ricky. She owned all his records, and photographs of him covered her bedroom walls. After the game her father asked Rick if he would mind posing for a photograph with his daughter, and, of course, he obliged. Kris added the photo to the collection on her wall with a handwritten addendum: "Nothing Is Impossible."

Her classmates all knew of her infatuation with Ricky Nelson. "The whole class was in unity with her and Rick," said one.

Kris was just a young girl in her first pair of high-heeled shoes when she attended David's wedding with her family. But about one year later, when the honey-blonde, hazel-eyed, seventeen-year-old beauty was picked as Marymount prom queen of 1962, it was Rick Nelson who showed up on her arm for the grand evening at the swank Cocoanut Grove, as the other girls whispered and giggled, barely able to suppress their awe. "That's all we talked about that night," said one classmate.

Before he started seeing Kris, Rick had never settled on any one girlfriend for more than a short time. But for a handsome and celebrated young bachelor, Rick did not take full advantage of all the opportunities he had. "David was the wild one," said one woman who dated both brothers. And after David got married, it was his Southern swain roommate, Charley Britt, who played compulsive womanizer, not Rick.

"Rick was sexually active," said Forrest Stewart, "not as much as one would think. But he was, and he was discreet about it. It wasn't something he was doing every night. He wasn't a sex-crazed maniac, as some people are. It wasn't the number-one thing in his life, let's put it that way. He'd probably rather sit down, pick a guitar, and play a song. But it was up there on the things he liked to do. It wasn't number one on the marquee. Music, listening to records, playing guitar, being with his friends. It had to be a girl he really liked a lot, that he really cared about and felt comfortable around before he had sexual relationships."

Rick and Charley Britt lived together in the apartment Rick previously shared with David only a couple of months. During

the summer of 1961, while Rick was on the road, his mother
went house hunting for her youngest boy and found a spa-
cious, Spanish-style villa poised on the knoll of a hill above
Nichols Canyon. She called Rick on the road with the news,
and he wanted her to arrange the real-estate purchase for him.

"Will you ask Dad to buy it for me, and I'll pay him back
when I get home?" he asked.

So, sight unseen, Rick and Charley moved into the Zorada
Drive house that would be Rick's home for the next twelve
years. The Nelsons' housekeeper came three times a week,
cleaned up, turned the piles of dirty clothes into fresh laundry
hanging in the closets, and fixed an occasional meal. Music
still consumed Rick, and, if he wasn't staying up all hours
strumming guitar at home, he might be found jamming with
a bunch of other visiting musicians. Dion DiMucci remembered spending an evening at Johnny Mathis's glamorous
home in the Hollywood hills (Howard Hughes built it for one
of his girlfriends), playing old Chuck Berry songs with Rick
thumping conga drums.

Football season did not unduly interrupt the parties for
roommate Charley. The Rams put him in a hotel the Saturday
night before games, but Sunday nights always swung. He often
brought along members of the afternoon's opposing team, like
Baltimore Colts quarterback Johnny Unitas and defensive end
Gino Marchetti. "Friday nights I'm not going to discount
either," said Britt.

Rick continued to periodically become absorbed with athletic challenges. When Britt first moved in, karate had captured Rick's imagination, and he worked on getting his black
belt. He used to practice breaking boards with his bare hands
and kept a box full of gravel beside his bed to toughen his
knuckles, a couple of well-known and especially flashy karate
exercises.

Sharon Sheeley remembered going with Rick, Glen Larson,
and her sister to a drive-in in Rick's convertible. Over his

objections, she insisted on having the top down, and a couple of large football-player types recognized him and sat on the hood of the car. When Rick asked them not to sit on his car, they began bouncing up and down on the fender and making obnoxious comments. He dispatched the recalcitrant behemoths with quick, efficient karate chops and returned to his seat. "Now can I put the top up?" he asked.

But karate was another one of those physical disciplines Rick attacked with a fervor until he developed adequate ability—in this case, getting his black belt—to feel that he had accomplished what he set out to, before his commitment dropped off. His interest in karate was also yet another parallel between his life and Elvis's. And, of course, his karate was featured on an episode of the TV show. But Rick soon lost interest in karate too.

He and Britt got along famously. Britt remembered Rick criticizing his playing—"You missed a tackle"—during a dinner at the house with dates. "I suppose you would have made that tackle?" Charley asked.

When Rick replied that he would have, Charley challenged him to even try to tackle him. The two excused themselves from the table and went into the bedroom. Standing next to a king-size bed, they took turns tackling each other as hard as they could and then returned to the dining room and their dates to finish dinner.

They shared phone numbers from a black address book. As he thumbed the pages, Rick would ask Charley if he was through dating someone, and Charley would answer, "I don't know—what does it say in the margin?"

Charley caught up with Rick in 1961 during the summer tour on his way home from Georgia, where he worked out on his own before Rams training camp. For the fourth straight year, Rick was playing the Steel Pier in Atlantic City and, as always, attracting huge crowds.

"We pulled up on the pier in a limousine," Britt said, "and

Rick's sitting in the middle and I'm on one side. Jack Ellena was sitting on the other side. He was a former Rams football player who would always travel with Rick. Rick, I thought, was always a little bit timid about what I thought were, hey, great situations. All these people are climbing all over the car. I look up and see this gorgeous chick about two people back. She smiles and I move my lips, 'Give me your phone number.' She starts writing it down. Rick has his eyes right on the floorboard. 'Charley, don't open that window,' he said.

" 'I'm going to open it just enough to get that phone number in here,' I said.

" 'Charley, don't open that window,' he said. But you know I did."

Charley joined the fraternity on the TV show, playing a frat brother named Charley. Ozzie liked his actors to portray characters with the same first name, a touch he felt heightened the realism he tried to achieve in the performances. "I wouldn't say it was the greatest acting in the world," said Britt, " 'cause Ozzie wouldn't allow that. If Ozzie caught you acting, you were in trouble." Indeed, Ozzie once severely chastised the mother of a child actor working on the show when he found out she had been sending her son to acting lessons.

"Ozzie, of course, was a football fanatic," said Britt. "He worked a lot of football players as extras and whatever on his show. He said these guys work great because you tell them what to do and they do it. There's no questions asked. All their lives somebody's been calling plays on them and they do it. There was no question about motivation, they just do it."

Ozzie loved to watch Britt play ball and would call him long distance on Rams road trips to talk over the day's game. Britt always graciously accepted Ozzie's armchair quarterbacking. Britt wanted to be an actor, and he was grateful for the contacts and experience Ozzie provided him.

In the summer of 1961, hot on the success of "Travelin'

Man" and "Hello Mary Lou," Imperial released *Rick Is 21,* an album featuring both sides of the smash single. The record company dropped Ricky in favor of Rick as a publicity gimmick. Rick always maintained that either name was OK by him. The LP was built on the strength of the two hit songs, strategically placed, one at the end of each side. Dorsey Burnette supplied "My One Desire," and Jerry Fuller contributed two songs in addition to "Travelin' Man." Dave Burgess of the Champs wrote two songs, including one of the LP's better efforts, "Lucky Star," and Gene Pitney provided a second song, as well as "Hello Mary Lou."

Jimmie Haskell put together what he called a Dixieland combo for "Do You Know What It Means to Miss New Orleans," the old standard Ricky crooned in *The Wackiest Ship in the Army,* which, along with another selection from Ozzie's days as a bandleader, "Stars Fell on Alabama," steer the indifferent album even further away from the sleek, engaging rock & roll sound of the two hits.

But albums barely mattered in the pop music world of the early 1960s. Rick maintained a huge following and took his show outside the United States for the first time in September 1961, when he toured Australia, where gigantic screaming crowds greeted him at the Melbourne airport and packed his appearances. Touring with him down under was Johnny O'Keefe, Australia's first homegrown rock & roll star who, like Rick, first vaulted to success on the strength of television performances.

And Rick's singles continued to sell and score on the charts. "A Wonder Like You," another Jerry Fuller song, repeated the globe-trotting motif of "Travelin' Man," and, backed with the jaunty Dave Burgess composition "Everlovin'," both sides scaled the lists into the top twenty in October 1961. In March 1962 Fuller put Rick back in the top ten with the lightweight but tuneful "Young World," backed by a surprisingly heavy

rock version of the George Gershwin classic "Summertime."
(Four years later, sixties garage band Blues Magoos would cop
the bass and guitar lick from Rick's "Summertime" for the
band's only major hit, "(We Ain't Got) Nuthin' Yet.")

His March 1962 album release, *Album Seven by Rick*, featured the familiar crew of songwriters—Dorsey Burnette,
Jerry Fuller, Dave Burgess, Gene Pitney, Baker Knight, even
Sharon Sheeley—but they had all done better by Rick before,
and it remained for the thunderous "Summertime" to carry
the album.

In August Rick again went top ten with a song he especially
deplored, "Teen Age Idol." Jimmie Haskell said that Rick found
the song egotistical—"Ozzie talked him into it," he said—but
more likely Rick found the yoke of the song's title increasingly
uncomfortable. He unerringly found the top ten again in December with a lithesome, bouncy Fuller song, "It's Up to You."

With a chart record exceeded only by Elvis, Rick hardly
lacked interested suitors as his five-year contract with Imperial drew to a close. Ozzie wanted to sign a new deal that
would guarantee Rick's future for many years and narrowed
his choice to only major labels that he felt certain could
maintain a long-term commitment. Decca Records had the
inside track, since the company was represented by Mickey
Rockford, who had worked in tandem with Sonny Werblin for
a number of years, representing Ozzie in his television deals.
The result was a twenty-year deal for a cool million. Nobody in
the record business had ever signed a pact remotely like the
one Rick inked with Decca Records.

Rick's failure to re-sign with Imperial after selling some $35
million worth of records for the label infuriated Lew Chudd.
He retaliated, according to Haskell, by forking over all the
remaining money he owed Rick in one $4 million lump sum,
most of which, consequently, went straight to Uncle Sam.

Other, more personal matters loomed larger in Rick's life,

however, as he had begun regularly dating the beautiful Kristin Harmon. His parents certainly approved and may have even taken a hand in arranging the match. "It was a Monaco kind of thing," said Sharon Sheeley, referring to the aristocratic pairing of Grace Kelly and Prince Rainer. Forrest Stewart remembered Rick asking his mother to invite Kris to dinner.

"I always felt that was an internal, arranged deal," said Joe Byrne. "Not on the nose that way, but it sure shaped up like that. Kris wanted him. She went after him. Kris is a very clever, very smart girl, and she knew what she wanted and she got it. She just outsmarted him."

Charley Britt also took credit for bringing them together. He first met the Harmons when the entire family visited the Nelson beach house shortly after he and Rick became roommates. Kris's younger sister, Kelly, developed a kind of schoolgirl crush on the handsome football player, and Charley used to spend time with her, horseback riding and such. He couldn't help but notice the attractive older sister and knew she was crazy about Rick. "I told Kris, 'I'm going to work this out,' " he said.

Charley, Rick, and Connie Harper were sitting around her office one afternoon considering the question of whom Rick should take to an upcoming party at his parents' house. Charley was going to be out of town and would miss the event. "Why don't you ask Kris to this party?" Charley asked.

"You mean go pick her up like a date?" said Rick.

"Yeah, pick her up like a date and take her to the thing," said Charley.

"Nah, I couldn't do that," Rick said.

"OK," said Charley, "but when I get back to town, I'm going to take her out."

"You couldn't do that," said Rick. "That would break Kelly's heart."

"C'mon, Kelly's just fourteen years old," Charley said. "She understands it's just like a friend thing. I'm going to take Kris out."

"OK, I'll take her out," he said.

He called sixteen-year-old Kris and took her out. "Neither ever looked at another person," said Britt.

"It was going to be approved by Ozzie, Ozzie's stamp," said Forrest Stewart, "so that was good for Ricky, because he wasn't getting Ozzie's stamp as often as he wanted. Rick was a rebel, but down deep I think he wanted his father's approval and that was a way to get it. She was the daughter of Mr. Football and she was a wholesome, very pretty girl and he liked her. He told me, 'God, if I ever have a child with her, I'd just love her for the rest of my life.' He really had warm feelings about Kris. I could tell he really cared for her. And the whole package. He felt real good about that."

Soon she started showing up at the TV show with Rick. "I heard they were dating before she came by the show," Bruce Belland said. "So there was already a relationship. They were seeing each other. I'm a big fan of irony. When somebody said, 'Have you heard Rick Nelson is dating Kris Harmon?' I said, 'The daughter of an All-American, all-star football player and sportscaster and the gal who played Joe Palooka's sweetheart in the films dates a teenage singing idol, son of the most famous couple in America?' My sense of irony liked that. Of course they're dating. Of course they're going to get married and have beautiful, talented children. Don't you understand, this is Ozzie and fucking Harriet.

"When she came on the show the first time, I do remember—and Rick probably would get embarrassed that I said anything—but he was with her like I had never seen him with anyone else. He was almost reverential in the way he treated her. She obviously to him was not just another chick to date. This was special."

Rick and Kris flew to Chicago with her parents in August to

catch the All-Star game and visit Ozzie and Harriet, who were appearing in the stage production of *Marriage-Go-Round* at the Tent House Theater. That Christmas, at a party at the Nelson home, their engagement was announced. Rick gave Kris a ring that was an exact replica of the one Ozzie gave Harriet—a diamond solitaire in an antique setting. They had been dating less than a year. "I'd had my fill of dates," said Rick in 1970. "I wanted a wife and children, the whole number. I didn't have one doubt about Kris. We really got along well."

Some friends suggested that Tom Harmon was not fully in favor of the marriage. Before the wedding, the Harmons insisted Rick take instructions in Catholicism, and he signed a paper pledging to have their children baptized in the church. The wedding was set for April 20, 1963, at St. Martin of Tours Church, by which time Kris was already pregnant. "Nobody really talked about it, but everybody knew," said one of Kris's friends.

David served as best man, and the ushers included the usual crew from the fraternity house and back lot: Charley Britt, Skip Young, Joe Byrne, Kent McWhirter, Karl Kindberg, and Jack Ellena. For the formal afternoon affair, they all wore oxford-gray morning coats and striped trousers. Attending Kris was her maid of honor, fourteen-year-old Kelly Harmon; David's wife, June Nelson; Kent's wife, Cynthia McWhirter; and her school friends Sheila Reeves, Gretchen Goemans, Candy Caballero, and Annabella Whitney. Several hundred fans kept vigil outside the church, while the couple exchanged vows in a thirty-minute nuptial mass. After a reception by the flower-covered pool in the backyard of the Harmons' Brentwood home, they left for a honeymoon in the Bahamas.

In August 1962, just before her second season on the show, June and David had a son, Danny. The adjustment of belonging to the Nelson family did not prove easy for June. She kept her maiden name in the credits—"June Blair appears as June Nelson"—and tension developed between her and Ozzie. Kris, on the other hand, jumped right into her new role as wife, off-screen and on-camera, when she joined the cast the following year.

"I thought of it as just a part," she said. "Everyone was terribly nice to me, and Ozzie and Harriet were the easiest in-laws in the world, totally nondemanding."

"He handled her with kid gloves," said Skip Young. "It was tougher for June to come on the show than it was for Kris. June was already an actress. She wanted to establish her own identity. There seemed to be a little jealousy of Kris on June's part. Ozzie tried to write the episodes as equal as possible so they wouldn't have any bad-news stuff going on between them. June was a professional, and she learned her lines and did whatever it was she was supposed to. Kris was a natural. She and Rick were a real good TV team 'cause that's the way they played in real life, laughing and hitting each other with pillows. They had a real rapport between them. With June and Dave, she never quite fell into the idea of being June Nelson on the show."

"It was a little difficult," admitted David. "My father did a wonderful job. For us, we had always learned that he was the director, even though he was our father. What he said on the set was not personal. What he said on the set was aimed at doing the best show he could possibly do and getting the best performance he could out of us. So we knew what he was saying to us on the set he was saying as a director to an actor. What he said after was father to son. He kept good lines for that, and it worked fairly well for the girls, too.

"But my problem with that, and Rick's too, was here we were husbands, and our father is dictating to our wives what he wants them to look like and what he wants them to do. Of course, when you get home, your wife turns around and talks to you [about Dad]. We both had to sit down and say to them, 'What he says on the set goes. He's the director, and you're an actress. You've got to make that definition and that split. It's not personal, and it should not continue into your personal life once you're away from the set.' He handled that very well, and I know it was a lot of pressure on him because there were a couple of times where I got a little upset."

Kris's lack of acting experience didn't bother Ozzie, who preferred that his performers stay as natural as possible. He was basically a radio director who directed with his ears, leaving the visual end of the show largely to the cameramen. "She was a little nervous," said David, "but she wanted to do it." She still made mistakes. One day she showed up with her hair cut short, after not finishing the scenes she had shot the day before when her hair was still long.

In less than a year, Rick had made the transition from a rollicking bachelor life with rakish roommate Charley Britt to devoted husband and father. Tracy Kristine Nelson was born October 25, six months after the wedding, at St. John's Hospital in Santa Monica. The slightly premature baby weighed four pounds and one ounce, the first Nelson girl in three generations.

After his marriage, Rick disappeared from all but his closest friends. "Other than work, I didn't see much of Rick," said his brother. He retreated into the comfort of domestic life, seeing his old roommate Charley Britt, the McWhirters, and occasionally Joe Byrne. Sometimes the couple would hit the town with other young professionals, like a triple date with Nancy Sinatra and her boyfriend, Tommy Sands, and Connie Francis with whomever she was seeing at the time. Once a month, the clan gathered at Ozzie and Harriet's for dinner. But wedding bells, by and large, busted up that old gang of Rick's.

Charley Britt did continue to socialize regularly with Rick. "I saw an awful lot of Rick after he got married," said Britt. "We continued to do things together. In fact, it was always a great breaking ground to take a new date up to Rick and Kris's house. The four of us would do what everyone else does, go out to dinner, stay home for dinner. We stayed real close."

He remembered a birthday party Kris threw for Rick where she drove up in a new Mercedes convertible with a sign reading, "Surprise! I Bought It With My Own Money." She had also made arrangements to fly the entire party directly to San Francisco for a night on the town.

Britt introduced Rick to golf, and he attacked the sport with his typical intensity. A native of Augusta, Georgia, home of the Masters Tournament, Britt had been a lifelong golfer, and he watched in amazement as Rick swiftly developed his game. "When we started playing golf," said Britt, "I saw him go from absolutely whiffing the ball—swinging at it and missing it—to shooting a seventy-five at Bel-Air. That was a period of about a year. He was playing as much as he could. On hiatus, we'd play quite a bit, but during the show, we played on weekends. We'd play down at Laguna. He'd play all he could."

He also worked on bodybuilding. With football-player friends like Britt and McWhirter, Rick spent much of his time around hunky physical specimens, and he beefed up with weights, able to press almost twice his own body weight. Bunny Robyn remembered running into him at the Beverly Hills Health Club on Santa Monica Boulevard. (Robyn, who grew tired of the music he recorded, sold his studio in 1960, although Rick continued to record at the new place, now called United Studios.)

Kris spent a lot of her free time painting. Rick encouraged her. "What happened," she said, "was that when I was dating Rick, he took me to his parents' home, and there I saw a Streeter Blair painting. Ozzie and Harriet love primitives too. I had no confidence, but Rick sat me down and started me off. I did my first painting as a good-bye gift to my parents when I left to marry. I called it *Our House*. It was of the house we lived in when I was twelve. My second painting was an engagement present for Rick—a train with each car depicting a part of our romance."

Streeter Blair painted primitive renderings of scenes from his boyhood in Kansas and became quite popular in California shortly after he began painting at age sixty in 1948. His work was widely exhibited in California galleries and museums throughout the 1950s, and he was scheduled for an exhibit at Beverly Hills's Sari Heller Gallery the week after he died in 1966.

Kris's mother, Elyse, started her career as a commercial artist and continued to paint as a hobby, long after her career as a model and actress took off. "My mother is a good portrait painter," said Kris, "so good that I felt I couldn't compete. But when I saw primitives by Streeter Blair, I knew that's what I wanted to do. I could never paint anything the way it was supposed to be. If my mother did oranges, they had texture and gloss, and they looked like oranges. I'd do an orange, and it would be simply an orange circle. But Streeter Blair's work demonstrated to me that it didn't matter if you were untaught. So I tried it."

Kris also continued to take ballet classes, something she had done since she was a small child. "I wanted to be a ballerina," she said, "and I keep fit by doing ballet exercises." She worked as a go-go dancer on a local rock & roll TV program called "Shivaree," alongside future actress Teri Garr. Her teacher, David Lichine, choreographed a number for an episode on "Ozzie and Harriet" called "The Ballerina," which featured a dream sequence where she and Rick performed an excerpt from *Swan Lake*. "All of a sudden, here's Rick—excuse me, Rick the jock who lifts weights and hangs out with Charley Britt—putting on ballet tights to dance a dream ballet sequence," said Bruce Belland. "He's gone on this girl. He will do whatever she tells him."

Not only did Rick perform with Kris, but he also did a

sidesplitting version of *The Nutcracker* with the fraternity
brothers that was to ballet what acting on the show was to
Shakespearean drama.

David grew interested in directing about this time. "I was
always fascinated with the mechanical end of making films,"
he said. He began directing an occasional episode, the first
one dealing with one of Wally's harebrained schemes about
getting publicity for the fraternity. He directed about a dozen
shows and began to develop ideas that conflicted with his
father. "After I made films where I saw actors had something
to contribute," he said, "that they weren't just cattle, we ran
into problems."

His father began to accuse him of not knowing his lines, not
caring about the show. "I was a conscientious actor," he said,
"and I knew my lines. But Dad was putting up some kind of
block, and every scene became a hurdle. He'd play some kind
of game where I'd have to blow the lines, and his prophecy
would be self-fulfilling. I never convinced him that I did know
the lines."

"I don't think anyone was aware of the tensions between
David and his father," said Kent McCord. "I guess it was a
question of proven success versus new ideas. You just don't
tamper with something that successful, when the formula has
worked that long." Rick didn't want to get involved and suggested David take it easy. "Our roles were completely reversed
from the early years," said David. "Now Rick was telling me,
'Why don't you just keep your big mouth shut?' "

June was unhappy too. She left the show after two seasons,
ostensibly to care for her young son, Danny, but also apparently chafing under Ozzie's bit. "For a while there seemed to
be a break in the family when June refused to go over to the
house," said Skip Young. She and David began seeing a psychiatrist.

The first Decca sessions took place in January 1963, when

an unexciting single of the old Ray Charles song "I Got a Woman" and a weepy country ballad, "You Don't Love Me Anymore," was recorded and, inexplicably, not released until two months later. Although Decca assigned Rick a producer named Charles "Bud" Dant, he mostly attended to paperwork and left the creative control in the hands of the old crew, including Haskell as arranger, Burton on guitar, Osborn on bass, and Frost on drums. Ray Johnson had primarily re-placed Gene Garf on keyboards, although on occasion they used a young pianist from Tulsa, Oklahoma, named Leon Russell.

To confuse matters further, Lew Chudd beat Decca to the market by a couple of weeks with a single culled from his tape files of "That's All," the ballad from *Songs by Ricky*, and "I'm in Love Again," a previously unreleased version of the Fats Dom-ino song probably recorded around the time of his second album. Perhaps because of the competition, neither single did very well, barely making it inside the top fifty.

Rick's first Decca album, *For Your Sweet Love*, turned out to be an undistinguished affair with, if possible, even less life and vigor than his last few Imperial albums. Outside of the title track from Jerry Fuller and a couple of contributions by Dor-sey Burnette and Joe Osborn, even the usual cast of songwrit-ers was missing, and Rick sounded as uninspired as he ever had in his career. Missing entirely was the sure vision that had guided his best records of the fifties.

But Rick did not stand alone among the surviving fifties rock & rollers who found themselves confused and lost in the changing styles of early 1960s pop. The fundamental sound of fifties rhythm & blues had evolved into gothic productions pioneered by Jerry Leiber and Mike Stoller, who began their careers at Bunny Robyn's Fairfax Avenue studio, and protégés like Phil Spector and Burt Bacharach. Producer Snuff Garrett represented the dominant mode of Hollywood rock & roll, with string-laden pop hits by Bobby Vee far removed from their roots in Buddy Holly's Tex-Mex rock & roll. (Garrett lofted Johnny Burnette into the top ten as a recording artist in 1960 with "You're Sixteen," as insipid a piece of pop fluff as Ricky ever recorded and which Burnette didn't even write.)

Elvis found himself mired in a morass of mediocrity, banished to making simpleminded movies and recording the attendant sound-track junk. The Everly Brothers had disappeared off the charts altogether, after watering down their high mountain rockabilly beyond recognition. Former rockabilly singer Roy Orbison was scoring on the charts with operatic melodramas.

Chudd pumped out no fewer than half a dozen Rick Nelson albums in the first year after the singer left Imperial, compilations of previously issued recordings that hit the market at a dizzying rate. When Decca released the company's second Rick Nelson single in May, "String Along" and "Gypsy Woman," Chudd matched them with another single out of his vaults, "Old Enough to Love" and "If You Can't Rock Me." But evidently he had begun to exhaust the quality of his Rick releases, since Decca slid into the top thirty with "String Along," while both of Chudd's sides barely nicked the bottom of the hot one hundred.

In August Rick recorded his first genuine hit for his new label, "Fools Rush In," a Johnny Mercer standard that Frank Sinatra recorded with the Tommy Dorsey Orchestra in 1940. Rick picked up his arrangement from the 1960 hit version by Brook Benton but made the song his own with a sprightly, percussive rhythm track vaguely reminiscent of "Hello Mary Lou" and an elegantly understated guitar solo by Burton.

"We did forty-seven takes of 'Fools Rush In,' complete takes," said session player Jerry Cole, a member of the Champs. "We were lying on the floor, and Ozzie walked in. They went in and listened, and Ozzie said, 'C'mon boys, take a few minutes more rest and then we're going to go in and cut some more.' So we did five or six more, and we were just beat. Rick would play high hat on Richie Frost's drums. But we couldn't make it anymore. I believe they took take three."

In December 1963, Rick put out a new album called *Rick Nelson Sings "For You,"* after the title of his new single. Chudd countered with another album of old scraps given the intentionally confusing title of *Rick Nelson Sings for You.* The single was another update of an old song, recorded by Glen Gray during Ozzie's big band era, and the record eased into the top ten. Between the success of "Fools Rush In" and "For You," it appeared briefly that Rick was on his way toward reclaiming some of his waning popularity. But actually it would be many years before he again had a record even close to the top ten.

In February 1964, while Rick was in the studio recording yet another big band classic—Ray Noble's "The Very Thought of You"—a new clamor could be heard on his car radio while driving home. The Beatles were singing "I Want to Hold Your Hand."

8
Love and Kisses

TIMES WERE CHANGING SO FAST that even an intelligent, well-read man like Ozzie found it difficult to keep up. His essential conservatism may have even led Ozzie to burrow in a little deeper, as the culture kaleidoscoped around him.

Nevertheless, his film *Love and Kisses* must have been so resolutely out of it when it was released in October 1965, it was probably a minor miracle—or at least a testament to the loyal bonds Ozzie maintained among the higher-ups at Universal Studios—that it ever got produced at all.

The play was already thin and dated when it first hit Broadway in 1962, produced and directed by the generally canny old hand Dore Schary. One reviewer called the Broadway show "a throbbingly trite cornball family comedy . . . about a sort of Ozzie and Harriet couple in a *Ladies Home Journal* fiction situation."

The three years that passed did not improve the clumsy situation comedy about the trials of a teenage marriage, the middle-class anguish of the parents, the boorish pomposity of an older engaged couple from the same family, and the contrived spats between the three pairs. But Ozzie bought the film rights to the Anita Rowe Block comedy and wrote, produced, and directed a film version starring Rick and Kris.

The young couple had brought a small measure of sex to the TV show, kidding with each other in a physical way, wrestling on couches, dumping popcorn on each other's heads, and in general acting with the spark of young lovers. Ozzie planned to showcase this frolicsome rapport in his motion picture.

As usual, Rick went along. But no twenty-five-year-old with a measure of self-respect could have failed to see how ridiculous his part was. He played an eighteen-year-old who gets married the day before his high school graduation, and Rick, with his beefed-up football-player physique, looked nothing like the teenager he portrayed. Kris, just twenty years old, passed marginally as the pert ingenue who moves into her new in-laws' home carrying a six-foot-tall stuffed animal.

"He didn't want to do it," said Joe Byrne, "but he got kinda roped into that between his wife and Ozzie. He was in the middle. He walked through it. It was awful. He did that for his wife 'cause she wanted to be an actress in a movie. And Ozzie wanted to do it, so he said OK. He was easy that way. If it was friends or family, he was vulnerable."

Rick stood on the edge of a professional abyss. His record sales ground to a near halt in the wake of the British invasion that revitalized rock music on these shores. He had grown sick of the TV show, a vestigial appendage of his youth he couldn't outgrow or shake loose. His marriage may have damaged his appeal with fans. With a controlling father having guided his every career move, Rick had little or no practice following his own instincts. He stood outside the swift currents of change in pop culture, high on a remote hill above Hollywood with his wife and daughter, hanging out with his football player buddies, a helpless, isolated figure. With no direction and no momentum, he didn't know what to do with himself.

He called it his "robot period—just wind me up."

The movie was little more than a Technicolor, big-screen "Ozzie and Harriet" episode with Jack Kelly of TV's "Maverick" and Madelyn Himes as the parents. Jerry Van Dyke played the role Bert Convy did on Broadway of the older sister's obnoxious fiancé, and Sheilah Wells handled the stuffy older sister. The stage production included no music, and a couple of songs were tossed into the mess, including the title track written by Sonny Curtis, a former member of Buddy Holly and the Crickets, who authored the 1961 Everly Brothers hit "Walk Right Back."

The laughs depended on silly gags like Rick falling over in his chair while dozing at the graduation ceremony or a falsie accidentally rolling out of Kris's overnight bag when she moves into Rick's room. For romance, the newlyweds begin their wedding night in separate berths of a bunk bed but coyly end up sleeping together.

The movie's big scene was that Ozzie Nelson specialty, a dream sequence, where Rick ended up in an elaborately choreographed bar brawl, staged by Jack Ellena. The stunts involved one six-foot-five, 250-pound actor jumping on Rick's back, throwing 230-pound Ellena over a bar and through a window, getting attacked by a knife-wielding assailant who misses his head by inches, and throwing another 210-pound actor through a door and down a flight of stairs.

As all this commotion was taking place, the camera focused on a couple of familiar faces sitting placidly at the bar. Skip Young turns to David Nelson and asks, "Doesn't he look familiar to you?"

"No, I never saw him before," replies David.

"It was a joke I suggested to Ozzie," said Young. Ozzie adlibbed the cameo into the shooting, much to the confusion of the script supervisor.

Shot on a seventeen-day schedule on Universal's back lot and a limited budget, *Love and Kisses* disappeared almost as soon as it was released. The *Los Angeles Times* reviewer struggled to say something nice. "About all one can say for *Love and Kisses* is that it is wholesome and not overbearing as so many teen films are these days. Whether the age group aimed for will go for it is doubtful because the story emerges no spritelier than a dull situation comedy on television."

"After we went to the preview," said Young, "I'm not sure that [Rick] thought it was well done. For one thing, the audience laughed at the credits—starring Rick Nelson, written by Ozzie Nelson, produced by Ozzie Nelson, directed by Ozzie Nelson. It got some all right reactions. But somehow it was more like an expanded episode of the show than a real movie with something for Rick to do other than what he does."

The Nelsons were getting left behind. After fourteen years, the TV show came to a merciful end. June returned to the cast for the final season—"I missed acting terribly, and we thought it would help the family situation," she said—and the series was shot in color for the first time; but nothing could stem the tide of time for "The Adventures of Ozzie and Harriet." Ozzie remembered the end wistfully in his memoirs.

"When we resumed filming our television show in the fall of 1965," he wrote, "we were no longer at General Service Studios but had moved our entire production out to the old Selznick Studios, on Washington Boulevard, which had become the Desilu Culver Studios. The move had been necessitated by a shortage of stage space at General Service, and although the Desilu people did everything possible to make us happy, we were never really comfortable there. We had been at General Service for 13 years, and after all that time it was difficult getting used to new surroundings and new faces.

"As for Harriet and me, we had been spoiled by the fact that General Service was only a ten-minute drive from home. In fact, on pleasant days I often walked it or jogged. Desilu

Culver, on the other hand, was a 35- to 40-minute drive, and that extra half-hour of fighting the traffic made a world of difference at the end of a day's shooting. It also meant getting up earlier in the morning.

"The show was unexpectedly canceled at the end of the 1965–66 season, but we always felt that it really ended when we left General Service."

The final episode of both the season and the series, "The Game Room," was filmed on January 1, 1966, and Ozzie claimed that since word of the cancellation from on high didn't come for a couple of months, the show disbanded without any kind of a farewell. David remembered his father telling the crew that final day that he didn't think the show would be back. "I believe Dad announced during the show that unfortunately we would not be coming back in the fall," David said. "He gave everybody a hint. He said he felt we were not coming back. He had not received official word, but it was his feeling we wouldn't be back."

Rick, as had been his custom, staggered awake that morning. He and Kris had hosted an extravagant New Year's Eve costume party at their home the night before, where Kris dressed as the Wicked Snow Queen and Rick came as Walt Disney, although he lost half of his mustache before the party began. The show had long ago ceased to hold any meaning for him. "He was sick of it," said Joe Byrne. "It was just a process."

His records too had shown little signs of life, and they performed accordingly on the charts. By the end of 1965, he had disappeared from the charts altogether. He released four albums during 1964 and 1965 with little to recommend them. *The Very Thought of You* was a lifeless event, and *Spotlight on Rick* recouped that nadir only slightly with his version of "I'm a Fool," later turned into a hit by those other celebrity children, Dino, Desi, and Billy, and a rocking version of Chuck Berry's "I'm Talking About You." *Best Always* featured "Lonely Corner," the first song he had recorded in years by Johnny

Burnette, who had died the previous year in a boating accident, as well as his final chart single for some time, "Mean Old
World," written by Billy Vera.

By the time he released *Love and Kisses* in October 1965,
Rick was reduced to recording such standard schlock as "Try
to Remember," from the long-running Broadway hit *The Fan-
tastiks*, and "More," the theme song from the movie *Mondo
Cane.*

To promote Rick's next single, "Fire Breathin' Dragon," not
only did Ozzie feature the song on two "Ozzie and Harriet"
episodes, but he lifted his ban on Rick's appearing on other
television programs. Ricky sang the number in November 1965
on "Shindig," ABC's prime-time rock show, and in January
1966 on "The Ed Sullivan Show." Regardless, the single failed
to chart.

"I think during that time, a lot of American artists dropped
into the background," Rick said. "You'd have to be English to
get airplay. I was always making records during that period
and it gave me the chance to go through different phases."

Meanwhile, the new sound of rock exploded around the
world. In the footsteps of the Beatles came a dozen more,
similarly armed British beat groups, and the reverberations
reached deep into this country. The Rolling Stones broke
through with "Satisfaction." The songs of Bob Dylan were
taken to the top of the charts by the Byrds, a group who
flourished right under Rick's nose in Hollywood. The Beach
Boys reinvented California, and pop music was in sudden full
flower, while Rick languished far from the limelight.

"After the series ended," he told the *New York Times* in 1972,
"I didn't know what I wanted to do. I didn't have to worry
about money or a job, but I didn't have any real interest in a
career. 'Ozzie and Harriet' had kept me working steadily for 14
years on a soundstage, so I wasn't in any real hurry to return."

James Burton left the fold. He had grown increasingly estranged from his old "running buddy" and didn't see much of

him at all after Rick got married. They had one run-in involving a Dorsey Burnette recording session on which Burton and Joe Osborn played. "It was the only time I ever saw him angry," said Burton. "He told us, 'I don't want you playing on other people's records. It's my sound. Your sound is my sound.' "

Burton got tired of sitting around, spending months at a time visiting his family in Louisiana and waiting for Rick to call. Osborn left to devote himself to studio work. Burton received an offer to join the house band for the "Shindig" show, and at first Rick didn't want him to accept, even if he would be playing off-camera. But Burton took the job rather than go stir crazy. "It was like he completely stopped doing anything," Burton said.

In February 1966, following a suggestion by Burton, the old "Louisiana Hayride" guitarist, Rick spent three days in the studio recording a straight-ahead country & western album, a radical departure from the dross he had been recording. It turned out to be the beginning of an almost frantic search for an artistic self. Over the next year, he would experiment with country music, musical comedy, fully produced folk rock, and fashionable mainstream pop and continue to make occasional public appearances with his band, singing his old hits interspersed with standard supper club fare of the era, like "Mame" or "Hello Dolly."

The country album *Bright Lights and Country Music*, released in May, included the first song of his own that he had recorded since "Don't Leave Me This Way" on his second album. Titled "You Just Can't Quit," the song was an unvarnished message to himself:

> *When the whole world puts you down*
> *And makes you feel like a clown,*
> *That's not it.*

You just can't quit.
Don't feel sorry for things,
'Cause can't you see,
I'm still me,
And I just can't quit.

He cannily captured the idiomatic feel of contemporary country, Burton's guitar and stinging Dobro, along with some help from guitarist Glen Campbell, giving the tracks a gritty authenticity that Rick's vanilla vocals couldn't quite match. But the sincerity was there. He pulled material from the songbooks of Roy Acuff ("Night Train to Memphis"), Jim Reeves ("Welcome to My World"), and Willie Nelson ("Hello Walls"), among others.

Artistically, *Bright Lights* served as a stunning reversal of field. It did not come out of a vacuum for Rick—Jimmie Haskell remembered him tuning the car radio to a country station the first day they met, and Joe Byrne recalled Rick considering recording a Hank Williams song instead of "I'm Walkin' " for his first record. But the idea of Rick Nelson as a country singer certainly came as a surprise to the general public.

Before the album was released, Rick and a band composed of Burton, drummer Frost, and Glen Campbell on bass made a concert tour of the Far East in April, playing dates in Tokyo, Osaka, Kyoto, Taiwan, Yokohama, Hong Kong, and Manila. He could still stir frenzy far away from home, drawing the old-time crowds at airports and capacity houses at concerts. Kris met him in Hawaii on the way home to celebrate his birthday, before she began performances of her own at Anaheim's Melodyland Theater.

Kris played Louise in a stage production of Rodgers and Hammerstein's *Carousel* that starred John Raitt for a two-week run in Los Angeles before taking to the road for most of the summer. Rick made it home in time to join the rest of his family for opening night. Although it was a small part, the *Los Angeles Times* reviewer at least noticed her: "Kristin Nelson makes a promising debut," she wrote.

"You Just Can't Quit," the first single from *Bright Lights*, made number one on Los Angeles country radio, and on June 10, 1966, Rick appeared on a country-music bill at the Shrine Auditorium in Los Angeles with a band he put together especially for the occasion. "I've liked country music as long as I can remember," he told Robert Hilburn of the *Los Angeles Times* backstage before the show. "I've always been a big fan of guys like Johnny Cash and Jim Reeves. Most of my early recordings were at least part country. I'm very excited about doing this show."

In addition to Burton on guitar, the band featured Junior Nichols on drums, Lynn Russell on bass, Bob Warford on banjo, Glen D. Hardin on piano, and Clarence White (who would later help transform the Byrds into a country-rock band) on rhythm guitar. In addition to songs from the album, he included other classic country numbers like "Take These Chains from My Heart," "Big Chief Buffalo Nickel," and "I Heard That Lonesome Whistle Blow," songs that he would record in August for a second country album.

Hilburn liked the show. "If he wants to concentrate more heavily on country music in the future," he wrote, "he can be a big success in the field. He has a feel for the music that comes across in the songs and his good looks don't hurt him."

But even before the dust could settle on his country music debut, Rick took another abrupt turn. In July it was Rick who followed Kris into Melodyland, playing with his father's old idol, Rudy Vallee, in *How to Succeed in Business Without Really Trying*. He took the role of Finch, the vicious, cut-throat protagonist of the musical comedy.

"It's a real challenge," he told the *Los Angeles Times*. "This aggressive kind of a guy is so different from me and the parts

I've played. But that's the way you learn, isn't it? By doing as many difficult things as you can.

"In the TV series, Dad used Dave and me as models for the boys and we played ourselves. That's not as easy as it sounds. Some actors can't do it. I've seen some try and get themselves really tied up. If you're playing a part, you're wearing a mask, you can get away with things, you can be as broad as you want."

Musical comedy was a time-honored aspiration of an older generation of pop vocalists. But while traces of an interest in country music could be detected in Rick's past, he had previously demonstrated no affinity whatsoever for the arcane art form or any kind of music this unhip, this square. Most likely, he saw the opportunity, as he did so many other past endeavors like flying on the trapeze or bullfighting, as a challenge to master.

"Singing in a show," he said, "is a different kind of singing than I've done before. It's almost a way of talking to music— you have to project the words for the story. If it's too pretty, it loses its effect."

The role of Finch made Robert Morse a star on Broadway. Rick left the *Times* reviewer slightly less impressed. "Without proper amplification, Rick Nelson's voice sounds thin," she wrote, "especially in the musical numbers. But he's an engaging, unmannered chap who only needs a bit more seasoning to find his place in musical comedy. He plays Finch straight without the exaggerated harshness that has tempted some young comedians who have played it."

"I thought he was great," said David. "Bobby Morse came and saw it and thought he was great. It was a different interpretation of the role because it was my brother. But I thought he did a great job."

David was also proud that he had spotted in the chorus line a young, fresh-faced blonde who didn't even have a line in the show and told Rick she was going to be a star—Goldie Hawn.

"I try to make Finch a real person," Rick told another interviewer, "not just a rat with no depth who spends all his time making significant 'takes' to the audience. That's all I could remember after I had seen the play—the leering expressions. Then, when I read the script, I found that there was something more to him.

"I'd like to do more theater and, if I can get time, to study acting. David and I have some thoughts for a film, which he would direct, that would be 'serious.' But, you know, I'm somewhat typecast because of the family show and the main barrier is to find somebody to take a chance with me. For somebody like me, if I'm going to do drama, I'm almost going to have to do it myself."

Charley Britt was taking acting lessons from Leonard Nimoy, who had yet to vault to fame as Mr. Spock of TV's "Star Trek." He introduced Nimoy to Rick at a party one night, and the two got into an animated discussion about the virtues of acting classes. Rick thought lessons useless and insisted that his imagination was an adequate guide in any role he might take. Nimoy struggled valiantly to convince him otherwise but ultimately couldn't budge Rick. At the end of the evening, before he left the party, Nimoy asked Rick for an autograph for his daughter. "Sure, Leonard," said Rick, happy to comply. "But this doesn't mean anything, right?"

Ozzie tried to develop various TV ideas for his sons, and some pilot scripts were written. "Oh, Brother" was a projected series that revolved around the exploits of two brothers, both former navy pilots, who run a charter airline service. One brother was supposed to be a documentary filmmaker and the other was a ladies' man. There was talk about a science-fiction western, where two modern-day motorcyclists get transported back through time to the old West and become cowboy lawmen. Ozzie also briefly flirted with a series called "My Uncle," which would star Burt Lancaster with Dave and Rick, but nothing came of any of these.

In August Rick squeezed in sessions for a second country album, while Kris took the stage at Melodyland again to play with Patrice Munsel in *The Sound of Music*. Three months after noting her "promising debut," the same *Times* reviewer cited Kris as "already an old hand on Melodyland's circular stage."

The next month Rick flew to New York to begin rehearsals and a grueling five-week production of *On the Flip Side*, a ninety-minute musical written for television by Burt Bacharach and Hal David. Songwriting teams didn't come any hotter than Bacharach and David, who were scorching up the charts with hit after hit by Dionne Warwick. Musical director Peter Matz came from television's "Hullabaloo." Built specifically around Rick, the show concerned a young rock & roll singer who, at the tender age of twenty-one, found himself perilously close to being a has-been.

A gospel quartet of heavenly hipsters led by another teen pop singer, Joannie Sommers ("Johnny Get Angry"), was dispatched from up yonder to come to his aid. After a series of misadventures through the bohemian underworld of New York nightlife, the angels return heavenward, leaving Rick with a hit record and a career on the rebound. Such was not to be the case in real life.

Although Bacharach and David provided him with one of their typical lilting, melodic flag-wavers, "They Don't Give Medals . . . ," Rick proved woefully inadequate to the demanding sweep of the Bacharach melody line. "He is who he is," said his costar Joannie Sommers. "Exact pitch, perfect timing—you can't use that with a man like that. He had a certain sound." A singer with a more acute sense of self would have known that, but robot Rick simply plodded through the paces.

Rick took time out from the production to join David as

surprise guests on "The Mike Douglas Show" on the last day of
the week Ozzie and Harriet served as cohosts. As part of a
circus routine with Douglas serving as ringmaster, David and
Rick appeared inside a two-man costume as Pansy the Horse.
They stepped out of the outfit and produced June and young
Danny from the wings to celebrate their parents' thirty-first
wedding anniversary.

Rick finished out a year of feverish activity by joining Vallee
again for *How to Succeed in Business* at the Circle Star Theater
in San Carlos, south of San Francisco, in November and by
taking the band south of the border for a round of appearances in Mexico in December, followed by a swing through
Canada in January. While he toured Canada, his uncle Don
and Connie Harper, Ozzie's secretary, who originally joined
up to supervise Ricky's fan mail, eloped.

Rick did return in time to attend the opening of Kris's first
art show at the Sari Heller Gallery in Beverly Hills. Jackie
Kennedy spotted a *Life* magazine photo of one of Kris's more
ambitious works, *When the Kennedys Were in the White House*
and inquired about buying the brightly colored primitive.
When the exhibit closed, Kris gave it to her. Not everyone liked
her work, however. The art critic for the *Los Angeles Times* put
it bluntly: "Her stuff is no good," he wrote. "I'm really against
rich ladies in this town who paint because it's something to
keep them busy."

In April 1967 *Country Fever*, the second c&w album Rick
recorded the previous August, finally came out, preceded in
August 1966 by a single that featured his sole self-penned
number on the album, "Alone." The single that was released
with the LP, "Take a City Bride," featured a B side not included
on the album that Rick also wrote, "I'm Called Lonely." With
"You Just Can't Quit," these songs formed a kind of semiauto-
biographical trilogy, as Rick sketched himself as a desolate but
determined loner. They were not intricately crafted, insightful
pieces of poetic introspection, but Rick, for the first time, was

beginning to allow glimpses of his feelings to creep into his music.

The sessions also produced a couple of numbers taken from old Sun Records by Elvis Presley. "Mystery Train," which was included on the album, smoked out of the roundhouse like the locomotive of its title, Rick tearing up the vocal. He sang the song with relish and some genuine abandon, obviously feeling completely at home with this piece of vintage rock & roll. His version of "Blue Moon of Kentucky," the same song he had trotted out for the kids at Hamilton High all those years before, never made it onto the album.

In June, with Rick about to leave for his annual summer tour, Kris learned she was pregnant with twins. Their daughter, Tracy, had already begun her show-business career that year with a part in a movie with Bob Hope and Lucille Ball, *Yours, Mine and Ours*, before her fourth birthday. Since Rick would be returning to Los Angeles every week to film his role as host for a summer replacement surf 'n' sun rock TV series called "Malibu U," he wouldn't stay on the road more than four days at a time. He started close to home with six days at the San Diego County Fair over the Fourth of July weekend and, before leaving California, stopped in the studio long enough to knock off two sides for a forthcoming single in one day.

Obviously, Rick couldn't find any musical direction on his own. Decca Records offered no help, disorganized and ineffective as the label was at the time. Frustrated and uncertain where to turn, he asked the company to provide him with a list of prospective independent producers, turning over the responsibility for the first time since he went in the studio with Barney Kessel as a sixteen-year-old. He picked Charles Koppelman and Dan Rubin, who had recently overseen the remarkable return to the top ten of Bobby Darin with the Tim Hardin song, "If I Were a Carpenter."

Rick liked one of the songs Koppelman and Rubin selected,

"Suzanne on a Sunday Morning," written specifically for the project by one of their staff writers, John Boylan, fresh out of college. Los Angeles session guitarist Dan Peake put together a band for the date, and the New York producers came to town to supervise the quickie session. The results hardly proved earthshaking, but Koppelman and Rubin managed to nudge Rick into the contemporary pop music world. Rick sang the clipped cadence of the lyrics in the upper end of his range, surrounded by plunking electric keyboards, swirling guitars, layered background vocals, and judiciously produced horns and harps. When the results bumped up against the bottom of the charts, Decca was ecstatic.

Rick performed the song on "Malibu U" in August, shortly after its release. The show combined the open-air setting of Dick Clark's "Where the Action Is" with the quick comedy takes of "Rowan & Martin's Laugh-In." Rick served as "Dean," introducing the acts that lip-synched hits while the bikini-clad Bob Banas Dancers pranced around on the sand. "All you need at Malibu U is a surfboard, a beach towel, and suntan lotion," Rick told the audience. "Now here's a word from our Madison Avenue campus," he said, introducing a commercial. Produced for television by the people who gave America *Teen* magazine and the annual Teen Age Fair, "Malibu U" pandered to adolescent TV audiences, and Rick looked uncomfortable and out of place wandering around that beach, microphone in hand. "At 27, Rick Nelson is probably a couple of years too old to be messing around Malibu U," noted the *Los Angeles Herald-Examiner* TV columnist.

Rick was lost. Not knowing what to do with himself, he tried anything, searching for a corner to turn that would lead him down the right avenue. It was the summer of *Sgt. Pepper's Lonely Hearts Club Band.* Outside his tightly circumscribed world, the new rock sound was the most exciting, dynamic art form happening, expanding its boundaries almost daily and leaving Rick far behind. He wanted to find his place in that world. Someone would have to help him. That someone turned out to be John Boylan.

The twins, Matthew Gray and Gunnar Eric, were born September 20, about the same time Rick entered the studio to record an album with "Suzanne on a Sunday Morning" author Boylan producing. Boylan was an unlikely colleague for Rick. Born in New York City and raised in Buffalo, the hip, urbane Boylan went to the fashionably leftist Bard College, where he roomed with comic Chevy Chase, who was dating actress Blythe Danner, and used to play in bands with Walter Becker and Donald Fagen, later of Steely Dan. From this hotbed of hipsterism, Boylan graduated directly into the offices of Koppelman and Rubin, and his trip to California to produce Rick was his first big-time assignment in the music business.

"Basically, Charlie's dictum was 'cut the catalog,' " said Boylan, meaning that Koppelman wanted Rick to exclusively record songs written by Koppelman-Rubin contract writers. "He gave me a list of tunes I had to cut with Rick. I was a fifty-dollar-a-week staff guy. I didn't have much say in the matter. Rick was ready to let Charlie carry the ball because he was so pleased to have anybody do something after Decca's apathy."

Rick began putting his vocals on *Another Side of Rick* the night after the twins were born. Boylan puffed a congratulatory cigar behind the console. Hope fluttered in Rick's chest. Boylan brought a glimmer of light into his darkness. He was someone in touch with the new social order, the swiftly moving currents of the pop culture. The album was a thickly produced collection of songs from Koppelman-Rubin songwriters with the modern touch: Tim Hardin, John Sebastian of the Lovin' Spoonful, Boylan himself, and his brother, Terry Boylan. Rick even contributed a pair of originals, one cowritten with Boylan, the other with James Burton. Jimmie Haskell and Boylan supplied most of the gaudy arrangements, but Jack

Nitzsche, the enigmatic whiz arranger of all the Phil Spector Wall of Sound sessions, also did a couple of tracks.

One evening Boylan called Denny Bruce, a drummer and Hollywood man on the scene, and asked him to bring some marijuana to the studio. "Rick's ready," he told Bruce. They smoked a couple of joints, and Rick didn't seem affected. "This is great," he told them, "but I don't want to work anymore. I just want to go home."

A little while later, the studio phone rang. It was Rick, calling from home, describing the extraordinary tricks the lights were playing on his eyes, tripping like a teenager stoned for the first time. "I can see what you guys mean now," he said.

The next night Bruce returned with more, and everybody got high again. They were working on a Terry Boylan song called "Blame It on Your Wife," a rather ridiculous piece of fluff about a farmer's wife. "Buy her a tractor instead," the chorus urged. Feeling the sway of the grass, Rick didn't want to sing the song and insisted, instead, on following his suddenly freed soul. "I want to sing the kind of thing I always wanted to, something I can close my eyes to with feeling, like Ray Charles." So Rick recorded "Georgia on My Mind" that night. His rather tame version got included on the album.

Bruce also participated with Boylan and Kris in an animated discussion of Rick's image problems. They decided to make a video of one of the songs from the album and, along with a couple of other musicians, trooped off to a local TV studio to produce an electronic portrait of the "new" Ricky, complete with handmade love beads Kris presented to all the participants.

"The biggest problem Rick had during that time was Kris pushing him," David said, "really pushing him to be part of the flower-child groups and stuff like that. She felt that he was out of date, and he should be more into the flower-power kind of stuff. Of course, she was dressing with a bandanna on her head. But Kris was always like that. She would come down in one thing and ten minutes later, go back upstairs and come down as an Indian princess. She was deciding whether she was going to be an artist or a manager. She got involved in Rick's music, making more suggestions than I think a wife should make about her husband's business."

She not only supplied one of her childlike paintings of a recording studio scene for the back cover of his next album, *Perspective*, but added a breathy French recitation to a song Rick and Boylan wrote called "Hello to the Wind (Bonjour le Vent)." Boylan returned to California, where he was producing folk rockers the Dillards and the sleek pop group the Association, who was doing the soundtrack to the movie *Goodbye, Columbus*. Boylan hunted up a bunch of songs by a relatively unknown songwriter named Randy Newman, along with numbers by the likes of Paul Simon, Harry Nilsson, Richie Havens, and a couple of his own, went into the studio with a typical cast of Hollywood sidemen and arrangers, and recorded *Perspective*, Rick's only 1968 recording, not released until almost a year later. Rick knew what the album sounded like.

"I was lost," he said. "For a while I said 'OK, you get me a song and a producer and I'll do it your way.' For a while, the producer was more important than the artist, which is kind of an unhealthy situation because the production should really enhance the artist. But with me, I was getting buried in it. Beautiful string sections, beautiful arrangements, but I sounded like I was that big," he said, closing his thumb and forefinger into a tiny gap.

Neither of the two Boylan albums proved particularly successful in the marketplace, and Rick grew to hate the overproduced records. But Boylan was influencing Rick's life in ways his football player friends like Britt and McCord were no longer doing.

"When I met him he had a sixteen-and-a-half-inch neck, he'd

been lifting weights, he had short hair, and looked like a football player," said Boylan. "Much to Harriet's chagrin, six months after he met me, he's got long hair, he weighs the same as I do, we're the exact same size, he's wearing jeans, boots, and he was into the sixties."

Harriet worried about Rick growing his hair, fearing—too late—he would start smoking marijuana. Little Tracy wondered aloud if Boylan was a beatnik. Boylan took Rick and Kris to the Esalen Institute in Big Sur, a Zen hideaway on the coast.

"It was a real eye-opener for him to find out there were a lot of people in the sixties looking to stretch musically," Boylan said. "Frankly, as soon as he found out about it, he wanted to be one of them. He was just so sheltered by the situation and by his own fame. The first show I went with him to was unbelievable. The band, except for James Burton, was sub par. James was phenomenal, and there were three pickup guys who could hardly play. He was doing 'Hello Dolly.' It was like the second song—'Here's a little show tune . . . [sings] Hello—thank you—Dolly.' "

Rick did almost nothing that year but stay home or play a little golf and some tennis. He listened to records. Boylan turned him on to people like Harry Nilsson and Fred Neil. Rick discovered Tony Joe White and John Hartford. He was opening himself up, but he was scared. "He thought it was all over," said Joe Byrne. "He thought he had peaked, and it was all over. He was hanging around, not doing a lot. He was trying to figure the music thing out. Where was it going? How did he fit into it or did he? That was his biggest fright."

In October Rick finally put a band together and made a brief tour of clubs on the East Coast. For the first time, Burton was replaced by Jerry Cole on guitar. Cole remembered that, even then, Rick hated flying so much he fortified himself with a couple of stiff screwdrivers before each flight. Onstage, Rick was going through the motions, singing his songs and cover versions of other familiar tunes like "La Bamba" in clubs with dirty jokes on the cocktail napkins. "I didn't know what I wanted or what direction to go musically," he said in 1973. "I didn't even know if I wanted to sing. But during this time it gave me a chance to be objective with myself because I had gotten tired of playing the same old songs in nightclubs.

"It happened one night while I was at the Latin Quarter playing to a hardware convention—all men. Suddenly I decided that I would rather be doing anything else than what I was doing on that stage. It became dishonest to wind myself up and perform.

"I felt like I was part of a freak show or something. People wanted to see if little Ricky had grown up or something. I didn't feel I was contributing anything musically and I wasn't getting any satisfaction personally, so I just stopped and tried to reevaluate things."

Rick returned home dejected. He didn't know what to do. Boylan took Rick down to the Troubadour one night to see the debut of a new band called Poco. The Troubadour was Hollywood's top showcase for the new, hip bands appearing at the Santa Monica Avenue nightspot almost weekly, and the Poco appearance was highly anticipated because Jim Messina and Richie Furay had previously belonged to Buffalo Springfield, one of the most innovative underground rock bands to emerge from Los Angeles.

"I remember seeing him sitting in the audience," said Poco bassist Randy Meisner. "It was like a big thrill. Rick Nelson's out there. Let's make sure we do a good job."

Rick left the club that night with a glimmer of an idea burning in his brain. Soon he would make his move.

9

Easy to Be Free

THE LINE OUTSIDE THE CLUB extended around the block. After years of playing around the world in arenas, auditoriums, and clubs of every description, Rick Nelson finally booked his first rock-club engagement in his hometown, Hollywood, and the Troubadour was packed to the rafters for the occasion. Rick had come a long way in the five months since he had seen the Poco show at the same club.

Rick put together the Stone Canyon Band around Poco bassist Randy Meisner, an affable, easygoing soul with a sweet, high voice. Producer John Boylan heard that Meisner had been fired from the country-rock group in a dispute over the final mixes to the band's first album. He called Meisner, and Meisner contacted his buddies from the band that first brought him to Los Angeles from Denver. James Burton was no longer available, having joined up with Elvis Presley.

"It came together almost from a negative standpoint," Rick explained. "I didn't know what kind of music I wanted to do. I couldn't verbalize it really, so I just got to thinking how I started, the kind of music I liked, and then I started looking for musicians who played along those lines. I was really fortunate in getting a unique type of style and one guy really led to another. The first guy I found was Randy Meisner."

Meisner grew up on a farm near Scotts Bluff, Nebraska, and as a kid used to imitate Elvis Presley records in front of a mirror in his basement. Soon he played guitar himself and, as a member of the Dynamics, was traveling throughout the Midwest working the road. He got married and started a family at an early age, but he continued to pursue his musical ambitions. He arrived in Denver to play a battle of the bands, where he linked up with one of the competing groups, the Soul Survivors, jumped ship, and moved to Los Angeles with his new band.

The group changed its name to the Poor, and they were not kidding. They took a one-bedroom apartment in East Los Angeles for eighty-five dollars a month. Meisner and guitarist Allen Kemp slept on the living room floor. They spelled the time by smoking prodigious amounts of marijuana and rehearsing during the day, with windows closed to dampen the noise, even in the stifling heat of the Southern California summer. They didn't have any cars, so they hitchhiked around town. Gigs were few and far between. "We all went vegetarian," said Kemp, "because it was cheaper."

When Meisner took the job with Poco, the Poor broke up. With drummer Patrick Shanahan, Kemp moved to a cheap three-bedroom house in Sherman Oaks, and Kemp got a job washing cars. One room was converted into something of a rehearsal room with egg cartons pasted on the walls. When Boylan contacted Meisner about working with Rick, the first call Meisner made was to his two former colleagues, Kemp and Shanahan, out in Sherman Oaks. Rick pulled up one afternoon early in 1969 in his Mercedes convertible with a guitar in hand. "We clicked," said Kemp. "Randy's and my vocals fit with his so well, we had great three-part harmony."

About two weeks later the band gathered in a rehearsal hall in a building Ozzie owned in Burbank and began working up a repertoire in earnest. Sometimes they rehearsed in the back room at Rick's house. Maury Foladare still acted as Rick's manager, but John Boylan stepped in on an unofficial basis. "Rick really needed help on the street," said Boylan. "I called Doug Weston and said, 'I want you to put Rick Nelson in the Troubadour.' He said, 'Well, it's chancy, but I'll do it.' We went into the Troubadour and kicked ass and took names."

Rick got the band's name from a remote area of the Los Angeles hills he used to drive by on his way to inspect two large parcels of undeveloped property Kris talked him into buying. He had to cash out some of his stocks from the trust fund to make the investment, and he passed Stone Canyon every time he drove up to look at the barren hillside he now owned. He thought it had more of a ring than Mandeville Canyon, which was where his property was.

Rick Nelson and the Stone Canyon Band opened a six-night run at the club on April 1, 1969, and although the curious, even skeptical crowds went away convinced, opening night did not go too smoothly. Steel guitarist Sneaky Pete Kleinow of the Flying Burrito Brothers called while the band was setting up to say he was fogged in at Las Vegas and could not fly out for the date. "I never heard of fog in Las Vegas, but that was his excuse," said Kemp. "I had to play lead guitar for the first night. Scared the hell out of me. I hadn't rehearsed any of that stuff. I was doing finger-picking stuff, and I had my guitar with medium-gauge strings on it. I didn't have time to change them or anything. I had to just take stabs at it."

Rick mixed choice selections from his fifties repertoire with some Dylan songs, a little Tim Hardin, and a couple of his own originals. The glistening three-part harmony, the raw drive of the band, and the revitalized Rick himself held the crowds enthralled. "Everyone was hypnotized," said Kemp. "They couldn't believe Rick Nelson was playing right there."

He no longer looked like the smart-mouthed kid from the TV show. Shaggy hair covered his ears, hung in his eyes, and framed his face with long sideburns that crawled down past his ears. He wore jeans and a long-sleeved, collarless undershirt. But the same beautiful blue eyes sparkled out of his fresh, handsome face.

The engagement proved to be a phenomenal success. Suddenly Rick found himself the beneficiary of all the credibility he had been missing. He was a bona fide rock & roll survivor, on his way to becoming the latest thing. Even *Rolling Stone*, that avatar of the underground music scene, glowed in its own wise-ass manner.

"And Rick—little Ricky not so little—well, he did just fine. Made his mom and dad real proud, and the next few days he was what everyone in Hollywood talked about."

"Before I went into the Troubadour," Rick told *Stone*, "I thought maybe I should change some of the words in the old songs, but then I got to thinking. At the time I did all those songs, I never put them down. When I did them, I really liked them. I never did a song I didn't like. In the long run it's better I didn't change the words. It's much more honest."

With fresh wind filling his sails, Rick and the band went into Decca's studios a couple of weeks later to try to record an old Brewer and Shipley song, "Bound to Fall," but never finished the track. Relations with the label were tenuous. Nobody from Decca even bothered to show up at the Troubadour, and Rick was angry and frustrated with the company. John Boylan characterized one top executive as "a bean counter," utterly dismissing his knowledge of music. Decca insisted Rick use its studio, and Rick hated the antiquated, confining setup. Boylan had a secretary call the studio to inquire about available dates. When she found a period booked solid by easy-listening maestro Bert Kaempfert, Rick called Decca back and told the label the only time he could get all his musicians together was the date of the scheduled Kaempfert session. The label reluctantly OK'd an outside recording studio session.

In May Boylan took Rick and the band into United Studios, along with country steel-guitar great Buddy Emmons, and in two hours completed a supple version of Dylan's "She Belongs to Me." Los Angeles radio jumped on the single, and Rick's career was springing back to life before his eyes.

"I went in and recorded that single without the label knowing," Rick said, "because I got preempted out in the studio. I said 'Well, this isn't a hobby to me, you know—this is what I do for a living.' So I just went in and recorded it. They all got mad because I said 'Just put it out, here's the single, just put it out.' "

Boylan brought folksinger Eric Andersen, a boyhood friend from Buffalo, up to Rick's house, and the two became friends. Andersen was a product of the Greenwich Village folk scene whose songs "Thirsty Boots" and "Violets of Dawn" established him in the mid-1960s as one of the outstanding new folksinging songwriters. He had just moved to California and was living near the beach in Venice.

"We hung out together, and he was a very funny guy," said Andersen, "hilariously funny. Probably the funniest person I ever met just sitting and talking with him, which was the total opposite of how he was with the public. If for no other reason, I'd go up just to laugh.

"Songwriting was something he took really seriously, something that really intrigued him. The idea that you could express yourself. It wasn't like doing other people's material. It wasn't like doing a script on TV. It was the idea that he was somebody himself, more than an image or a face to the public. He started to get inner stirrings about his own expression."

Rick loved Dylan's work. He sang a number of Dylan's songs

at the Troubadour and used to play the *Blonde on Blonde* album constantly. That same month Dylan released his country-rock masterpiece *Nashville Skyline*, and Rick was beside himself. Dylan's album actualized the vision Rick was trying to pull together with the Stone Canyon Band. His own country-rock hybrid seemed to have found the crest of a new wave in rock.

"We rehearsed four or five days a week," said Rick. "We improvised and experimented and listened to a lot of other people's work, people like Randy Newman and Tim Hardin. Then one day I heard *Nashville Skyline* by Bob Dylan and I knew where I wanted to go. I listened to that album for days. The songs were so simple, yet cryptic at times. I wanted to sing songs like that and, if possible, also write like that."

He drafted Tom Brumley to take the steel-guitar seat in the band. Rick saw Brumley playing with Buck Owens on TV, and the sedate country-music veteran fit right into the blend. Brumley was happy to depart the Owens organization. "We were financially badly off under him," he said, "in that we didn't get much money compared to him. We started as nothing and became top entertainers, but the pay remained behind that fame. In fact, we were on duty with him and only had to play. We were constantly traveling, and, in the long run, I found our music was becoming bad. When we went into the studio to make a new single, you had no time to be creative but just had to play a prearranged part.

"I didn't know what kind of music Rick was doing then, but I went looking for a rehearsal. It was easy for me to play steel with Buck, as pure country and western playing had become a routine. With Rick, all was new, and I had to start almost at the beginning. The first dates I played with Rick were to a far younger audience than I'd ever played to, and the kids just weren't familiar with the steel guitar, not the way country people are. They'd see this guy sitting at what looked like a coffee table and wonder what the hell he was doing."

With the success of "She Belongs to Me," which slowly climbed into the top forty over a remarkable eighteen-week life span on the charts, Decca wanted an album immediately. "The only thing we could think of to do quick for an album was to go live at the Troubadour," said Boylan. "I called Westin again and said, 'Let us back in; we want to record live.' He said, 'You can come back anytime you want.' "

At this point John Boylan disappeared from the picture. He said Decca didn't want him involved because of money problems stemming from their deal with Koppelman and Rubin, and it didn't matter that Boylan had left them to establish himself as an independent. "There is no way Rick could have stood up for me with Decca without sabotaging the momentum of what was going on," said Boylan. "The only thing for me to do was take a hike."

Allen Kemp had a different explanation for Boylan's sudden disappearance. He thought Kris and Boylan were having an affair. "I think she and Boylan had a thing going for a while," he said. "I think Rick found out about it, and that's why he stopped being the producer." Kemp frequently saw Boylan's car parked outside her La Cienega art gallery and studio. Whatever the truth is, one thing was clear: Rick and Kris's marriage was not a glass road anymore. She would spend days at a time at the studio, and their relationship veered away from exclusivity. "Rick's exploits on the road are fairly legendary," said Boylan.

"It was almost like she didn't want him to do well," said Kemp. "They were kind of competitive. She was trying to be an artist. She had her little gallery. When we started going on the road, Rick and I would sit on the plane together, and he would tell me all about the numbers she would pull right before he was getting ready to leave, so he would be all upset about going on the road. He messed around on the road sometimes, and I think she did when he was gone. Their relationship wasn't that close. They had a lot of trouble."

His life was changing in many ways. The Mercedes was traded for a Volkswagen van. He questioned the wisdom of the war in Vietnam—although he didn't protest—and spoke out in an interview favoring the legalization of marijuana. In fact, he began to smoke grass regularly, becoming something of a connoisseur of hashish. He maintained a certain paranoia about it, preferring to let the other guys in the band carry the pot and keeping his stash buried in his yard. Eric Andersen took him to see the Rolling Stones at the Forum and turned him on to mescaline, and they repaired to Rick's parents' Laguna Beach home after the concert. "He was seeing purple waterfalls coming out of walls," said Andersen. "There was this religious fanatic on TV. It was an evening of psycho-Dada."

Charley Britt was still around. He had been married and divorced a couple of times, and his football career had ended after brief stints with the Minnesota Vikings and the San Francisco 49ers. He did some acting and stayed friendly with Rick and Kris. In fact, earlier that spring Kris was cast in the lead role of *La Creation*, a production by the Ballet Society of Los Angeles, under the supervision of her longtime teacher, David Lichine, who couldn't find a suitable male dancer to play opposite her. She insisted Charley try out for the part, even though he knew absolutely nothing about ballet.

He was reluctant. "She put her friendship on the line with me about it," said Britt. Kris could be very determined when it came to getting her way, so Charley went down to a rehearsal. Lichine loved his athletic grace and strength, and before he could think about it, Charley had agreed to "memorize" the ballet. He learned his part. Leslie Caron, who had danced the female lead in Europe, came by a rehearsal and danced with him one afternoon. On opening night at the Wiltern Theater, a star-studded audience waited in its seats as

Charlton Heston gave some introductory remarks. Lying on the stage next to Kris behind the curtain, Charley looked over at his costar. "Kris, I cannot believe I am going to do this," he whispered. But do it he did.

Kris and Rick also acted together in one of the first made-for-TV movies that spring, playing husband and wife in, ironically, *The Over-the-Hill Gang,* a comedy-western that starred Pat O'Brien, Walter Brennan, and Edgar Buchanan. The corny film got some of the highest ratings of the year when it was broadcast in the fall, but it really was already a project from Rick's recent past, not connected to the rapid forward momentum of his musical career, which was gaining ground virtually every day.

For professional guidance, Rick turned to his childhood friend Joe Sutton, who had left the public relations business to manage an unknown Neil Diamond. Sutton, a suit-and-tie type who represented the conservative end of the business, signed on as manager, acted as a liaison with the label, and ended up with coproduction credit on the live album, recorded in October at the Troubadour.

"I always felt that if Ricky could have loosened up a little," said Sutton, "he could have been the most incredible performer ever. He was so warm in person, and when he got onstage, he just presented his music. He didn't open himself up. I guess that was the game plan. If he could have shown onstage what he was offstage—the warmth and the sense of humor—it would have been great."

"Joe was a conniver," said Allen Kemp. "He was a strange person. He didn't really come out with a lot of ideas. He's the one who kinda kept Rick on his clean-cut image, the American thing. Joe was sneaky."

A young TV writer named Steve Martin was trying to make the transition to stand-up comedy and opened the late October shows at the Troubadour. The Wally Heider remote recording truck captured the proceedings on tape, and the shows were, once again, crammed to capacity. *Los Angeles Times* reviewer Robert Hilburn gave the show a qualified approval.

"After all this time," he wrote, "Rick Nelson is still trying to find himself musically. His appearance at the Troubadour showed signs he may be getting close to that discovery."

Backstage opening night, Ozzie came downstairs and immediately started offering his son advice, telling him to fix his shirt. "Rick visibly stiffened," said Eric Andersen. "Rick got really formal fast. He didn't dig it at all. It was like somebody stabbed him."

Rick Nelson in Concert, released in January 1970, showcased the crisp, clear sound of Rick and the Stone Canyon Band. Brumley pushed every song with his steel. Meisner and Kemp stacked their vocals on top of Rick's in angelic harmonies that took flight every time the three voices melded. The program combined Rick's oldies, like "Hello Mary Lou" and "Believe What You Say," fresh and almost urgent in the new context, with three Dylan songs; one song each from Doug Kershaw, Tim Hardin, and Eric Andersen; and four compositions by Rick himself. Andersen wrote the liner notes. The neophyte songwriter crafted songs that stood up for themselves admirably among such formidable company. One song in particular sounded especially natural and poignant, "Easy to Be Free," a title cribbed from an unlikely perusal of Hermann Hesse's *Siddhartha*. He cast his plaintive whimper against a gentle declaration of independence, a topic prominent in Rick's thoughts at the time ("Did you ever wonder why people tell you not to try?").

"I looked at his songs," said Andersen. "I would say things to him. But I thought he had a really beautiful melodic sense. He had a good way with words. He had a special feeling for the language."

"This has been the real new work," Rick said of his songwriting. "It's a new thing, a new discipline you have to obtain.
It's real hard for me to just sit down, pick up a pencil and start
writing. I guess it's a throwback to school homework. When I
started doing my homework I always thought 'What would
happen if I didn't do it?' I found out. You get poor grades. But
I can always put off the song. I've written quite a few, but only
when I was in the mood. I guess eventually I'll have to
change."

Rolling Stone record reviewer Lester Bangs went wild for the
album. "This album is an unmitigated delight," he wrote, "a
strong set of authentic American music. Clearly now, the dude
who can sing songs like 'Hello Mary Lou' is also a member of
that great company which includes the likes of Bob Dylan,
Buffalo Springfield and the Byrds. Listening to this album, and
recalling Nelson's early work, the extent of his influence on
styles of composition and delivery of above artists becomes
obvious, and now he has returned the favor with a brilliant
collection of gutsy originals and exquisitely rendered favorites
by Dylan, Kershaw, et al. And the big, rich country sound of
the guitars here show how thoroughly Rick has digested the
lessons in rock ensemble sound of the Byrds and the Springfield.

"The opener, 'Come On In,' sets the mood perfectly. It is a
sanguine handshake of a song that draws you in and sets you
perfectly at ease. When that great steel guitar takes off on its
first rippling solo flight, the exhilaration is doubled as you
realize that this music is as technically impeccable as it is
congenial. Mention should also be made of Rick's announce-
ments of songs and general comments to the audience; he's so
nervous and shy it's almost embarrassing, yet absolutely
charming.

"The rest of the album is just as comfortable and inspired as
that great beginning. 'Mary Lou' features a vibrant steel guitar

excursion by Tom Brumley that I would trade for almost any album by hip L.A. country-rock groups. Somehow Rick's music seems more authentic, as if he and his band had been hiding out in Okie bars all these years paying dues and assimilating the pure draft beer ethos of this music."

With this album, Rick once again planted his feet firmly in the forefront of contemporary rock music, a rock & roll Lazarus back from the dead in less than a year.

One person who must have been watching Rick's remarkable resurgence was his old idol, Elvis Presley, who was planning his own return to live performances in Las Vegas. His wife, Priscilla Presley, told a story in her memoirs: "At dinner one evening Elvis said that he was concerned about his hairstyle, and I mentioned I'd seen a billboard of Ricky Nelson on Sunset Boulevard. His hair was long with a slight wave and I thought it was extremely appealing. I innocently suggested that Elvis take a look at it. 'Are you goddamn crazy?' he shouted. 'After all these years, Ricky Nelson, Fabian, that whole group have more or less followed in my footsteps, and now I'm supposed to copy them? You gotta be out of your mind, woman.' "

The Stone Canyon Band continued to rehearse as much as every other day at Rick's house. Rick always showed up late, even with rehearsal no further than down the hall, while the band hung out shooting pool. "We'd wait around for two or three hours," Allen Kemp said. "He'd always take a shower first, then come and go, 'Hi, guys.' " He loved being part of a rock group and used to discuss dropping his name from the billing and simply going out as the Stone Canyon Band.

Rick and the band made a relative flurry of television appearances. He swapped lines on "Louisiana Man" with his old sidekick Glen Campbell on Campbell's show. He sang the same song with its author, Doug Kershaw, and Johnny Cash on Cash's network variety show and appeared on the summer replacement for the Cash series, "Johnny Cash Presents the Everly Brothers Show," produced by his old friend Joe Byrne. Although he never mentioned it to Byrne, Rick harbored hurt feelings that Byrne didn't use him as host instead of the Everlys. He was on a Bobbie Gentry special, sang and did a skit with the host on the Jim Nabors show, played a medley of his old hits on the Andy Williams program, sang Dylan's "Tonight I'll Be Staying Here with You" on the Miss U.S.A. Beauty Pageant, and performed on a show hosted by Mama Cass, "Get It Together."

Kemp used to go over in the evenings to play acoustic guitar with Rick, informal sessions that would last until four in the morning. One night they went down to his parents' house in Laguna, took a few uppers, and stayed up all night playing guitars. Kemp dumped an ashtray on Harriet's immaculate sofa and burned a large hole he couldn't cover. Harriet put him at ease the next morning. "Don't worry," she said. "I've been trying to get Ozzie to buy me a new one."

Rick rarely got up before noon. Kris kept a different schedule, getting up in the morning with the three kids. "She would just disappear," said Kemp. "She'd get up early and go down to the gallery. She could stay down there if she wanted."

Kris did a lot of expensive redecorating. She spent $30,000 on a remodeled kitchen that was eventually pictured in *House Beautiful*. David remembered her slamming down the phone on an accountant and going ahead and ordering the new carpets regardless of what the accountant said. "They spent money," said Kemp. "She probably drained him. She was always looking for something like that to do. Every day it was, what can I do to spend money? It didn't seem to show that much. You'd see a big new kitchen stained glass thing or a big new dining table show up. All of a sudden, new carpeting."

Rick, on the other hand, barely noticed money. Half the time he didn't even carry pocket change. Stores always recognized him and were happy to forward a bill if he forgot his wallet again and didn't have credit cards with him. An accountant paid the bills he never saw. It meant nothing to Rick to drop $600 on a red-white-and-blue fringed leather jacket, although he was not as a rule extravagant. But that was more a matter of taste than means. Kris was a little different in that regard. "She liked to doll up," allowed Kemp.

In March 1970 Rick and the band did twenty shows at U.S. military installations in England, Germany, and Spain. Kris went along. "They did a lot of shopping," said Randy Meisner. "I couldn't 'cause I didn't have any money." Nobody enjoyed the trip that much. The band members were all strapped for cash, and the long bus rides didn't help cheer anybody up. Without any equipment managers, the musicians had to depend on servicemen to help load and unload the instruments and amplifiers. The audiences at the bases were small and unappreciative.

"They expected me to be as I was 12 years ago," said Rick, "with short hair. When we walked onstage the first night, the guy in front of the stage turned his chair around so his back was to the stage. Someone else shouted 'Where are your mini-skirts?' It was terrible. And we'd gone all that way. It's rough trying to play to a man with a cigar hanging out of his mouth and his back to you."

Back in the states, the band hit the road on a tour of colleges and small clubs in major cities. Rick hated flying and customarily took some kind of downers before boarding a flight. "He couldn't wait to go on the road half the time, just to get away," said Kemp. "That's when he got more appreciation. At home, he was just a guy. On the road, he would get his old treatment. He would be Rick Nelson. At home he was Eric. She called him Eric or Ricky. I've seen her quite a few times be cold, cold as ice. He never, ever, in front of anybody stood up to her. She'd get real snotty and leave. She'd come in while we were rehearsing and say something like, 'I'm going down to the gallery—I don't know when I'll be back.' "

Customers at San Francisco's Basin Street West could hear Kris clearly from backstage during intermission at one show screaming, "Where the fuck is my old man?" Even in the face of her most fiery tirade, though, Rick could remain calm.

When the band returned from Europe, Meisner quit. His wife and three children were still in Nebraska, and her patience with his musical career had run out. "We weren't really making that much money," said Meisner, "and being away from the family a long time, things were kind of eating at me." Meisner went to work as a parts manager at a local John Deere farm equipment outlet. "He was having problems with his wife," said Kemp. "He quit, and Rick was pretty upset about it." Tim Cetera, younger brother of Peter Cetera of Chicago, replaced Meisner.

The band entered the studio in June to record a new album, one that would exclusively showcase Rick's burgeoning songwriting skills, *Rick Sings Nelson.* Without Meisner's high harmonies, the vocal sound sorely lacked the celestial choir quality. But that was the least of the album's deficiencies. The bland, unexciting songs themselves provided the basic problem. For an album that based its entire concept on the songwriting, that represented a grave obstacle. If Rick plumbed his inner feelings to come up with these songs, he found little to connect with in the way of wrenching emotion. He did not inhabit the songs but stood outside like a detached observer. "He wanted to be a songwriter, come hell or high water," said Kemp.

The package itself announced the seriousness of the venture. With a die-cut cover that revealed a hand-lettered record label bearing Rick's picture, the album also came with a fold-out poster of Rick posed in the $600 red-white-and-blue fringed leather jacket. The *Rolling Stone* reviewer tried to be kind: "How is Rick Nelson as a songwriter?" he wrote. "Well, so-so. He's got a fine touch for softer country-rock like 'Anytime' or 'The Reason Why,' but he also dabbles in pseudo-allegorical Doorsy dreck-rock on 'Mr. Dolphin.' Perhaps the latter offers us a clue as to why Rick has shied away from a funkier style—when he tries, he sounds simply awful."

In September, just before the album was released, he took the songs into the Troubadour for a live trial. Robert Hilburn of the *Los Angeles Times* caught the show. "Unfortunately," he wrote, "the country-rock numbers have little freshness. The songs such as 'Mr. Dolphin' and 'California' have melodies that are too familiar and lyrics that are too uneventful. Nelson is better off, on the upbeat portion of his show, sticking to his old hits or some other contemporary material.

"The softer songs, however, are a different matter. Nelson showed a fine vocal sensitivity on 'How Long' and 'Life,' two songs which reflect a good feel for lyrics. On both numbers, he set aside his electric guitar in favor of an acoustic guitar. They were his best offerings."

For all his years as a musician, Rick started writing songs in earnest only with the Stone Canyon Band. He had trouble with the discipline and lacked the intellectual predilections of a natural writer. For Rick, it was work, and it didn't come easy. A song like "Easy to Be Free" gave a glimpse of a gift, and he was determined to make those skills blossom.

Meanwhile, back in Nebraska Meisner was getting mighty tired of working the parts counter at John Deere. After about three months, he put together another band to work occasional gigs and keep his hand in. Soon he found himself playing five nights a week and dragging himself to work the next morning. Kemp kept trying to convince Rick to invite Meisner back, but Rick wouldn't agree. "No, it's not a good idea," he would tell Kemp. Finally, he caved in, and Kemp called Meisner, who flew back to Los Angeles and rejoined the band.

The sessions for the next album were scattered between road trips. Rick also had not finished writing many of the songs. So the band would lay down the instrumental track and sit around while Rick wrote lyrics to already finished tracks. Rick played piano on a number of the selections, and Jimmie Haskell supplied some unobtrusive string arrangements. Haskell had come a long way from whipping boy for Lew Chudd and won Grammy awards for his work with Bobbie Gentry ("Ode to Billie Joe") and Simon and Garfunkle ("Bridge Over Troubled Water").

The album was a curious mixture of songs. Rick extended his winning penchant for covering Bob Dylan songs with sensitive versions of "Just Like a Woman" and "Love Minus Zero/No Limit." He romped through the Shirley and Lee oldie "Feel So Good." He gave a surprisingly barrelhouse feel to "Honky Tonk Women," a song that would remain in his repertoire for the rest of his life. Years later, when Rick was introduced to Mick Jagger at a party, he stammered out a compliment, telling the Rolling Stones vocalist he thought "Honky Tonk Women" was one of the best, if not the best song ever written. Jagger smiled condescendingly. "We liked some of your stuff, too, Ricky," he said.

Rick wrote a tight, commercial piece called "Gypsy Pilot" that verged on autobiography:

> *When I was a young boy,*
> *My mama told me 'Son,*
> *You gotta get it together.*
> *You know you're the only one.'*
> *So I tried to see the sunshine.*
> *I tried to feel the rain.*
> *But I just couldn't get it together.*
> *I was feeling too much pain.*
> *So I got myself a guitar*

When I was just a kid.
I played rock and roll music.
And I'm so glad I did.

A psychic told Rick about reincarnation, telling him he was an old soul named Eric the Red in his final earthly life. Rick treated that idea in the song "The Last Time Around." Another song, "Thank You Lord," took an even more directly spiritual approach, and perhaps the most affecting song of all on the album, "Life," could have come from Zen Buddhism. These ethereal concerns have no precedent in his work, and Rick certainly lacked the intellectual underpinnings to draw the fine-point detail of the concepts he toyed with in those songs But his intuitive grasp and simple approach to the complexities may have ended up making the songs all the more accessible.

"When I wrote 'Life,' " he said, "I was feeling very low, but by the time it was completed, I was really lifted. It was one of those songs that just came to me one night and the whole thing took me less than an hour. I knew how I wanted it to sound even before we went into the studio to record it, and it was my idea that Decca should release it as a single before it came out on an album."

The song came out on a single in January 1971, with a number from *Rick Sings Nelson*, "California," on the other side. The gentle, soft-rock sound of the song, along with the philosophic abstractions, made it an unlikely candidate for top-forty airplay, and the single failed to make even the bottom of the charts (although "California" was a hit in Australia).

The album was completed in June, and while the band sipped champagne and listened to the final playbacks, the record was named *Rudy the Fifth*, after the bottle of champagne. The cover photo, by Kent McCord, captured Rick in his new look, with his hair hanging down around his shoulders, surrounded by a fur coat. The public failed to respond. While *Rick Sings Nelson* spent a grand total of two weeks on the charts, rising no further than 196, *Rudy the Fifth* didn't make the charts at all.

But Rick was in charge of his music. For the first time in his life, he was making his own decisions, guiding his ship with his own hand and following his own vision, however weak and scattered.

"Now I'm the happiest I've ever been," he told the *Los Angeles Herald-Examiner*, "especially with a group like the Stone Canyon Band. It's really nice to go into a place where people are expecting to see what happened to the kid they saw grow up on television, Little Ricky, then we blow their minds with our music.

"And I've gone along with that image. It would be a dishonest thing to make a prime factor of trying to overcome it. It's something I did and, at that time, was a good thing. I'm not embarrassed about the early songs. Every song I recorded I was really into at that time. But that's what a lot of people were into. I never copped out on the songs. I never did a song I didn't like.

"I really don't even mind if people want to think of me as 'Little Ricky.' Of course, nobody wants to be 'little' anything. But those days were more of a plus, more of a help than a handicap. It helps to have people know who you are. I feel sorry for guys who have to go from one hit record to another to have people recognize them.

"A gold record now would mean all those early hypes would be taken away. It would be given to me on the merits of the record and not of a kid singing on television."

He spoke with the voice of a man coming to terms with his past but still yearning for the acknowledgment he felt was his due. He was not as comfortable with his past as he appeared, but that discomfort would be soon put to use, producing that gold record now he so avidly sought.

As he did when he first linked up with Rick, Randy Meisner got another call from John Boylan. This time, Boylan wanted him to join a couple of other musicians to back Linda Ronstadt, whom he was both producing and dating at the time, in a nightclub engagement in the San Francisco Bay area. Meisner, Glenn Frey, and Don Henley hit it off so well they decided to form a band. Once again, he left Rick, this time to fly with the Eagles.

10
Garden Party

A CONCERT PROGRAM COMBINING Chuck Berry, Bo Diddley, the Coasters, the Shirelles, Bobby Rydell, Gary U.S. Bonds, and special guest stars Rick Nelson and the Stone Canyon Band guaranteed a sellout for the Richard Nader Rock & Roll Revival October 15, 1971, at Madison Square Garden. But nobody at the Garden that night could have had an inkling that it would turn out to be one of the most famous concerts in rock history, celebrated in song and acquiring an integral place in Rick's own legend.

Nader, a Long Island–based promoter, made a name for himself promoting these rock & roll revivals, beginning two years earlier with a sold-out concert at the Garden starring Bill Haley and His Comets. Ironically, Rick had never played a concert in New York City, and it had been a long, long time since he faced a crowd the size of the twenty-thousand-seat Garden.

"Nor had he performed on what we call a package show with other rock and roll stars," said Nader. "When he had his hits in the late fifties and sixties, he was a solo performer, and his schedule didn't allow him to go out and do long, extended tours around the country. He was featured at state fairs and events of that nature. He'd get out on a weekend, do a city, and fly back. So he wasn't a regular rock and roller that went out and did these package shows. So it was really foreign territory for him to come in and do that show. It took a lot of convincing to talk him into doing it."

"It was a case of being talked into," remembered Rick, "and myself talking to myself into doing the show. A fellow named Richard Nader used to promote a lot of 'Rock and Roll Revivals' and I can remember hearing the word 'revival.' It sounded like someone had passed away and they were raising him up from the dead. It was a kind of weird terminology that went against what I was doing at the time. I had just formed a band, the Stone Canyon Band. I was writing songs and performing them and everything. But I got to thinking.

"For about two or three years, Nader would come to different shows and try to talk us into doing these. Then, when I finally got the band together, I thought, well you know, maybe it'd be a good place to be seen and have a band seen. I'd never played at Madison Square Garden and there were a lot of people there. So I figured, why not? But deep down, I had my doubts about it. I really did. But I'd never seen a rock and roll revival. I had just heard about them.

"So we went back and learned all the old songs in chronological order and came out and did them and there was just this kind of nonacceptance. My hair was a lot longer and I think maybe the physical appearance, combined with the new band—I had a steel guitar player at the time. I didn't realize what was all part of the game. You're supposed to come out and look like you're from the '50s and you had the exact same format musically, which I didn't. But I figured as long as I was there and I was singing the songs, it wouldn't make much of a difference. But it was just a weird experience."

Guitarist Allen Kemp remembered holding similar reservations. "At sound check," he said, "everybody else was looking the same and doing just their strict old hits. He refused to do just that. He wanted to do something different. I remember looking out through this doorway from the dressing room and you saw everybody coming in, the audience, dressed in old fifties penny loafers, white socks, and hair combed back. I thought, 'Oh, no. We're in trouble.' "

"Rick looked great," said Nader. "He had long hair at the time. He didn't really know where he was. He was trying to capture the psychedelic look and at the same time maintain his roots in rockabilly. He wanted to be contemporary, but there was just too much roots in rockabilly."

The audience and band warily appraised each other at the start, leery of the impending culture clash. Those in the crowd not dressed in nostalgic 1950s gear wore the standard East Coast garb of the time, bell bottoms and T-shirts. Rick and his musicians came decked out in Hollywood hillbilly, spangled western wear and boots, shaggy haired and looking very California. But the crowd loved the performance. At first.

Rick tore into a procession of his old hits, some, like "Poor Little Fool" and "Lonesome Town," worked up especially for the occasion, feeding the Garden crowd the pure nostalgia they came to hear. But when Rick took off his guitar and stepped to the piano for the next-to-last tune of his twelve-song set, an incident took place in the remote seats of the far upper balcony that changed the tone of the evening for him and the band.

The cheap seating sections near the rafters, painted blue and referred to as blue heaven, were a notorious nesting place of rowdies looking to raise hell at hockey matches, basketball games, and rock concerts. The security guards chose this moment to clear an entire section of drunken fans in these rear seats, and the crowd raised a lusty roar at the police action. These boos coincided with Rick's sitting down at the piano to play "Honky Tonk Women," a number from his *Rudy the Fifth* album and a recent hit by the Rolling Stones. Some of the people down front took the balcony booing as a cue to express displeasure at this departure from a rigid oldies program and picked up the boos. "There is no such thing in New York as a quiet boo," said Nader.

Rick came offstage shaken. "It was shivering," said Kemp, "all these people booing. We were all upset. Rick kept saying, 'I knew we shouldn't have done it.' " A few minutes later, a security guard came into the dressing room and explained the real reason for the booing, and the mood in the band room changed to a relieved giddiness.

About six months later, a song jelled in Rick's head. He stayed up all night finishing it. "I ended up writing it on one piece of paper," said Rick. "I didn't want to get up. It just started happening. I really heard the instrumentation exactly as I wanted it to sound like and, at the end, I had a Carl Perkins–type ending on it. It was just all there."

"I remember falling asleep listening to Pop play the piano," Rick's daughter, Tracy, recalled, " 'cause the music room was right below me. And one morning I went downstairs to go to school at about seven, and I knocked on the door. It took a while for him to answer. I said, 'What are you doing, Pop?' He said, 'I got up about three in the morning and I've been writing this song, "Garden Party," and I've been writing all night. I haven't been able to stop. I just felt compelled to write it.' Later on we used this as an example of what it means to be an artist. Sometimes things just came through you. He said that night he felt he was given a gift. The music just came through him."

In May 1972 Rick and the band went into the studio to record "Garden Party" and a few other songs. He got the band members to agree to stick to the story about what had happened that night at the Garden. No mention would be made of the police clearing out drunken fans to ruin the drama of the story. Rick knew he had something. He insisted the record company release the cut as a single immediately. Decca Records had been merged with other labels into a conglomerate called MCA Records, and undoubtedly many of the new company's executives didn't even know they had Rick Nelson under contract. The record wouldn't have gone anywhere without some extraordinary cooperation from the record label. His cousin Willy Nelson now managed him. Willy Nelson, son of Ozzie's older brother, Al, had been a singer himself and also had been part of a vocal group that appeared on TV's "Shindig" called the Shindogs. He also worked in management with Del Shannon and Brian Hyland.

Cousin Willy went to meet with Rich Frio, vice president in charge of marketing at MCA, to discuss the single. "He poured out his heart to me," said Frio, "what Rick's feelings really were, what the record meant. It put everything in perspective for me. I was in a very powerful position at the company. While Willy sat there, I put together a conference call with all thirty of my promotion men. I told them I was going to go to lunch with Willy Nelson at the Universal commissary, and when I got back from lunch, I wanted them each logging in with at least one radio station. Lo and behold, when I got back, the calls were coming in."

What Frio put in motion didn't stop until the single of "Garden Party" climbed all the way to number six on the charts. It was one of the most unprecedented comeback hits in the history of rock music.

Rick was right. "Garden Party" was a gift. Nothing in his body of work remotely hints at the emotional resonance and the depths of sensitivity he reached as a songwriter on this number. He sculpted the record's sound with a sure, certain hand, using nothing more than the tick of the drummer's high hat to drive the track, accompanied by a couple of acoustic guitars, a lazy, prominent bass figure, and a few curling accents from steel guitar. This model of simplicity sets off the laconic vocal and the Dylanesque lyrics.

The mood is mildly scornful, and the resolute conclusion—"If memories are all I sing, I'd rather drive a truck"—echoes a line Rick often employed in interviews. But, at last, on "Garden Party" Rick used songwriting as a way to express his closely guarded feelings. Not surprisingly, he does not raise his voice in anger or engage in biting sarcasm. It is a timid but determined cry for self-respect, and the issue revolves around a key to his own sense of identity—his lifelong battle to be taken seriously as a musician.

"I know what they think," he told the *New York Times* earlier that year, before he wrote and recorded the song. "But in the old days I sold a lot of records over a period of time, and you can't sustain that by being just another pretty face. A lot of people equate me with guys like Frankie Avalon and Fabian, but my thing wasn't built on that foundation. I know and like Fabian, but to me he contributed absolutely nothing to music."

(Fabian, on the other hand, said he met Rick only once, when they ran into each other at an airport, and he remembered Rick looking down his nose at him.)

"Sure, in the beginning I used to fake it on guitar," Rick continued. "I was too scared to play, and anyhow no one could hear you with everyone screaming. But in time I learned to play and enjoy it. Also I had guys like Joe Osborn in my band [Osborn went on to become a top studio musician, lending his bass to records like Simon and Garfunkle's "Bridge Over Troubled Water"], and later Glen Campbell and James Burton on guitar. Jim, incidentally, is on lead guitar today with Elvis. We had some fantastic musicians at that time, and you'd be surprised at how many English groups—like the Beatles and the Rolling Stones—admitted they were influenced by some of our early records."

Music began for Rick as a way to escape the oppression of

the family TV show, except that Ozzie found a way to usurp even that. Rick nevertheless doggedly pursued the craft, pushing himself and growing rapidly with experience, making his records far better than they needed to be. He knew how good those California rockabilly sides were, and he knew he never got credit for his accomplishments. His TV fame and teen-idol image confused the issue. With the Stone Canyon Band, he finally began to stand on his own, even if he was still propped up in part by his past. "Garden Party" was a ringing declaration of independence.

"I've always enjoyed playing the guitar and listening to music," he said. "When I was 16 I looked around for something I could do on my own. The rest of the show was totally my father's idea and we were all part of it, but music was my own thing."

In December 1971 Rick and the group took the stage at Nashville's Ryman Auditorium for a one-song performance on the Grand Ole Opry, the signal honor the country music establishment can extend. His old pal Johnny Cash was also on the program that night, and Kris Kristofferson staggered into their hotel suite, tequila bottle in hand.

Before leaving for his first public tour of England in February, Rick participated in a major piece of image breaking with a dramatic appearance on the television series "Owen Marshall, Counselor at Law." In an episode that aired January 27, 1972, Rick played Vietnam veteran Gar Kellerman, an ingratiating hospital attendant accused of rape. Kellerman had an alibi from his wife and the evidence was too flimsy for prosecution, so he was sued in civil court by his victim (played by Stephanie Powers). Her attorneys—Arthur Hill as Owen Marshall and Lee Majors as his associate—uncovered evidence of previous assaults by Kellerman, but the victims were too scared to testify. In a powerful scene slightly reminiscent of "Perry Mason," Marshall forced Kellerman to confess on the stand, unwinding frantically as the silent victims one by one took seats in the back of the courtroom. A long way from "Ozzie and Harriet," the role required Rick to come out of the nice-guy character he had played his entire life for this emotional climax. He convincingly fell apart on the stand, bellowing and grimacing in a display of turmoil no acting assignment had ever before required of him. Producer John Epstein was responsible for the offbeat casting.

"Epstein gave me the script and said I had one hour to decide whether I could do it," Rick said. "I said yes without reading that courtroom scene at the end. I think if I had read it, I would have been too scared to do it."

Rick also played the part of a strolling minstrel in a musical special produced by Sid and Marty Krott called *Ful-de-Rol*, which was broadcast in February, continuing to move away from the static video image that followed him from childhood. Later in the year he walked his way through a small but pivotal part in an episode of "McCloud," the series about a popular small-town cop written and produced by his old friend Glen Larson of the Four Preps, on his way to becoming one of Hollywood's top TV producers. His character, Jimmie Roy Taylor, was a rock singer with a shadowy past, and the script left the dialogue largely in the hands of other parts; the show did feature a couple of truncated concert sequences where Rick got to sing his new hit record, even though a prime-time crime show may not have been the most appropriate or effective TV exposure for "Garden Party."

Ozzie, meanwhile, was making plans to return to the small screen. He produced a pilot of a show called "Ozzie's Girls," where Ozzie and Harriet rented out the boys' old rooms to three female college students. He let slip to the press hints that his sons might make guest appearances, but they never did, even when the show finally aired as a series during the 1973 season.

As portrayed the previous year in *Esquire* magazine, the Nelson family was in disarray. Even the customarily cheerful Harriet bemoaned the situation. "We're just as confused as everyone else," she said. "And we used to be so sure about what we wanted, what was good. We're three separate families now. It's kind of sad."

But it was left to David to scourge the family's public image with his angry, somewhat bitter assessment. "A lot of families are trying to make a transition, in morals and values, from the '50s to the '70s," he told writer Sara Davidson. "In our family, there was no generation gap, and I think it's too bad. Because I was a little old man at 13. I was polite, tried never to offend anyone, and I felt this great responsibility, because I wasn't just me—I was a quarter of a thing. Whatever I did, I felt the burden of three other people and all the crew who worked on the show. I wasn't a truck driver's son who could go out and bust people if he got mad.

"Let's say the Nelson family as the great American pastime is sinking," he continued. "Ricky is likely to dive in and try, until his last breath, to prop the whole thing up. I'm likely to stand on the rocks watching, with my arms folded, and say 'I told you so.' "

After the show was canceled, David started a company that leased lighting equipment and tried to establish himself as a director. He made a few episodes of a TV series called "O.K. Crackerby," starring Burl Ives, and helmed three low-budget feature films that came to nothing. David even directed a documentary on his brother titled *Easy to Be Free*, which featured live footage interspersed with interviews and which eventually ran on a few independent TV stations in 1973. He was still trying to eke out a place for himself in the highly competitive world of professional filmmaking, as determined and driven in his field as Rick was in his. "I can't listen to my father forever," he told *Esquire*. "He can't direct my life and career indefinitely. The cord should have been broken years ago, but at 30 years old I was still on that show saying 'Hi Mom, Hi Pop' every week." Rick, on the other hand, appeared to be on the verge of finally breaking free of his tangled past.

In February he made his first public tour of England. Rick always held a special feeling for England, because the TV show never aired in that country and his records were successful solely on their musical merits. Rick, Kris, and the band arrived in London a week ahead of the first concert so Rick could appear on the live music TV show "The Old Grey Whistle Test," where he forgot the lyrics to Dylan's "Love Minus Zero" halfway through his rendition.

It was an especially severe winter in Britain, and across the country power workers were staging strikes that resulted in the first date at Manchester being canceled. But the ecstatic reception at the Royal Albert Hall wiped away the bad taste lingering from Madison Square Garden; Londoners including Cliff Richard, Paul McCartney, and Olivia Newton-John gave Rick a hero's welcome. In a throwback to the fifties, fans actually ripped the clothes off his back. He and Kris managed to spend a day with George Harrison, who was instrumental in convincing Rick to make the brief tour, before the show, but a car crash on the way to the show prevented the Beatles guitarist from seeing the concert. Harrison briefly rented a house next door to Rick's Nichols Canyon place and used to drop over and shoot pool.

The shows remained stiff and almost rote, Rick whipping through the songs with little more than a muttered "thank you" in between numbers. "I always found that very strange," said Allen Kemp. "He could never relax. He was so inward and so shy, he never let the audience really know him. Each night didn't spark anything different. It was like, 'Here's another song.' I don't know how many times I heard that. There was a time where he was into snorting a little mescaline. He did so much better shows as far as talking. He'd kind of just go off rambling. At least every night wasn't the same old thing. But he stopped doing that. It was getting out there. It was too psychedelic."

In June the single of "Garden Party" took off, right alongside the first single by Randy Meisner's new band, the Eagles, "Take It Easy." A major breakthrough was in the works, but Rick stumbled going through the door. He couldn't finish an album to follow the single. It would be a fatal six months before the *Garden Party* album was released.

"We had some problems in the studio," said Kemp. "There was some stuff that wasn't finished. He was finishing writing stuff in the studio. He would have a verse, no chorus, and didn't have vocal parts arranged. Doing stuff in the studio costs time. Lot of sitting around. He wasn't happy with some of the words. He'd go back in and change them. A lot of the other stuff is meaningless. 'Garden Party' was starting to go, so we needed an album. He had all these little ideas of songs. Then he really wanted to go in and have all the rest of the songs be his."

He rerecorded an old Chuck Berry song he had previously recorded on *Spotlight on Rick,* "Talking About You," and cut another song Kemp wrote with Meisner, although Kemp remembered having to give up the publishing to get the song included. Otherwise, the rest were strictly Rick Nelson compositions—and a dreadful lot they were. "Palace Guard" was the worst kind of vapid Dylan imitation. "Nighttime Lady" was a weak, clichéd love song. "Are You Really Real?" doesn't even sound like a finished song.

Rich Frio wanted Rick to cover the 1960 Jimmy Jones hit "Handy Man," but Rick firmly refused to do any nonoriginals. The same song turned out to be a hit for James Taylor, who handled the tune in the same kind of soft-rock style Rick could have given it. When the album was finally released after Thanksgiving, the company searched in vain for a second

single to try to bring some much-needed attention to the LP,
finally settling on an edited version of "Palace Guard," which
climbed slowly to number sixty-five on the charts and rapidly
disappeared. The comeback, so fiercely struggled for, faded
away.

"You'd think MCA would've been happy," said Rick. "They
had themselves a big seller. In fact, though, I created a monster with 'Garden Party.' Just when the record was doing real
well, I got this call from Mike Maitland, the MCA president. I
thought he was calling to congratulate me, but instead he tells
me 'You spent too much money, you need a producer.' I
couldn't believe it. Not only did they stop promoting the
album, but they also wanted to limit my freedom. I had always
worked best when I had a free hand, and now that was going
to stop. It was clearly the beginning of the end of our relationship."

Trouble also hit the band. The final straw came when Willy
Nelson offered the musicians a seven-year contract. The musicians wanted a raise from the $350-a-week salary ($150 a week
when they were off the road). The group had been spending
spare time rehearsing with a couple of additional musicians,
with an eye toward recording as a unit on their own. The
proffered contract called for control over the members' outside activities. "We got to feeling like 'Garden Party' was maybe
a fluke," said Kemp. With the exception of Brumley, the band
resigned en masse, moved to Aspen, and changed the name to
Canyon, before breaking up for good.

"I think he [Rick] was pretty pissed off," Kemp said. "We told
him on a flight back from Dallas to L.A. one night. He said he
understood. I talked to him a little bit after that. I was just then
starting to write my own material. I told him out front I didn't
want to be a backup musician the rest of my life—I wanted to
take a stab at doing my own original thing. He understood. I
think."

The timing couldn't have been worse. The *Garden Party*

album had hardly been out more than a month. In a few weeks Rick was due to appear on February 27, 1973, at the Houston Astrodome, followed shortly by a Carnegie Hall concert in New York. Rick, who didn't fraternize with musicians, didn't have a clue where to turn to put together a new band in such a rush. His inevitable luck held out, however, and a new band walked into his life within days.

"They had been talking about it," said Rick, "and they wanted to form their own group, all except Tom. Tom was very happy with what we were playing. I've always let them do what they wanted to do and it was a mutual agreement kind of thing. No hard feelings or anything. It happened just before the album came out and it could have been very difficult to promote the album but I got together with the new band in about three days. It was incredible—such super musicians and singers. That was my main worry, that I'd fail vocally to be able to match what was going on.

"We were playing a date at the Houston Astrodome. It's kind of frightening anyway, just to drive by there. It's so huge. So that was my next date and we just had to get it together. We had a week and a half between that and trying to get the band together, so it was kind of thrown together. But everyone really came through."

Dennis Sarokin was a scrambling, aggressive, street-smart New Yorker who combined his first name with his brother's to come up with the stage name Larden when the two put together a folksinging act that worked Greenwich Village in the mid-1960s. Dennis and Lary Larden belonged to a band called Every Mother's Son that picked up a 1967 top-ten hit with "Come on Down to My Boat," before dissolving. Dennis moved to California to work in a big-budget feature film that fizzled and was hanging out, doing little or nothing, early in 1973, when a friend who worked at MCA Records called and told him Rick Nelson needed a band.

He hurriedly threw together a rhythm section with Jay DeWitt White, a down-home Texan whom Sarokin had seen play in a bar band once or twice, on bass and drummer Ty Grimes from Birmingham, Alabama. They auditioned for Rick at Studio Instrument Rentals and got the job. Sarokin was under the impression that nobody else tried out.

"We didn't do anything to set the world on fire," he said. "I certainly wasn't a sensational guitarist, but I guess he liked my attitude, my session-player mentality, and my arranger chops." The band's first date was the Houston Astrodome. The second took place at a small San Jose nightclub, and the third job was playing Carnegie Hall. Sarokin took a leadership role right from the start, suggesting Rick include "Lonesome Town" at Carnegie Hall, backed only by acoustic guitar.

The prestigious Carnegie Hall show did not sell out, and Willy Nelson resorted to giving away free tickets so the house would be full. Andy Warhol's attending the show, however, delighted Kris.

The "Garden Party" hit did have the effect of boosting Rick's concert appeal, and he moved out of the small clubs and college campuses he had been playing into larger facilities and higher-paying engagements, although a stand at Disneyland hardly put him in front of eager fans but relegated his performance to just another fairgrounds attraction, something to spell the time between the waits for the rides.

He stayed home as much as possible to spend time with his three children but hit the road for three or four days at the end of every week. Rather than book a string of dates to accommodate an extended tour, he and the band would fly first-class to a cluster of dates, return home, and go back out again toward the end of the week.

"Back then, I used the term 'weekend warriors,' " said Sarokin. "We'd usually go out three days on the weekends, 'cause Rick was real into the family and the kids were young.

He was very active with things like Daddy's got to be home Wednesday, which was the ballet recital. So we'd fly out, play Rochester, New York; Syracuse, New York; Philadelphia; and fly home. Then we'd go out the next weekend and do something that was two miles from Philadelphia, which would eat up a lot of bucks. But he chose it because it suited his lifestyle. He liked to get out on the road, but he liked to get back and be there for the family."

In April he started recording an album with the new Stone Canyon Band, and work progressed slowly. Sarokin wrote a song on the way home from the Carnegie Hall concert called "One Night Stand," scribbling the lyrics in a phone booth while waiting for a flight. He based the song on an experience of his own during the New York stay, but Rick knew all about the song. There were always women on the road for him.

Sarokin ended up with four of his songs on the eventual album, along with a collaboration between him and Rick. He also worked as a kind of assistant producer to Rick, whose laid-back, indecisive ways contrasted sharply with Sarokin's East Coast hustle. His chores often extended beyond the studio. "I'd have to go to his house to drag him down to the studio," Sarokin said. "It was like chaperon duty."

In addition to contending with Rick's chronic lateness, Sarokin found himself making musical decisions usually left to the producer because of Rick's inability to take charge. "For a guy who liked to be at the helm, captain of the ship," he said, "he was not always at the helm. I would go out there and say, 'OK, Rick, what are we going to do?' He'd say, 'Let's cut the track.' I'd go and tell the guys, you do this, you play bass, I'll play acoustic, arrange it all for the guys, and lay down the track. I'd come back and say, 'Is that all right?' He'd say, 'Uh, yeah.' I'd say, 'What do you want to do now?' He'd say, 'I dunno.' 'OK,' I'd say, 'I'm going to put on a stereo acoustic now.' I'd come out and say, 'How's that?' He'd say, 'Sounds good. How does it sound to you?'

"So that was a great compliment, knowing that he trusted me, and that worked well. We developed our rapport. The other guys would be off, and I'd be in the studio all night, arranging something. But it got to the point with his vocals where I could go out there and listen to a thousand takes and choose which the best ones were, but I couldn't go out there and motivate him to do it in one take. He was very, very introverted when it came to doing vocals."

Rick recorded a song, "I Don't Want to Be Lonely Tonight," by his old associate from the early days, Baker Knight. They hadn't seen each other in years when Knight went by his house to show him some songs. "I was nervous," Knight said. "It was a nice meeting, but I didn't get much. It wasn't like the old times. He was more standoffish, even shyer, not wanting to make any comments. I don't know how to put this. He was just uncomfortable with it all. I was glad to leave."

Rick and Kris moved to their Laguna Beach house early that year, selling the Nichols Canyon place to Randy Meisner, who was finding both fortune and fame with the Eagles. Before six months had passed, they moved again, to a yellow-and-white frame, fourteen-room house on an acre of land, tucked away on the hillside above Studio City in the San Fernando Valley. Built fifty years earlier by a woman who prized privacy, the house was turned around so the front faced the garden and the back looked out on the road. "We'll stay here," said Kris in 1973. "We tried living in our beach house at Laguna, but we seemed to spend our whole day commuting by freeway. But we needed space for the children and we refuse to live in Beverly Hills. I won't even shop there—it's just not my kind of place. I found this house just as the owner was putting a 'For Sale' sign up in the yard. This is home. How lucky we are."

She busied herself redecorating the Farm, as they dubbed the new home. A seven-foot dining-room table was made out of a piece of parquet dance floor from an old ballroom in London, old on top, new on the bottom. The ten-foot living-room table, on the other hand, was an antique Kris put a new top on. An eight-burner, three-oven 1927 Magic Chef stove was reconditioned for the kitchen. A large American flag hung above the couple's bed, a housewarming gift from Kris's brother, Mark Harmon, then following in his father's footsteps as quarterback at UCLA.

At the bottom of the hill, a stable and corral housed their two horses and goat. More than forty miles of trails led all the way to the beach. Corn, tomatoes, beans, and other vegetables grew in the backyard, and four dogs ran free around house and yard. A tire swing hung from a tree. Rick's brand-new, bright-red Ford Pantera, one of the fastest production cars Detroit ever made, was parked out front. Delighted with his new-found role as gentleman farmer, Rick even took to getting up in the morning to do chores.

Kris continued to paint and run her gallery. "It won't be open nine to five every day, but for people to drop by and catch me if I'm here," she said. She planned another exhibit that December, and her simple paintings were commanding as much as $5,000 apiece. Luci Baines Nugent bought one of her works. "She asked friends to bring her to meet me in the studio after she saw something I had done in a home in Beverly Hills," Kris said. "After she left, President Johnson's secretary called and bought a painting she had seen in the studio and told the president about. Later, Luci's secretary and friend called and commissioned me to do a painting of the Johnson farm in Texas. I have a five-page letter from Luci written in longhand, thanking me for the painting."

Kris could count on the confidence of an oldest child, even if she admitted to having problems asserting herself while growing up in the male-dominated household of the Harmons. She could also flare up a fiery temper. "Probably I'm exposing a bad side of my personality to admit it," she said, "but when something strikes me wrong, I just go bananas. I go berserk. I'll go out of my way to fight something that seems wrong and to set things right. I'm not reticent about that at all."

In January 1974 MCA Records finally released *Windfall*, almost six months after the album was completed. "Lifestream" and "Evil Woman Child," a single culled from the sessions and released the previous September, failed to make the charts, and the label didn't appear enthusiastic about the album either. "Rick had been with Decca forever," said Sarokin. "It just got to the point where the label was tired of him. They had the back catalog. They didn't know what to do with him. It just wasn't clicking, and the company didn't know what to do with him. And you had people running around saying, 'Hey, we sold twenty million records and "Poor Little Fool" was the biggest thing.' But the nuts and bolts of tho situation was people at Decca said, 'You sold records for people twenty administrations ago, and it's not selling now.' "

While the Eagles were soaring with a country-rock sound that was essentially only a variation on the sound Rick had etched with the original Stone Canyon Band, Rick himself turned toward a more relaxed, more country sound almost entirely at odds with the prevailing trends in the rock scene. The album never made the charts. *Rolling Stone* record reviewer Greg Shaw gave *Windfall* a rave, but he qualified it: "After building his stature through the last three albums," he wrote, "Rick has allowed Dennis Larden, formerly of Every Mother's Son, to write or cowrite most of the album. Ironically, Larden writes as if he was imitating Rick's style and the result is a batch of second-rate Nelsons."

Rick began the year with a six-day run at Los Angeles's Knott's Berry Farm, scene of his impromptu tryout with the Four Preps all those many years before, where he was nothing more than an extra added attraction at an amusement park. The gains of "Garden Party" were rapidly falling by the wayside.

He headlined the late-night TV show "Don Kirshner's Rock

Concert" in January and performed seven songs, including three tracks from the new album. He appeared on "The To-night Show" the next month and told Johnny Carson that he and his wife were expecting their fourth child sometime later that year. He also took another one of his idiotic acting assign-ments, appearing as Country Boy White, a country-rock singer unjustly accused of murder, on "Petrocelli"; he sang "One Night Stand," the new single from the album, during the opening scene. He may not have been a candidate to play Shakespearean tragedy, but he continued to play these thinly disguised roles of himself in prime-time potboilers. He told *Women's Wear Daily* he liked the idea of playing Lord Byron in a movie, then admitted he really wasn't up on poetry and didn't know that much about Byron's past.

Drummer Richie Haywood joined the band in April and made the trip to Holland, where Rick and the group per-formed on Dutch TV for a UNICEF Children's Relief Fund program. In the Netherlands, *Windfall* was enjoying a run at the charts, and the television appearance there helped push the single, which, along with "Garden Party," appeared on a Dutch album, *Artists Helping UNICEF.* Haywood left the band after only a few months to join Little Feat.

Rick and the band appeared at the second annual Willie Nelson Fourth of July Picnic, along with a star-studded cast from the country music field that included Waylon Jennings, Jerry Jeff Walker, Michael Murphy, Jimmy Buffett, Lefty Fri-zell, and a couple of dozen others. Leon Russell served as the master of ceremonies, and the event was filmed for broadcast later on TV's "The Midnight Special."

Like sacrificial lambs, Rick and the group closed out the three-day festival just after sundown the final night. By then, the festival site had completely run out of water, and the crowd of fifty thousand had been alternately drinking beer and throwing up all day long. Rick looked around for a drink of water, and someone in the crowd flipped him a can of beer, a projectile that banged hard against his delicate Martin acoustic guitar. "It was like someone had thrown a grenade onstage," said Dennis Sarokin. When Rick recovered from the fright, he cracked the can and took a deep drink.

They tore the place up, mixing rock & roll oldies, straight-ahead country numbers like "Louisiana Man," and selections from *Windfall*. A large number of the women in the crowd signaled their approval by doffing their tops and baring their breasts, a feature of the event that did not make it onto the TV special.

Sam Hilliard Nelson was born on August 29, but there was little time for celebration. Rick's increasingly hectic touring schedule was causing tension at home, and in November his father underwent surgery for liver cancer. Rick kept a crowd waiting at the Bottom Line in New York until he got word the operation had been completed but, typically, didn't give the band a hint of what his problem was. Doctors diagnosed the cancer as fatal. Ozzie, the lifelong health fanatic who never smoked or drank and made a daily practice of swimming two miles in the ocean outside their Laguna Beach house, went home to die. Vital, vibrant Ozzie, the human dynamo and wheelhouse of his family, struck down by cancer—devastating. "We were both concerned about Mom," said David, "and what was going to happen. My father right up to the end told us what he wanted us to do." David sat in dazed silence in the Laguna Beach house while his father read the will aloud. Rick canceled many dates to stay close at hand during his father's illness.

When he finally died on June 3, 1975, at the age of sixty-nine, Ozzie left behind an estate of nearly $1.3 million, including more than $160,000 in cash. He left the estate entirely in a living trust controlled exclusively by Harriet. He provided nothing special for his sons, who were equal partners with their parents in the old TV series and would presumably be endowed in their mother's will. "Death, no matter how you look at it, is a difficult time period in anyone's life," said David. But even after all the years of adulthood, Ozzie's death left his sons without a fundamental touchstone in their lives.

Three months after his father died, and three days after being granted a divorce from his wife, June, David married Yvonne O'Connor Huston, a stunning model. Life at home for Rick too was rocky going, especially after returning home from an extensive summer tour and virtually not working the rest of the year. Kris tried her first New York art exhibit in September and made a brief acting appearance on TV's "Adam 12," starring Rick's longtime friend Kent McCord. They made a public appearance with all four children at the installation of Rick's star on Hollywood Boulevard, right outside Wallich's Music City, where he had spent so many hours shopping for records years before. During the hiatus, Rick and the band got involved in a surprising recording project.

"If you think I'm crazy, you ought to meet Rick Nelson," Keith Moon told a newspaper interviewer. The drummer for the Who could boast one of rock music's best-known reputations as a wild-eyed lunatic, having trashed more hotel rooms than he could remember and once driving a car into the swimming pool of a Holiday Inn. Rick kept his most outrageous behavior out of the public eye. "He could be coaxed behind closed doors," said Sarokin. "He could be really silly, and he had a lot of guts. He was not afraid of doing things, and he was not one to be outdone."

Rick ended up singing on Moon's inept solo album, *Two Sides of the Moon*, and his band members joined an all-star lineup that included Joe Walsh on guitar and Flo and Eddie on additional background vocals on two badly garbled Rick Nelson covers, "One Night Stand" and "Teen Age Idol." Rick and Moon shared muddled lead vocals on "One Night Stand."

"Yeah, Keith thinks I'm crazy," Rick told the *Los Angeles Herald-Examiner* in 1975. "And he's probably right. I think everybody has to be a little crazy to be in this business. But the story behind the song I did for his album is kind of funny. Keith came out to see me at the Palomino Club, heard me do the song and approached me about doing it for his first solo album. I recorded a vocal of the song for Keith so he could phrase it and he ended up using my vocal on his album."

For Rick's own next record, he released a single of "Try (Try to Fall in Love)," a song from an obscure folksinger called Cooker, and "Louisiana Belle," an original from guitarist Jerry McGee of the Ventures and the new Stone Canyon Band drummer Eddie Tuduri. With the instrumental track swathed in silky strings, "Try (Try to Fall in Love)" sounded like bathetic dross more fitting for a lounge act, but Rick was clearly losing any sense of direction "Garden Party" may have given him. "Obviously he was picking at straws for material," said Sarokin. "I don't know where he was coming from." The single failed miserably.

"I am the ultimate judge of what I do," Rick said. "As a composer and singer, I have to please the public, but the experience of music begins and ends with me. If I go against my own feeling, the music is dishonest and it doesn't work."

Of course, first he had to know his own feelings, and as the public and record company continued to ignore his latest offerings, his confusion mounted. He always worked best under the influence of a strong guiding hand—an Ozzie, a John Boylan—and the label began to feel the need for some outside influence on his recordings, too.

He turned to his old colleague Jerry Fuller, who had gone from "Travelin' Man" and writing all the other records for Rick to become a successful record producer.

Fuller wrote and produced "Young Girl" for Gary Puckett and the Union Gap. As a staff producer at Columbia Records, he supervised hits by Mark Lindsay, O. C. Smith, Andy Williams, and Johnny Mathis and signed Mac Davis to the label. In 1973 soul singer Al Wilson made a number-one record out of Fuller's song "Show and Tell." He signed a deal to produce an album with Rick and dredged up a schlocky Australian rock ballad as a single called "Rock and Roll Lady."

"It was such a fiasco getting it on tape," said Fuller, "I waived my right for the album. I had held out during negotiations for the album, but I called back halfway through the single and said, 'Forget them.' It was pulling teeth getting it on tape. He wanted to use his band, and I didn't want to use his band, except for one guy, the steel-guitar player, Tom Brumley. The others were too strung out. They had a little fun there in the studio, and I was totally against that."

Fuller objected to the musicians smoking pot during sessions and would leave the studio. Rick and the band would try to keep their smoking under wraps, but Fuller was disgusted. "I couldn't get what I wanted out of them," he said, "and I wanted to use my own musicians, studio musicians."

Rick gamely plugged the single with a lip-synched performance on Dinah Shore's afternoon TV talk show, but the record was a commercial disaster. Bouncing around between studios and scheduling sessions between live dates, he attempted to finish an album. He recorded another version of the old Elvis Presley song "Mystery Train" and worked hard on a simpering ballad called "On Dreams Alone." "He fell in love with the song," said Dennis Sarokin, "but the band was in terror of doing the song. Not because we couldn't play it, but Rick just could not read it. It was real slow and impossible for me to stay awake. Rick kept saying, 'I know it will be good.' We beat it to death."

The album was never finished. "It was like fishing for that one song," said Sarokin. "There wasn't a lot. Other tunes were coming in. Rick just seemed kind of spooked by material.

Deep inside, he wanted to write another 'Garden Party' or he wanted me to write him another 'Garden Party.' "

With seven years remaining on his contract, MCA dropped Rick from the label. Flushed with the success of the Who, Elton John, and Olivia Newton-John, the company had little time to devote to an obviously floundering Rick Nelson. Once again, Rick was lost, wondering which way to turn, and, for the first time in his career, he was without a recording deal.

11

Rick Nelson Now

RICK HAD BEEN SEEKING new management in 1975. His career was in the worst shape ever. He had no record contract, and he barely worked the previous year. He had exhausted virtually his entire nest egg, and the checks from his television residuals and record contract had dried up. Their beach house was up for sale. He spent his days playing basketball with the twins. Rick met with some of the biggest managers in the entertainment business at Kris's urging. He saw Jerry Weintraub, riding high at the time with John Denver, and talked to Ken Kragen, whose main client, Kenny Rogers, verged on the big time. But he was suspicious of these moguls he referred to as "shiny suit guys," possibly because they came recommended by his troublesome wife.

"She was very involved during that time period," said David, "as far as advice to Rick. Kris was very competitive, period. She is a Harmon, and if the Harmons can be competitive against the Harmons, you can imagine how the Harmons can be competitive against someone else without a Harmon name on it. But that comes from Tom. Elyse was one of those people who had a career and also was a wife and a mother and seemed to be able to handle that role. She unfortunately didn't pass that on to the rest of the girls, because they've had a very difficult time."

A decade earlier, teenage air-conditioner repairman Greg McDonald found himself called to the Palm Springs home of Colonel Tom Parker, the notorious manager of Elvis Presley. The Colonel's wife was a semi-invalid, and soon McDonald was going back to take her shopping and chauffeur her on various errands, generally ingratiating himself into the Colonel's good graces.

He frequently referred to himself as Colonel Parker's adopted son and spent a lot of time serving as a kind of all-purpose gofer to the aging rock patriarch. McDonald amused the crafty, eccentric Parker, who accepted the young man as a casual protégé. The Colonel earned a colorful reputation in show business circles as a wily, unscrupulous promoter who built Elvis into the biggest phenomenon in rock & roll through a combination of cunning, chicanery, and greed. No matter how many millions of dollars passed through his hands on the way to Elvis's coffers, Parker still retained the huckster's touch he had picked up during his days working in carnivals. The Colonel loved to kibitz respectful neophytes like McDonald. Advice was one of the few things he gave away for free.

In the early 1970s, McDonald began promoting rock concerts around Palm Springs and occasionally even as far away as San Bernardino, about sixty miles east of Los Angeles. He originally sought out Rick Nelson as a potential attraction for one of his concerts.

He spoke with Jack Brumley, brother of Rick's steel-guitar player, who was handling bookings after Willy Nelson left. The two wound up talking about going into partnership to manage Rick, and McDonald drove to Los Angeles to meet with Rick.

Rick didn't make the meeting. Kris had temporarily thrown him out of the house in one of their increasingly dramatic domestic rifts. He missed a second meeting because of another battle with Kris. But the charmed third time, they did meet.

Rick liked the scrappy, ambitious twenty-six-year-old who boasted the vague association with Colonel Parker. While the big-time managers with the star clients may have appealed to his wife, Rick saw their grand plans for his career as a threat to his own control. The inexperienced McDonald, without an agenda of his own, would be someone easily enlisted to do Rick's bidding, and the unofficial link with the Colonel only heightened McDonald's appeal to Rick.

McDonald met with Nelson family business manager Wally Franson and found out that Rick was broke. For the first time in his life, Rick needed to go to work for a living, and with an overhead hovering between $30,000 and $40,000 a month, he needed to work hard. Bookings were thin, and, when he could get them, his going price ran around $1,500 a night.

The first order of business was to arrange a new record deal, although Rick Nelson did not exactly pass as a hot property in the record business. But Epic Records artist and repertoire executive Gregg Geller was a fan. "He brought a lot of things with him," said Geller. "He had a legendary status, and it wasn't that long before he had 'Garden Party.' The Eagles and Fleetwood Mac were very big at the time, and I heard a direct connection. The deal was not real expensive."

Geller said he didn't know what to make of McDonald. "He seemed to be a real novice at the record business," he said. McDonald also allowed Epic to believe the Colonel would somehow be involved in managing Rick. At the company's annual convention at Los Angeles's Century Plaza Hotel in July 1976, Epic announced signing a major act, the Jacksons, and mentioned in passing a few other incidental acquisitions, including Rick Nelson.

The label feted Rick, McDonald, and the band at an expensive industry luncheon at the prestigious New York restaurant 21, where McDonald sat around smoking cigars and telling Colonel Parker stories, and Rick waved and smiled, doing what he called his "Eleanor Roosevelt number." Epic label chief Ron Alexenburg toasted Rick as a person who was "already a star, but is going to be a superstar." It was a promising beginning to a new association.

Geller decided to pursue the connection he heard between Rick's music and Fleetwood Mac, who vaulted the year before from a British blues-rock band with a cult following into multiplatinum territory with an album Geller described as "nouveau rockabilly" produced by Keith Olsen. McDonald pleaded with Olsen to produce Rick's Epic debut, and, although his schedule was tight, the idea appealed to Olsen, a Los Angeles–based producer-engineer of long standing, suddenly greatly in demand because of the success of Fleetwood Mac. Olsen, a quick, pugnacious character with thousands of hours' experience in the studio, saw a professional door opening for him after many years of waiting for a break like the Fleetwood Mac album. He was not about to waste time making yet another ineffective, unsuccessful record.

"What I had in mind, I think, made a lot of sense," said Geller. But Rick, used to getting his own way, didn't take to outside direction well. He didn't want to yield control. At the same time, he didn't want to command either.

"He always wanted to be a rock star," said Keith Olsen. "The guy was nuts. He could never make up his mind on anything. We would be working on arrangements. The band was playing the way I wanted, and I would say, 'So, Rick, what do you think?' And he'd go, 'Uh, Keith, uh, I don't know. What do you think?' And it would go on like this for hours. After a while, instead of asking him, I would look at his face. I finally found out that the only way to find out if he liked it or not was if he kind of did a little curl in the corner of his mouth. That would show that deep down inside he was making a decision."

Olsen wanted to make a rockabilly record and even brought in a session player to overdub slap bass. But he had problems with the project from the start and rapidly lost interest. He didn't like the songs and found Rick resistant to recording outside material. He thought the band barely competent and tried to convince Rick to let him use seasoned studio musicians. He distrusted McDonald. "I didn't think anybody had any respect for him," Olsen said. With Rick insisting on using his band and the material Olsen thought mediocre, the sessions were doomed. He also found Rick strangely absent, even when he wasn't smoking the Thai sticks he carried in a Samsonite attaché case.

"It was real hard to communicate with Rick," Olsen said. "He was basically a closed-off person. It's real hard as a producer to differentiate between the producer and the artist when the artist is expecting you to be both. I was supposed to be the artist, and he was just going to sing it. He was going to be the vocal sound."

Olsen was an exacting producer, and he became thoroughly frustrated by the band's not meeting his expectations and by Rick's listless attitude. He left four partly finished tracks and went away to produce the sophomore album by a hot heavy rock band, Foreigner, who would sell many millions of albums under his supervision. The task of finishing the album reverted to Rick himself.

"Keith was a great producer," said guitarist Dennis Sarokin. "Still, Rick didn't let go of everything. Even when he let go on paper, he didn't let go emotionally. He didn't do his homework. I thought it was sort of a blowout."

McDonald went to work pumping up the booking schedule. Although Rick had an official booking agency, McDonald found its efforts ineffective and spent hours daily on the phone, filling the calendar himself and leaving only the paperwork and the commissions to the agency. Dealing with Rick could be somewhat exasperating for a conventional business manager since, after all his years as a star, Rick insisted on things being a certain way.

He talked to McDonald about something he called "the price of happiness." That meant he didn't care if it cost him virtually his entire gross revenue to travel first-class on commercial airlines, instead of more cost-effective means like rented buses. He would also not stand for any tampering with his show. He wanted to do his music his way, and he rebuked any attempts to compromise his myopic vision.

McDonald weighed a $500,000 offer from a Las Vegas hotel, but Rick immediately rejected the proposed contract. He had no interest in putting together what he called "a flower and feathers show" that would require him to perform with the house orchestra, wear a tuxedo, and make snappy small talk with the audience. "I'm not going to act like someone else onstage," he said. He turned down a lucrative offer for a proposed popcorn commercial that would have instantly solved his financial problems and passed on another pizza commercial his brother, David, brought him. All he wanted to do was take his four-piece rock & roll band out on the road, away from Kris, and sing his songs in front of audiences that came to see him. There he could be Rick Nelson the way he liked it best.

"For me, it's really satisfying," Rick said, "not satisfying, sustaining. It rejuvenates me and it's not work or anything like that for me to be doing this. I really like just about everything about it. I like being places and the traveling. I hate getting up in the morning, to be honest with you. That's what happens to me. I cannot get up in the morning. So that's what I don't like most of all. I guess I don't go to bed at night because what happens when you entertain, when you perform, is that sometimes it's like two or three o'clock in the morning and you don't really come out of that. It's not like you can go home and totally readjust. It takes a while. I always contend there should be a halfway Holiday Inn house somewhere from the airport to the house, so that everyone can just sort of go home and be halfway sane. This is my reality and it's just a very difficult adjustment to make when I go home."

In February 1977 Rick opened his first Nevada showroom engagement at the Sahara Tahoe, a hotel and casino on the south side of the mountaintop resort of Lake Tahoe. Popular with the ski crowd and a more informal, youthful audience than Las Vegas, the hotel featured more rock-oriented performers than the Vegas counterparts, and Elvis held the house attendance record. At Tahoe Rick could be himself, do his regulation show and not run afoul of hotel management.

"If I played Vegas," said Rick, "I wouldn't change my show. Come out in a tuxedo and do all that? I wouldn't feel right doing that. I would definitely get my clothes cleaned every night and pressed. I wouldn't wear a tuxedo. We played up in Tahoe at the Sahara and I was frightened 'cause it's a big room and it's a big Nevada nightclub really and I went up there with my band, which I don't know if it had been done before, and played. It went over real well and that's why I think I can do the same thing in Las Vegas."

McDonald brought along the Colonel, who played roulette in the hotel casino. Kris sipped drinks at the backstage bar. David and his new wife, Yvonne, attended the shows, as did Harriet Nelson and Tom and Elyse Harmon. The hotel lobby and casino was festooned with bright orange signs reading "Rick Nelson Now." Lorrie Collins Carnall and her husband, Stu Carnall, who lived in nearby Carson City, made a brief, uncomfortable visit backstage. Rick hadn't seen his teenage girlfriend in almost twenty years. Neither had much to say to each other, and Lorrie thought her husband's presence upset Rick.

He made two more inane acting appearances on TV series in March. He played a baseball pitcher who lost his hand in "A Hand for Sonny Blue" on "Tales of the Unexpected" and appeared as Tony Eagle, a rock star and target for assassination, on "The Hardy Boys Mysteries," a dumb show heavy on teen appeal, written and produced by Glen Larson of the Four Preps, now one of Hollywood's top TV producers. Neither performance was going to win Rick any awards for dramatic excellence, although he did look properly perplexed as the baseball pitcher whose new hand retains the murderous personality of its former owner.

In August, more than a year after recording began, Epic finally released *Intakes*, the first new Rick Nelson album in more than three years. After the sessions with Olsen the previous summer collapsed, Rick took the helm and slowly completed the album as producer himself. Progress ran painfully slow. With recording sandwiched between road trips and Kris banning all music work from their home, sessions were difficult enough without Rick invariably showing up hours late. After all these years, he still operated on Nelson Standard Time, and the results were tremendous frustration on the part of his associates and many wasted dollars. And when he did get to the studio, he worked slowly.

The album barely mattered. Rick showed little signs of life, and the material was mediocre at best. Although the basic tracks for the four cuts produced by Olsen were all well recorded, Rick supervised the ham-fisted mix, which hardly compared with Olsen's customary scrupulous work in this crucial stage of recording. (Olsen said he usually spends ten hours mixing for every hour he records.) Dennis Sarokin provided a couple of songs, as did bassist Jay DeWitt White. Rick recorded a lackluster Baker Knight number, "I Wanna Move with You," and three songs from other outside sources, Gallagher and Lyle's "Stay Young," the old Brenton Wood hit

"Gimme a Little Sign," and Tim Ryan and Bob Yeomans's "You Can't Dance." Epic selected the latter two pieces as singles but came up empty-handed with both.

Rick wrote two songs himself that could have easily been inspired by his wife: "It's Another Day," a wistful description of a deteriorating love affair, and "Something You Can't Buy," with its chorus "And you get back what you've given, and love is something you can't buy."

Kristin filed for divorce in October, asking for custody of all four children, alimony, and a full share of community property. Rick had returned home earlier to have Kris pick him up at the airport and deposit him at a new house she had rented and moved him into during his absence. He actually liked the new place, but their differences were temporarily resolved and he had returned home shortly thereafter. This time, however, Kris retained counsel and set legal wheels in motion to formalize a permanent split.

He went ahead and played with partner Dean Martin, Jr., in a celebrity tennis tournament sponsored by the rock group the Eagles and took off for a small tour in November, but he managed to work things out with Kris to the degree that when he appeared on network TV in January 1978 to present an award on "The American Music Awards," she was standing by his side.

Financial problems pressed him on all sides. At home, money, not love, was the issue. Kris dropped divorce proceedings on the contingency that Rick hire her divorce attorney as business manager to conduct an extensive audit of his finances, with an eye toward getting rid of Greg McDonald. The result showed Rick actually owed McDonald money.

The band was also unhappy with their take. Dennis Sarokin was frustrated and disappointed with *Intakes*. Rick came back from a party where he met Paul McCartney, who professed his admiration to Rick. "Did you ask him for a song?" Sarokin inquired. Sarokin wanted Rick to pull together his rock-star friends—McCartney, George Harrison, James Burton—and have them write and produce individual tracks for an all-star *Rick Nelson and Friends* album. "Then we would have an album none of us could fuck up," Sarokin said, "the Rick Nelson album everybody's been waiting for and we could quit playing the surf-and-turf rooms in Buffalo and Syracuse." But it was never to happen.

The band was also furious about stalled session pay from the Epic album, and Sarokin took the matter to the union. The case went to arbitration, and the matter was settled in favor of the musicians. But the discontent in the band eventually got to oven Rick, who liked to maintain an all-for-one attitude. But his generous facade was beginning to wear thin.

"What happened, even before we were doing that," said Sarokin, "obviously the vibes in the band were bad. We'd go into the rehearsal hall and Rick was late, chronically late, all the time. Sometimes we were fine. We'd have another beer, go out for tacos. We'd come back and he's sitting there. 'Where'd everybody go?' he'd say. 'Are you ready now?' But obviously, when the vibes were bad, every second was a ticking time bomb. He got down to this real attitude thing. 'What's wrong guys?' he'd say. 'You know we're not doing well, and I'm losing money on the road.' All of a sudden, he's talking from this other side. 'I've been fighting for you guys and what am I getting? You guys are fighting me and holding out for more money.' He's throwing it in our faces."

Sarokin blamed Greg McDonald. "The guy was deceptive to me from day one," he said. "We had a raise due. He'd say, 'You're not getting the raise, but we're doing this bunch of gigs and you're going to get a bonus.' Then it would be 'But guys, look, we're not working—do you know how much Rick is making?' I know how much we're grossing. It's not our choice to be on a retainer [when the band wasn't booked], which was nice at the time. But we made more money when we worked. At that point, the difference between three hundred fifty dollars a week when we worked and seventy-five dollars when we didn't was a lot of bucks."

The final straw for Rick came at a record company show-case at the Roxy in Hollywood, where Sarokin mugged his way through the background vocal on "Poor Little Fool." A couple of the label executives kidded Rick backstage about his guitarist's antics, and Rick blew a fuse. The next day he called Sarokin and fired the band. He told Sarokin he could no longer afford to pay the musicians. "I had to get rid of the horses," he explained to Sarokin. "The kids were heart-broken." Of course, with his first appearance ever in Las Vegas looming only a couple of weeks ahead, he had to get another group immediately.

Guitarist John Beland got a call from Jack Brumley asking Beland if he wanted to put together a band for Rick to take to Vegas. Beland did not feel comfortable in his current gig, playing with Dolly Parton, since the Los Angeles session player was the only member of the band who didn't come from Nashville. Rick Nelson had been one of his earliest musical heroes, and he knew Burton's solos from the early records by heart. Beland jumped at the chance. He tabbed drummer Billy Thomas and bassist Thad Maxwell and met for a rehearsal with Rick at Hollywood's Studio Instrument Rentals.

As they considered possible material for the Vegas show, Beland asked Rick if he wanted to do "It's Up to You" and ripped off a note-for-note copy of the original solo. McDonald had been concerned that Rick would refuse to emphasize his old hits onstage and would instead insist on playing songs by Dylan and other contemporary writers. Beland unconsciously began to echo McDonald's arguments.

"Greg and I were very supportive of Rick and his old hits," said Beland. "Rick had fallen into a kind of rut, like a lot of the stars from the sixties, where he was trying to compete with what was going on at the moment musically. It was really in vogue for everyone to walk around and downplay artists' old hits, even Rick's. He was surrounded by band members that made him feel like those hits were something of the past and had no relevance to what was going on today. He was embarrassed with them."

Along with guitarist Don Preston from the Leon Russell band, Elvis's former background vocalists the Sweet Inspirations, and steel guitarist Tom Brumley, the new band took a revamped show to Vegas that, for the first time in a decade, consisted exclusively of Rick's classic numbers, with "Garden Party" thrown in without the slightest irony. If this signaled a return to his roots, it was also the beginning of a journey for Rick to discover himself again.

He was still at a loss about what to do on records, and with the dismal showing of *Intakes*, his position with Epic hardly allowed him to object when the company suggested he make his next record with an experienced producer. The label assigned Al Kooper to the project. An original member of the sixties New York underground rock band the Blues Project, founder of jazz-rock pioneers Blood, Sweat and Tears, and keyboardist who played on the Bob Dylan classic "Highway 61 Revisited," Kooper was a cunning hipster who made a million-selling album (*Supersession*) out of some late-night jams with guitarist Mike Bloomfield and produced the 1970s' most popular FM radio track by an American rock band, Lynyrd Skynyrd's "Free Bird."

To get acquainted, Kooper joined the band at the Aladdin Hotel in Vegas, sitting in on keyboards. His initial game plan was to re-create the original Rick Nelson sound and reunite Rick and guitarist James Burton. But Burton wanted nothing to do with the project. Kooper's next idea, while making sound commercial sense, turned out to be a wacky, left-field way to approach making a Rick Nelson album. Kooper decided to make a record that cast Rick in the same slick format that Linda Ronstadt was currently employing with immense success. "That seemed like a good formula for him in my head, those kind of albums," Kooper said. "So we just followed that formula."

He gave Rick a pair of tapes with about sixty songs and told him to choose the ones he wanted to record. Kooper used Rick's two guitarists, Beland and Preston, but supplemented the band with a gang of Hollywood heavyweights like Dr. John and Michael McDonald of the Doobie Brothers on keyboards, Jeff "Skunk" Baxter from the Doobies and Steely Dan on guitar, and Bob Glaub from the Linda Ronstadt records on bass. Kooper, an irrepressible wit, and Rick got along wonderfully. Sessions were full of semiobscene, playful banter.

"It's like taking a great leak and finding out you're going in your pants," Rick told Kooper at one point during the sessions. "You know what I mean? You've never done that?"

"I've done it in my sleep but never in my pants," answered Kooper.

"You haven't lived," said Rick. "The golden shower—*s-s-s-s*— in the boot."

Never before had Rick so totally turned over the responsibility for making his records to another person. Rick flew back and forth between Los Angeles and Vegas to record his vocals, while Kooper went ahead and worked on the tracks in his absence.

"On the day we started the vocals," said Kooper, "he sang the first song and it was awful, really bad. I said, 'Jesus, I thought he could sing these songs.' I really had to work hard to get the vocals out of him. He didn't just get up and sing them and that was it. Every line was murder. But he had it in him. That was the strange thing—it was there, but you really had to work as a producer to get it out of him."

The songs included the old Steve Alaimo hit "Every Day I Have to Cry Some"; a gorgeous but obscure Bob Dylan tune, "Mama You Been on My Mind"; an uncharacteristic piece of New Orleans funk from writer Allen Toussaint, "What Is Success"; the Little Feat rocker "New Delhi Freight Train"; and some Texas blues & boogie from ZZ Top, "Gettin' It On."

The title of the album, *Back to Vienna*, came from an utterly bizarre, off-the-wall song about psychiatric pioneer Carl Jung, "Carl of the Jungle." "He didn't know what it was about," said Kooper, "not a clue. He just liked the song."

The album sported a sleek, glossy production, peppered with the pings of electronic syndrums. After recording at the Record Plant in Los Angeles, largely without Rick around, Kooper took the tapes to complete the final mixes at Causalito's Record Plant. Rick never missed a moment of the mixdown. In the hands of a skilled producer, Rick fashioned a record that was a startling departure for him. Enough time and care was taken to push the budget toward $175,000. The album did not sound remotely like anything Rick had ever done before. But the big surprise came when the record company heard it.

Epic refused to release the album.

"I was horrified," said Kooper. "When you produce records, you work really hard. It broke my heart."

"That album was a joke," said John Beland. "Everybody in the world who could play a note of music was on the album. There were all sorts of characters coming and going. Everybody was doing a ton of dope, and the songs were really out there. Al Kooper was a strange guy. He would hire all these monster players and when they would leave, later on that night he would replace their instruments with him playing on it. The budget went through the ceiling. Rick just showed up and sang. His input on it was zilch."

"Certain companies sign you up and then you audition for

them," said Rick. "It's ridiculous. You have to prove yourself to
them before they'll even allow a record out. I really don't
understand that. The company wanted Al Kooper to produce
me and I went along with it. We delivered the album and they
said 'It sounds like an Al Kooper album.' It doesn't make a
whole lot of sense. I thought that was what they wanted."

His marriage was disintegrating rapidly. Kris could flash
blazing anger or icy cool, but the playful warmth of their early
years together was long gone. She held strong opinions about
Rick's career and expressed them without reservation. Rick
ignored her as much as possible. One of the things he liked
best about touring was being away from Kris.

Kooper remembered that Kris was a big problem for Rick at
the time. She may have called off the divorce proceedings, but
she could still be contentious. Any reconciliation was obviously shaky.

"He was having a lot of trouble with Kris," he said. "That
was sort of like the bane of his existence. He couldn't afford to
split up with her. I think that's basically what it was, because
she was one of those gals that would just go for it, Hollywood
style. She really made his life miserable. She would come to
the studio and come to the reception desk and say, 'Rebecca's
here to see Rick.' If he went to see who it was, she would say,
'Oh, you just go and see if any strange girl comes?' She was
jealous to the max."

On the road, Rick readily justified any suspicions she held
about his fooling around with willing female fans. Not that
Kris was the model of a virtuous wife herself, but she would
go to extreme lengths to keep him sleeping alone.

"At Vegas," said Kooper, "she would find out what time he
got offstage and call him after the second show and keep him
on the phone for three hours so that he couldn't score. She
did this every night. It was pathetic. I was a bachelor, so I was
saying 'C'mon, let's have fun,' and he'd just get hung up on the
phone until like five in the morning."

At home in Los Angeles, John Beland got used to hearing his phone ring after midnight. "I'd get these calls late at night," he said. "He'd start humming the theme from *Jaws*—duh-duh, duh-duh, duh-duh. I'd go, 'Kris, huh?' He'd go, 'Yep.' I'd go, 'You want me to come on over?' He'd go, 'Uh, yeh.'

"So I'd come over and babysit. She had locked him out of the main part of the house, and he had this music room downstairs. We would just hang out down there until the sun came up, playing records, playing the guitar, shooting the breeze.

"They were having problems. She was drinking a lot. I think Kris was frustrated because out of the Harmon family, she was the low one on the totem pole. Everybody else was real successful, her brother, her sister, her father. She never did get her acting career off the ground. Maybe there was a little jealousy there. It got to be pretty bad. There were a couple of scenes.

"I know she drank. Rick did a little bit, too. Rick didn't really drink. Pretty much just a little coke here and there. But I remember being at the house one night when they brought out the scrapbook. We were all up late. They polished off a bottle of tequila like it was ice water. There were some pretty bad scraps on the road. She would show up at some of the gigs. It was pretty bad.

"Kris was running around with some people at the time. Hey, so was Rick too on the road. I think what burned Rick was that when Rick messed around, it was on the road. But when Kris messed around, it was at home. I think that added a lot of pressure. No names mentioned, but she was seeing people that Rick knew, and that was a drag for him."

Other people did mention names. Among those of Rick's friends linked with Kris were basketball player Gail Goodrich, who was named in a newspaper article as one of the celebrities to own one of Kris's paintings, and singer and graphic artist Dean Torrance of Jan and Dean.

"Greg and I used to have a joke," said Beland, "every night

on the road. Rick would do what we called 'the Rick Nelson fade.' There would be a bunch of people around having a party and Rick would say, 'I'll be right back.' He'd go in the bedroom and call Kris and talk for two hours on the phone with her. After seventeen, eighteen years of marriage, what do you talk about for two hours on the phone?''

Happy times at home were getting few and far in between. Of course, Rick toured out of town as much as possible. But he loved being a father, even if he didn't spend much time with his children off or on the road. And Kris maintained her flair for the extravagant celebration. It was nothing for her to drop $10,000 on a party. On one of their birthdays, the twins were told they were being taken to the dentist, only to find themselves at a surprise birthday party at a recording studio. The two teens had taken up bass and drums, and their equipment was waiting for them. Beland played guitar and the Pointer Sisters dropped by to add some background vocals on the first recording session by Matthew and Gunnar.

Kris did not know the meaning of the word *thrift* when it came to parties. She spent $25,000 for a party in Malibu, where she rented a beach house for three weeks to throw a party on one night. The same night, Rick played Simpsonville, Kentucky, and earned $5,000.

Rick signed with booking agent Jim Halsey, who operated a Tulsa, Oklahoma, agency specializing in country music, and dropped the Stone Canyon Band from his billing. Greg McDonald pushed Rick's price up slightly and packed his schedule more fully, but his financial picture didn't improve dramatically. He was still playing small clubs and dinner theaters in secondary markets, working out-of-the-way cities where he still qualified as a major attraction and could draw crowds. He also started renting a private Lear jet for travel. "Sometimes it costs more to start Rick's jet than the fee he gets," McDonald claimed. But if Rick didn't spend the money on jets, Kris would spend it on parties.

Ten years later, still America's favorite family, 1963.

Ozzie and Harriet's first granddaughter, Tracy Kristine, six months old, poses for her first publicity photo, June 10, 1964. *(UPI)*

Love and Kisses: The food-fight scene from the movie written and directed by Ozzie, 1965. *(Universal)*

Rick costars with Rudy Valee in the stage
musical *How to Succeed in Business
Without Really Trying*, 1966.

With Cindy Bush and
Kam Nelson (no relation),
Rick as the dean on the
ABC-TV summer
replacement show
"Malibu U." in 1967.
(ABC)

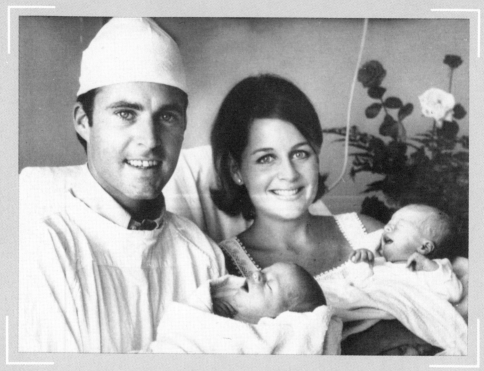

Star draws a pair: Rick and Kris with one-week-old twins Matthew and Gunnar, September 28, 1967. *(AP)*

In the studio with Linda Ronstadt, producer John Boylan, and folksinger Eric Andersen, 1968. *(Courtesy of John Boylan)*

Kris and her painting *When the Kennedys Were in the White House*, which she gave to Jackie Kennedy, 1967. *(UPI)*

Stone Canyon Band: Allen Kemp, Rick, Pat Shanahan, Tom Brumley, and Randy Meisner, 1970. *(Courtesy of Allen Kemp)*

Rudy the Fifth: Rick with the long hair that shocked the Madison Square Garden Rock & Roll Revival crowd, 1971. *(Courtesy of Allen Kemp)*

The twins and Tracy: Appearing on a Nelson family
Christmas card, 1971.

Stone Canyon Band number two: Jay DeWitt
White, Rick, Dennis (Larden) Sarokin, Tom
Brumley, and Ty Grimes, 1973. *(MCA)*

Rick and Kris at home, 1973. *(New York Times)*

On "the farm," Rick feeds the horses at their Studio City home, 1973.
(*New York Times*)

Rick plays an evil hippie pied piper on
"The Streets of San Francisco," 1973.
(*ABC*)

"A Hand for Sonny Blue": Rick is the baseball pitcher and subject of a bizarre hand transplant on "Tales of the Unexpected," 1977. *(NBC)*

Back to Vienna: With producer Al Kooper,
who supervised the unreleased Epic
Records album, 1977. *(Gary Nichamin)*

''Big Train from Memphis'': With Johnny Cash and Carl Perkins at a
Memphis recording session, 1985. *(Dave Darnell)*

Arriving at London's Heathrow Airport with fiancée Helen Blair, two months to the day before their death. *(AP)*

The wreckage of the DC-3: Burned from tail to cockpit, January, 1, 1986. *(UPI)*

An unidentified woman consoles Harriet Nelson at her son's memorial service. *(AP)*

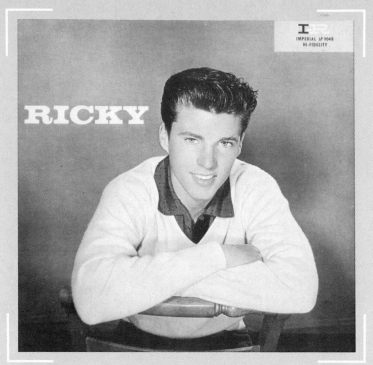

Ricky: Cover of first album, 1957. *(EMI)*

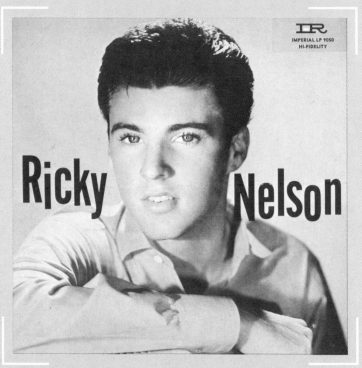

Ricky Nelson: Cover of second album, which contained
''Poor Little Fool,'' 1958. *(EMI)*

Ricky Sings Again: Cover of his fabulous third album, 1958. *(EMI)*

"Be-Bop Baby": Cover of first Imperial single, 1957. *(EMI)*

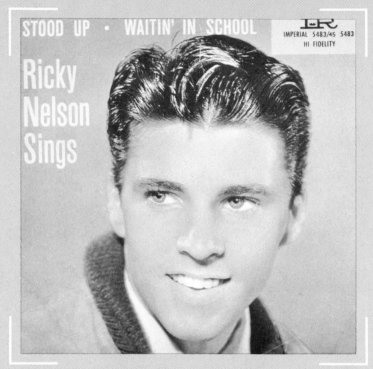

"Stood Up": Cover of second Imperial single, 1957. *(EMI)*

He filmed a TV documentary in September at the Monroe, Louisiana, State Fair called "Rick at the Fair," combining live performance footage with interviews shot backstage and around the fairgrounds. Rick had become a regular attraction at fairs around the country. "There's more communication in fairs," he told the TV interviewer, " 'cause usually the people are right there. You can reach out and actually touch them and everything. In a nightclub, it's a whole different thing. I think people go to a nightclub just to go to a nightclub. At a fair, I think a lot of people are there to see you, so right away it's a different feeling. Also, they're going out to have a good time outdoors, and I just like the feeling of the whole thing." The show was never picked up for broadcast.

In December Rick headlined the Tulsa International Music Festival, a country-music show produced by his new booking agent and featuring many acts from Halsey's roster of clients. Steel guitarist Tom Brumley remained as Rick's sole, tenuous connection with the country-rock sound of the early Stone Canyon Band, as Rick veered increasingly toward a return to the fundamental rock & roll sound with which he started.

Acting at the suggestion of the record label, Rick, Beland, and McDonald took off that December for Memphis to record a new album. He left all the other band members behind, without any specific plans other than to go down to rock & roll's hometown, soak up the Southern atmosphere, and wing it. It was the first time Rick recorded outside of Hollywood and a sentimental journey to the town where Sun Records artists like Elvis and Carl Perkins cut the sides that spurred Rick into rock & roll in the first place.

In the heart of winter, Memphis can be a dreary, snowy, rainy city. With Elvis dead a little more than a year, the city was beginning to discover its pride as the birthplace of the music. The recording scene had dried up since the heyday of Memphis soul came to an end with Al Green in the early 1970s. But Lyn-Lou Studios, a converted grocery store, was trying to pump new life into the town's tired music scene.

Nashville producer Larry Rogers hired the studio house band, Shiloh, to back Rick and Beland, and during the first day, someone made a comment about Elvis. Rick began mimicking Elvis singing "That's Alright Mama," the first record Elvis recorded at the old Sun studios on Union Avenue. Before long, they completed a version of the song in earnest, and the Memphis album was underway. Ironically, it would be the only track from the sessions to be released as originally recorded.

Rick and Beland stashed a bottle of cocaine in the bathroom and would dash out between takes for quick pick-me-ups. The drug was becoming a regular part of Rick's routine; he used to carry his coke in an empty ginseng capsule, ever at the ready. Beland remembered parking out in front of Elvis's old mansion, Graceland, around four in the morning, snorting blow, and making bad jokes about Elvis, although Greg McDonald denied this ever happened. The Colonel did issue an invitation for them to actually stay at Graceland, but Rick thought that too bizarre and passed.

One night Rick and Beland drew a kind of cartoon that everybody thought was hilarious, which was hung up on the studio wall. It showed an airplane with its windows cracked and a man's face pressed against one of the panes. The caption read "Buddy Holly, Moment of Impact."

"It was just this weird humor that we had going for the whole album," said Beland, "and it made recording a lot of fun. Between laughs we'd say, 'Let's go out and do something' and 'Speaking of Buddy Holly, let's try "Rave On." ' It was really cool."

They used a sixteen-track machine and bathed Rick's vocal in old-fashioned tape echo. Beland had an arrangement for the old Bobby Darin hit "Dream Lover," left over from his work with Australian singer Lee Conway. Dennis Sarokin had once suggested the song to Rick too. They cut a supple, dreamy version of the song, and Epic slated the track for a single release.

With the impromptu sessions producing some of Rick's finest, most relaxed work in years and the single scheduled for release in February 1979, fortune smiled on the project and offered just the lucky chance needed to break the single big. With about ten days left before the scheduled broadcast, at the last moment Muhammad Ali bowed out of his role as guest host on "Saturday Night Live" and the producers gave Rick his spot.

In its fourth season, "Saturday Night Live" was rewriting the rules of television. Not only had the show's extraordinary popularity boosted little-known cast members like Chevy Chase, Dan Aykroyd, John Belushi, Bill Murray, and Gilda Radner into stardom, but the show also had become the single most important showcase for popular music on TV. The cream of the rock music world played the show for peanuts—the Rolling Stones, Elvis Costello, Paul Simon—looking for the cachet and the exposure. Rick made appearances the previous year on "The Midnight Special," sang "Mystery Train" on "Dick Clark's Live Wednesday," played a sleazy reporter on the TV movie *Three on a Date*, and did a guest shot on has-been–laden "The Love Boat," but nothing of this importance had come his way since he turned down the Sullivan show twenty years before. Rick, Beland, and McDonald flew to New York to begin a week's worth of rehearsals, and they invited the Memphis studio guitarist from Shiloh, Bobby Neal, to join them.

"For the whole week, it was crazy," said Beland, "like 'M*A*S*H.' They were all smoking dope and everything you'd think they would be doing. Belushi was incredible. For the first five days we were there, nobody knew where he was. They sent somebody out looking for him, and when they found him, he had this raincoat on and looked like a bus had run over him. He was wasted. He was gone. And, sure enough, when showtime came, I don't know what they gave him, but he came out and looked great. He was funny."

"This is probably the first time most of you have seen me in color," said Rick, as he walked out onstage and rolled into a three-song opening performance of "Hello Mary Lou," "Travelin' Man," and "Fools Rush In." His performance was a triumph. He not only played in skits like the bogus public-service announcement for the national manufacturers of helium, the TV quiz show send-up "Quien Es Muy Macho?," and a hair-salon bit with Bill Murray, but he participated in one of the show's all-time classic pieces, designed specifically for Rick.

The writers worked hard to come up with a sketch that would play off Rick's own TV persona. Writer Al Franken suggested a skit called "Ozzie's Dead," which Rick didn't think was funny. But what they finally came up with may well be Rick's finest comedic performance.

Shown in black and white, Rick entered a typical TV set kitchen, poured himself a glass of milk, sat down at the kitchen table, and announced, "Mom, I'm home." In walked Jane Curtin dressed as June Cleaver. Rick had wandered into the Cleaver household of "Leave It to Beaver" by mistake. Bill Murray as Eddie Haskell and Belushi as the Beaver made an appearance. The camera moved to Dan Aykroyd doing his Rod Serling impersonation.

"Submitted for your approval," he intoned, "a sixteen-year-old teenager walking through Anytown, U.S.A., past endless Oak Streets, Elm Streets, Maple Streets, unable to distinguish one house from another for he's just entered a strange neighborhood, a neighborhood known as the Twilight Zone."

Still looking for the Nelsons' house, he went from the Cleavers' to the Andersons' of "Father Knows Best," to the Ricardos' of "I Love Lucy" with Gilda Radner doing an exquisite Lucy ("You're not Ricky," she shrieked), to a final stop at the Williamses' residence from "The Danny Thomas Show." While not exactly "Ozzie's Dead," it was an irreverent and effective parody of Rick's televised youth and a brilliant use of his seldom-seen self-effacing humor.

Rick finished the show with a sterling performance of "Dream Lover," a single he expected to land on the desk of radio programmers across the country in Monday's mail. It would have been one of the biggest coups Rick had managed in many moons, but the Epic Records artist and repertoire department interceded.

For some unknown reason, a&r executive Bobby Columby pulled the single back from distribution in the eleventh hour so he could add a conga drum to the finished track, which delayed the release for a critical five weeks. It was probably the strongest single Rick had made since "Garden Party," but without the explosive power of the "Saturday Night Live" performance behind it, the record died a quick death.

They returned to Memphis in April to finish the album, having asked Bobby Neal to join the band on a permanent basis. Tom Brumley was let go after ten years of working with Rick. Steel guitar was no longer going to be a part of Rick's new spare, stripped-down rock & roll sound. The completed album, titled *Rockabilly Renaissance*, featured songs like Buddy Holly's "True Love Ways," John Fogerty's "Almost Saturday Night" and "Rockin' All Over the World," Stealers Wheel's "Stuck in the Middle with You," Smokey Robinson's "Lay Back in the Arms of Someone," and the Valentino's "It's All Over Now." The songs were rife with the informality of the sessions, and Rick never sounded better. While undoubtedly out of step with the fading disco sound and ascendant new-wave rock of the day, *Rockabilly Renaissance* was a brilliantly executed piece, with Rick totally at home with the music.

Memphis galvanized his determination to return to the pure rock & roll sound of his youth. "I can record my music and I don't have to sound like anybody else," he told a reporter. His years of declining popularity didn't affect his self-confidence. As long as an audience would turn up to hear him play, Rick Nelson could do what he wanted—sing his songs with a rock & roll band.

Epic Records, however, didn't care for *Rockabilly Renaissance* anymore than it did *Back to Vienna*. Once again, the label refused to release the album, and the company and the singer mutually agreed to part ways.

12

The Loser, Babe, Is You

ERROL FLYNN BUILT HIS MULHOLLAND DRIVE RANCH on eleven-and-a-half acres at the then-staggering cost of $125,000 in 1941. The hilltop lot alone, with its panoramic view of the San Fernando Valley, ran him $35,000, but it was Flynn's dream house and he built it to match his extravagant personality.

The actor known for swashbuckling roles led an even more raucous life offscreen. Reputedly a Nazi spy and part-time homosexual, Flynn was an alcoholic womanizer, renowned as one of Hollywood's most prodigious seduction artists. He built his mansion with secret passageways, peepholes, a two-way mirror in the bedroom, mysteriously connecting upstairs rooms, and dozens of little sexual jokes like trick chairs that released large, quivering penises at the touch of a cushion.

"She snuggled on the side of the hill," he wrote of the house in his memoirs. "Inside, in most of her rooms, there were mirrors that brought the beauty of the valley into the house. The swimming pool was almost in my living room. Outside was a riding ring, below on the hillside a tennis court, and a little ways off I had stables for cockfights."

The sprawling Tudor-style home boasted a hexagonal hall-way, a glass-enclosed dining room overlooking the pool, a mammoth living room running the entire length of the front of the house, huge open fireplaces in both the living room and the den, a massive bedroom with built-in mirror above the bed, and a bathroom that originally hosted side-by-side his-and-hers toilets. Ozzie Nelson played tennis with Flynn on the hillside court.

Flynn lost the property to back alimony in 1955 and lived his few remaining years in an alcoholic haze at a Hollywood hotel. When Rick and Kris Nelson bought the seven-bedroom house in April 1980, it was owned by country star Stuart Hamblen, a one-time cowboy who began recording in 1928. A brawling, boozing, rugged man who frequently played bad guys in cowboy movies, Hamblen converted to Christianity under the spell of evangelist Billy Graham in 1949. He ran for president on the Prohibition Party ticket in 1952 (although his friends knew him to take an occasional drink regardless) and was best known for his song "This Ole House," a big hit for Rosemary Clooney in 1954.

Semiretired at the time, Hamblen and his wife, Susie, still broadcast their weekly religious radio show, "Cowboy Church of the Air," out of the Flynn house—where he covered up all the peepholes—when Rick and Kris purchased the estate, cut down to four-and-a-half acres, for more than $750,000.

This would be the staging ground for the final act of the travesty their marriage had become and a lonely Xanadu where Rick would spend his remaining days, like a sorrowful prince in exile.

The same month he moved his family into the Mulholland house, Rick began work on his first album for Capitol Records. He signed a two-album deal with the label in late 1979 for a decidedly modest $25,000—$12,500 per album—but he looked forward to a fresh start, pointed in a new, comfortable direction from the Memphis sessions.

"When I was with Epic Records," he said, "everybody there had different ideas what I should be doing. I was trying to listen to them all and it wasn't a workable situation."

Initially, Rick was approached by Capitol's country-music division with an eye toward having Rick cut a Nashville version of "Be-Bop-a-Lula." But he demurred, and it was decided he should do his work in Hollywood. The next idea Capitol presented to Rick was to see if he could get John Fogerty to produce an album with him. It was not a new idea. The first time it came up was two years earlier, before the Al Kooper sessions.

Although they had never met, Rick knew and admired Fogerty's work as leader of Creedence Clearwater Revival, whose string of nine consecutive top-ten hits in the late sixties and early seventies drew directly from the California rockabilly tradition Rick established. Fogerty even recorded his own version of "Hello Mary Lou" on Creedence's final album, and Rick would cut Fogerty's "Almost Saturday Night" and "Rockin' All Over the World" for the unreleased Memphis album.

What Rick didn't know was that Fogerty was stuck in the middle of a crippling, eight-year mental block. After losing his life savings in an offshore banking deal in the mid-1970s, Fogerty blamed his record company for the bad financial advice. He became embroiled in a series of complex lawsuits and had not released an album in more than five years, although he still went into the recording studio every day. Deep in the grip of a crisis of confidence, he would erase the tapes he recorded the day before first thing every morning. Often as an exercise during this period, Fogerty would record versions of Rick's old hit "Stood Up" to try to shake loose the cobwebs and battle off the demons that plagued him. Producing an album with Rick didn't seem like a good idea to him at the time.

"I had never produced anyone but me," said Fogerty, "and

I had a big problem with the idea I would be controlling anybody else's say-so. I never look at a record as a one-time project or a ten-minute deal. I look at it as a record, a big deal out of somebody's life or career. If a record's just a record, then what's 'I Want to Hold Your Hand' or 'Heartbreak Hotel' or 'Proud Mary'? I'm sorry. If you do it right, it's a lot more momentous. I took that weight on even thinking about doing a record with Ricky Nelson."

Fogerty turned down Rick's request for a meeting, but somehow wires got crossed and Rick flew to San Francisco to confer with Fogerty at his East Bay recording studio. "I'm sure he was looking for somebody else," said Fogerty, "somebody to go, 'Here, you take this and you do it. Show me what I'm doing wrong or show me what to do right. You just take it. Do what you always do for yourself—or Creedence—and do it for me.' "

Rick's sustained good looks at age forty stunned Fogerty, and the two noodled on guitars for a few minutes before talking. Rick explained what he wanted to do was make a record that used modern technology to re-create the feeling of old rock & roll. "He was saying that, but he didn't know how to do it," said Fogerty.

Fogerty had admired Rick since he started listening to rock & roll but wasn't prepared for Rick's attitude about him. "He thought I had a direct line to the rockabilly soul," said Fogerty. "He had a higher opinion of me than I did of myself." Nevertheless, he passed on the project. Rick didn't ask again when Capitol suggested it.

Rick heard an import copy of "Tired of Toein' the Line," a song by Johnny Burnette's son, Rocky Burnette, at that point unreleased in the United States. He thought it could be a hit record and quickly threw together a session to cut his own version. To produce the record, Jimmie Haskell was contacted, but the event proved far from a sentimental reunion.

"It was a strange session," said Haskell, who was called the afternoon of the session. There was no rehearsal, and recording lasted through the night. Rick's version dropped the booming guitar and horn lines in favor of a slower, more country version. Rocky Burnette heard Rick's version over the phone, and he held no ill feelings toward Rick for trying to beat him to the American charts with his song.

"After all my dad's and uncle's songs he did," said Burnette, "I was thrilled to death. It was like a continuation of the whole thing."

Capitol Records, on the other hand, didn't quite hear it the way Rick did. They never released the recording, and Rocky Burnette went on to have a top-ten record in the United States with his version three months later. Times had changed since Lew Chudd used to get Rick's records out of the studio and on the streets in three days.

Finally, Rick and Capitol settled on Jack Nitzsche to produce his first album for the label. A record-business veteran, Nitzsche also came with a wild reputation as a madman, almost as well known for unpredictable behavior as the reclusive and eccentric producer Phil Spector, whose classic sixties Wall of Sound recordings with the Crystals, the Ronettes, and others Nitzsche arranged. Nitzsche's girlfriend, actress Carrie Snodgress, once charged he raped her with the barrel of a gun, although the case was eventually dropped. "I wish I had done it," Nitzsche told friends.

His musical credentials were truly formidable. In addition to his pioneering work with Spector, he played piano on Rolling Stones records and toured with Neil Young. His arrangements graced the records of the industry's biggest names, and his film soundtracks included *The Exorcist* and *One Flew Over the Cuckoo's Nest*. Nitzsche needed the Nelson album to complete a four-album production deal with Capitol, and he could claim some contemporary credibility with albums he produced by new-wave rockers like Mink DeVille and Graham Parker.

But Nitzsche's unreliability reared its head as early as the first session. At the time, Nitzsche was known by his associates to be fond of snorting heroin. According to one person present that first night, he passed out, head down on the console, during recording. Rick, on the other hand, kept excusing himself with a member of his road crew to take numerous, mysterious trips to the bathroom. Nitzsche complained to friends that Rick couldn't come to even a minor decision without conferring privately outside the control room with his road manager, whom Nitzsche mistook as a coke dealer. According to one of Rick's colleagues, Nitzsche spent the better part of an hour in the bathroom with Rick one night, trying to convince him to try sniffing a little heroin. Despite their chemical incompatibility, Rick and Nitzsche liked each other and got along well.

"Jack would come to the sessions and fall asleep," said one insider, "and the guys would just go ahead and make the record." Kris occasionally showed up at the sessions too and sat in the corner for hours, looking stoned and miserable. Rick complained that Nitzsche was never straight enough to even know he was making a record.

Beland left the band to join the Flying Burrito Brothers before the album sessions started. The new band revolved around Memphis studio player Bobby Neal, who took his place in a long line of Rick's musical collaborators, beginning with James Burton. Old Hollywood hands like drummer Micky McGee, bassist John Davis, and keyboardist Charlie Harwood rounded out the instrumental lineup, with Pat Upton, who wrote the 1960s lounge hit "More Today Than Yesterday" for his group, Spiral Staircase, adding harmony vocals.

Nitzsche provided songs by contemporary songwriters like John Hiatt, Ry Cooder, and Graham Parker. Rick's cousin Kathy Nelson, Don Nelson's daughter who was beginning her own career in the music business, brought in a song by an unknown Billy Steinberg, who later became one of the industry's leading writers with hits like "True Colors" for Cyndi Lauper and "Like a Virgin" for Madonna.

Throughout the year, Rick stayed on the road when he wasn't in the studio, keeping a backbreaking two hundred-plus date schedule that took a severe toll on the band. John Beland got divorced. Charlie Harwood shaved his head and a beard he had had for twenty-five years and got a divorce too. Micky McGee had a nervous breakdown and went to live with his parents in Phoenix. Both Harwood and McGee joined Beland in the Flying Burrito Brothers and did not come back with Rick. "That was Greg McDonald's philosophy," said road manager Alan Bush. " 'You want to go? Good-bye. Don't count on coming back.' "

With monthly living expenses running close to $30,000—including almost $6,000 in payments on the new house—Rick had to tour. He faced a constant cash-flow struggle, and the pressure to make his payroll, pay his expenses, and keep Kris in the lap of luxury and the four kids in expensive private schools left him no alternative but to take any crummy booking that would guarantee his minimum price. He played a bowling alley in Grand Rapids, Michigan. He took $1,800 from a date in Bloomington, Indiana. Bush remembered getting beaten up and held by his ankles out of a projection-room window by some tough guys working for a New Jersey promoter when Rick drew fewer than two dozen customers to a theater seating several thousand.

Kris wanted Rick to give up music and concentrate on acting. He got a part as onscreen narrator of a sweet, partly animated children's show, "A Tale of Three Wishes," but took it no more seriously than he did the old episodes of his family's TV show, studying his lines in the car on the way to the set. He liked touring and performing music, despite the grueling itineraries, and he could earn enough money to almost make ends meet.

"Rick just said to Greg, 'I want to live in this house,' " said Alan Bush. " 'I want to drive my car. I don't want anybody to call me and say my bills are late. . . . You take care of it.' So they'd take some real questionable shows."

The stages would be makeshift, the sound systems inadequate, the lights barely operational, but virtually any promoter willing to put up the deposit could book a Rick Nelson engagement.

Even out of town, Kris dogged his steps. "Kris was real good at calling just as we were getting ready to leave for the show," said Bush. "He wouldn't say, 'I can't talk to you now, I've got to go to my show.' He would talk to her. Sometimes we might be at a venue that was forty-five minutes away from the hotel, because we parked by the airport instead of the venue, so we could get out early the next morning. He got on the phone with her. She talked to him for about forty-five minutes. I screamed at him to get to the show."

He rarely complained. "Kris called him one time and gave him a real bad time," Bush said, "and he talked to her just real plain. As soon as he hung up the phone he said, 'I don't believe this woman.' It was the maddest I'd ever seen him. He raised his voice."

In October 1980 the inevitable happened. Kris again filed for divorce. She did not move out of the house, only to an upstairs room on the other side of the building. But what ensued wasn't merely divorce. It was war.

All attempts to negotiate a preliminary settlement agreement failed. The financial picture was grim. According to statements by Rick's business manager, there was a bank overdraft of $30,000 and pressing debts of more than $135,000. He borrowed $50,000 from a bank and another $50,000 from Harriet. Lawyers ran up bills on both sides every day. Kris saw a psychiatrist three times a week. All this was crashing down on Rick in January 1981, when Capitol finally released his album *Playing to Win*, his only hope for a professional break-through that could solve his disastrous economic condition.

Rick hired public relations expert Oscar Arslanian to represent him, and the former Capitol Records executive got results. Instead of being referred to as a "former teen idol," Rick now began seeing the word "legendary" precede his name, so often the band began to call him "Ledge." "We absolutely maximized a whole new media outlook at who Rick Nelson was," said Arslanian. "He was regarded by the electronic media as a matinee idol."

Rick himself took a new attitude about promoting his record. He became actively involved in getting himself known at Capitol, visiting executives in their offices and attending company events, a stark contrast to his aloof and distant relationship with Decca and MCA or Epic. He did interviews by the dozens, gladly trotting out the same old answers to the same old questions. He also tried to tie himself in with what was going on in the music scene at the time, although he never listened to the radio or kept himself up to date.

"They talk about new wave and punk and all that," he told the *Los Angeles Times*. "It's really an extension of the way I started. It's gotten back to three and four pieces and things like that, which I feel very close to. The Graham Parker song, it sounded like a song I would have done when I was starting out."

The album burst out of the speakers with the roar of electric guitars that introduced "Almost Saturday Night," the Fogerty song Rick had previously recorded during the Memphis sessions. He updated the Burnettes' "Believe What You Say," although the pumped-up, fuzz-toned remake hardly holds a candle to the original. He struck a nearly sarcastic attitude on John Hiatt's "It Hasn't Happened Yet" and rocked merrily through Graham Parker's "Back to Schooldays." Some tracks suffered from the worst arena rock clichés of the era, but, on the whole, *Playing to Win* presented Rick in a thoroughly believable modern-day light, nothing ground-breaking but fresh and compatible with his essential character.

"The album was going to be called 'It's Rock and Roll to Me,' " said Rick, "but the idea was shelved because Billy Joel brought out a thing with the same theme. I just want to make records that sound like me. I've been through so many people telling me 'Go this direction' and then changing their minds the next day."

The tentative title came from one of his two originals on the album, "Call It What You Want," a jaunty, Rolling Stones–style romp.

His other original, however, provided the LP's most prophetic song, "The Loser Babe Is You." The message was clear.

> *I know you think I'm crazy,*
> *Burnt out, lazy,*
> *Winning days are through.*
> *Am I mistaken?*
> *Have you been taking*
> *More than you can use?*
> *By the way,*
> *The loser babe is you.*

In February Rick and Kris signed a temporary agreement in which Kris was granted custodial rights to the four children and $3,600 a month in spousal support. In addition, Rick was obligated to pay property taxes, income taxes, auto insurance, private school tuitions, attorney fees, and doctor bills. He didn't have marital problems; he had money problems.

Tracy, seventeen, was a serious and sober young lady. A senior at the exclusive Westlake School for Girls, she did well academically but experienced social problems at school. "She was the misfit," said one of her friends. "When you are concerned with learning and other people are concerned with having parties, you're going to be." She studied dance and thought of going into ballet or becoming a veterinarian or writer. She stayed at the Flynn mansion with her father, regardless of the temporary divorce agreement, and did not get along all that well with her mother.

Kris rented a house in nearby Studio City, and the twins ostensibly took up residence with her, although they too spent as much time up the hill at the Mulholland house as they could get away with. Matthew showed alarming signs of failing at Harvard School. He was not invited back for the ninth grade. Sam was spirited off to the care of his Harmon grandparents, Tom and Elyse, in Brentwood. Kris's sister, Kelly, had been taking care of the young boy every afternoon and all day on Saturdays for the previous year anyway.

"I raised my youngest brother, Sam, pretty much," said Tracy. "It taught me a lot, most of all patience. Why did I? Well, my parents were gone so much of the time. So when I saw Sam needing answers to things, I was always there. He's a lot like I was when I was little, which is really fun to watch. My other brothers aren't. They're like Mack trucks. They're young Adonises—or so they think. They've never really liked me very much. They like me as a person, but not as a sister because I tend to tell them what to do and they don't appreciate it."

The children grew up with parents that were rarely around and, when they were, often zonked out. After the split, they battled over nickels and dimes that didn't exist. Rick and Kris lived in a fantasy, into which the only reality that intruded was ugly. The children could barely depend on anybody outside themselves. This was a long way from "Ozzie and Harriet."

As family matters crushed down on Rick, the new album opened doors for him. Radio totally rejected the record. But the press stood in line to conduct interviews, and television wanted him everywhere. A documentary titled *Portrait of a*

Legend—starring the Ledge himself—was filmed. He did "Almost Saturday Night" on "The Tonight Show" and exchanged banter with guest host David Letterman about the mirror above his bed in the old Flynn house. He played "The Midnight Special," "Good Morning America," and "Solid Gold" and taped an interview with David at the Mulholland house for Tom Snyder and "The Tomorrow Show."

In March he played for a star-studded house at the Roxy on Sunset Strip, Hollywood's top rock club and record industry showcase. He looked sharp in a pearl-white blazer, his black hair combed back off his forehead to reveal those chiseled features, and the band delivered a razor-edged performance. Nitzsche showed up backstage so bombed Rick expressed concern. One of the stars attending the show that night, Sally Struthers, fresh off TV's long-running "All in the Family," got worked up about the idea of developing a series for her and Rick.

Nothing ever came of her enthusiasm. Nor did anything come of the entreaties of the powerful William Morris Agency, who wanted to sign Rick and represent his acting career at the time. When asked by interviewers why he didn't pursue acting more seriously, he always made some comment about not being able to concentrate on two careers at the same time. But the truth was that he hated to get up in the morning, and acting would have also kept him in Hollywood and near Kris Nelson.

For years, road work took a strain off their marriage and allowed Rick his dalliances. "I love pussy," he told a friend. "That's why I tour so much." He laughed about his wife once catching him in bed with a girl wearing a cowboy hat, boots, and nothing else. Now going on the road meant relief of a different sort, a break from depositions, conferences, and meetings with accountants and lawyers, as the legal battle over the dissolving marriage escalated. He wanted to stay on the road as much as possible and would have Greg McDonald book additional dates while the band was still on tour.

In June Kris changed attorneys, and her new lawyer took an aggressive stance. When Rick filed a motion seeking custody of the children, her lawyer answered with drastic accusations:

"Respondent has a severe drug problem, which is encouraged not only by his managers, but by the entourage of musicians and groupies who always surround him. The children are aware that Respondent [Rick] constantly takes cocaine, Quaaludes, and many other drugs, and have expressed great anxiety and concern that they are unable to speak with him or do anything at all for him when he is under the influence of these drugs.

"Respondent allows wild parties to take place in his home at all hours during which drugs are always taken. Respondent is constantly on the road, but strangers are allowed to come in and out of the house freely, even when he is not at home. The children, especially Tracy, are literally in physical danger when they visit the home because of the number of drugged and unpredictable persons who are constantly in the house.

"Respondent is on the road touring in excess of one half a year. The short time that Respondent is at home, he does not get out of bed until the evening, and has virtually no contact at all with the children when they are visiting. Respondent hires an ostensible 'houseman' named Joseph, purportedly to supervise and help him with the children. However, Joseph is Polish, cannot even speak English, and does nothing at all for the children. For example, the children are not served meals in the Respondent's home and are required to find ways to get their own food.

"Respondent is virtually mesmerized and entirely controlled by his business manager and personal manager. Both are aware of and encourage Respondent's drug problem, and his personal manager in fact secures drugs for Respondent."

Rick's attorney responded in equally strong language. "Petitioner [Kris] consumes excessive amounts of alcohol and combines alcohol and Placidyl [a barbiturate]. . . . Petitioner's sudden desire for custody of the children is based not on the welfare of the children but on her desire for a larger home and greater financial support. Further, when the boys were with Petitioner, your declarant's [Rick's] houseman, Chester, was required to drive to her home, make breakfast for the boys, drive them to school, pack their lunches and drive them home from school. Petitioner's care of the children during marriage was virtually nonexistent. . . . Petitioner is a regular user of large amounts of cocaine and uses various other drugs which prevent her from properly caring for the children when under the influence. . . . Petitioner is an uncontrollable spendthrift who is incapable of controlling her spending or admitting this problem. Her spending problem interferes with Petitioner's ability to parent causing her to constantly be out of money, unable to provide for the children or seek additional support."

Chester Golasinski went to work at Rick's house after the previous houseman [Joseph] lost the family grocery money in a poker game at the Gardena card parlors. A strong, handsome Polish immigrant, Golasinski spoke halting English but adored the children. When he first came to work, Kris and all the children still lived at the house. He stayed in a small room at the house and was on duty virtually around the clock. "Everything," Golasinski said, describing his duties. "I cleaned the house. I made the food for the kids, for him. Drive the kids to school."

Golasinski said Rick stayed almost entirely in his bedroom, coming into the house only occasionally. Rick slept during the day, newspapers and tin foil on the windows to keep out the sunlight, covering the panoramic view of the San Fernando Valley. Sometimes he didn't get out of bed for days on end. He subsisted on hamburgers, ice cream, and Pepsi-Cola. If the children were staying at the house, he only ran into them in the hallways on his rare forays out of the bedroom. They grew accustomed to not seeing their father much, even on his infrequent and brief stays at home. A tailor visited the house, so he never even needed to go out shopping for clothes.

Rick told the children the divorce was their mother's fault. The children witnessed Kris's explosive temper, as she threw things while Rick remained calm. According to court documents, she once broke his car window and, on another occasion, smashed one of his gold-record awards.

Alone, Rick would stay in his room and watch TV or play piano. He would go grocery shopping at two in the morning at the twenty-four-hour Hughes market and occasionally ate Mexican food at Casa Vega, which stayed open past two specifically to accommodate him. "He wouldn't leave the house if he hadn't shaved," said Alan Bush. "He'd shave, have his hair combed, have makeup on, his summer tan in place."

Golasinski was under the impression Rick used a lot of drugs. He thought the children suspected their father's problem but never actually saw him using. Greg McDonald, one of the few regular visitors to the house, told Golasinski that Rick was as isolated as Elvis Presley grew to be in his final years.

The divorce battle raged, as Kris and her lawyers kept trying to discover some hidden wealth and Rick's true earnings. A statement from his business manager showed a net loss of almost $30,000 on Rick's personal income for the year of 1981. Although he grossed more than $900,000 touring that year, the net remaining after expenses showed about $55,000. His earnings on record royalties and song publishing amounted to a little more than $64,000, and his total personal income barely broke $200,000. It was not a lot to show from almost 250 nights of work as a headline entertainer. Even so, while most people can live quite comfortably on that amount, by the time Rick paid his living expenses, including more than $37,000 in alimony and extensive attorney fees, he was in the red. Experts recommended Rick file for bankruptcy, but he refused.

Rick never learned to be realistic about money. All his life, his finances were handled by other people, and he never bothered with learning the details. He barely knew how to write a check. He did not know what it meant to not be able to afford something, and his constant touring created enough cash flow that he could live on the float.

He left home on tour practically every week, returning to sleep day and night. On at least a couple of occasions, Kris showed up at the house while he was out of town and raided the house for furniture and other belongings. His mansion came to be sparsely furnished. He grew estranged from David and his mother and saw them only on special occasions like Thanksgiving—and not always even then. According to Alan Bush, Rick "couldn't get it together" to leave the house for Laguna Beach before late in the evening and simply abandoned plans for a family Thanksgiving that year. He skipped a planned appearance on the Christmas TV special hosted by David and Harriet. Although they used the excuse that Rick couldn't make the show because he was touring, Rick actually was at home and just didn't get out of bed.

Into this solitude came Helen Blair, a pretty twenty-five-year-old who met Rick at a Southern California nightclub engagement. "She was a groupie," sneered one of his friends. She followed the show around various southern California stops. When she and Rick crossed paths again at the Riviera Hotel in Las Vegas, she came to stay, moving into the big house and, instead of opening up his life, closed him off even more. She changed the phone number and hovered around Rick constantly, careful to stay quiet in the background, but never far away. She became the intermediary that handled all communication with Rick. The children did not especially care for her, and his friends wondered what Rick was doing with her.

"He told me that he needed someone like her," said one, "someone that would give up her own life and devote herself totally to him."

"She was the kind of person," said Golasinski, "who tried keeping Rick all for herself. After then, nobody came to the home. After then, things were absolutely separate. Everything was crazy. She was a nice person, but she was so jealous about Rick. She was crazy."

Helen Blair came with at least one major drawback—a severe drug problem. One associate recalled leaving her at the hotel rather than taking her to the nightclub where Rick was playing because of her condition. "She was incoherent," he said. Helen and Rick had become codependents in a classic pattern for addicts. The situation grew so distressing to McDonald that he arranged for an intervention, where a number of Rick's old friends like Kent McCord descended on him at once and pleaded with him to seek treatment for drug abuse.

Rick went back to work for promoter Richard Nader, producer of the infamous "Garden Party" concert at Madison Square Garden more than ten years earlier. His meager drawing power as a solo headline act was well established, and Rick could count on getting good crowds only in smaller cities. As part of a package concert, Rick could play to larger crowds for more money in major cities again. Nader was now putting on his rock & roll revival shows all around the country, and Rick topped a bill that included Bo Diddley, Tommy Roe, the Drifters, and the Shirelles at the Cotton Carnival Music Festival in Memphis before a crowd of twenty thousand on Mother's Day in 1982.

In October that same year Rick returned to Australia for the first time in twenty years for a seventeen-date tour that lasted almost the entire month. He was greeted by a phalanx of reporters and photographers at the Melbourne airport and made a couple of network TV appearances in advance of the first show, recalling his previous visit. "We performed in old wrestling stadiums," he said, "and I was on the same program as Johnny O'Keefe. But I had a great time. I loved it."

O'Keefe, Australia's first homegrown rock & roll star who tried without success to make hits in America, died a few years earlier, but his daughter, Vicki O'Keefe, was scheduled to open a few of the concerts on Rick's current tour. Australians still treated him like the big star he used to be back home. He loved Australia. For one thing, it was practically as far away on the planet as he could get from Kris.

Kris kept her lawyer working overtime, on Rick's back immediately if he was so much as a few days late in his payments. She sent private investigators to serve him with warrants, only to have them find the gates locked or Rick not at home or somehow unavailable for service. Charges and countercharges flew back and forth. Rick fell so far behind in his own attorney's fees, he issued her a deed of trust on his home for $85,000 to secure her payment. They signed a twenty-nine-page settlement in December 1982, more than two years after Kris started proceedings and more than $300,000 worth of lawyer bills later. Rick agreed to pay $4,000 a month support to Kris, a figure that would jump to $7,500 a month for three years beginning either after one year or when the house was sold, whichever came first. He could begin to put the divorce behind him. All he had to do was keep coming up with the money.

His bitter evaluation of his former wife: "A waste of skin," he said.

"I'm sure our marriage would have survived if it wasn't for drugs," Kris said in 1987, after going through rehabilitation.

He began plans for his second Capitol album. There was brief talk that the record would be produced by Lindsey Buckingham of Fleetwood Mac, but nothing came of that. More serious was the proposal by Paul McCartney. The former

Beatles songwriter suggested he take Rick to Memphis, park a recording van outside the old Sun Records studio, and cut a rockabilly style album with Rick on that hallowed ground, with a cover photo to be taken outside. But McCartney and Capitol, who had lost McCartney as a recording artist to CBS Records, could never come to terms. Instead, Capitol turned to old hand Nik Venet, who used to run across Rick in the early days in Hollywood.

Venet had a distinguished history as a record producer. He helmed the original Beach Boys records, produced a slew of hits by the Lettermen and others for Capitol in the 1960s, and supervised the first hit record by Linda Ronstadt when she was the vocalist with the Stone Poneys. But he had been largely inactive for many years, and the Nelson project represented a return to action for the veteran producer.

Sessions for the album were held intermittently, depending on Rick's tour schedule, throughout 1983. "We used Ocean Way Studios," said Venet. "We used the old original studio he used. I tried to find the only studio that still had the floor he originally recorded on. Ocean Way still had the tile floor."

Recording did not go smoothly. "Rick Nelson had a pace that was unnerving," said Venet. "There is slow. There is medium. There is fast, and there is Rick Nelson time. Rick Nelson would set a song up like a guy sets up a shot for a film. He would make rushes of the song. Instead of takes, they were rushes. He would wait to hear rushes. He would come in and want to change a bar. And I don't mean mechanically, with a razor. No. We couldn't punch it in. We started from the top."

Venet said that Rick often heard things that weren't there. He thought Rick's drug intake made him unnecessarily scrupulous. Rick's associates allowed they thought Venet spent a fair amount of time himself with his nose in a bottle.

"Helen Blair and Rick Nelson were joined at the hip," said Venet. "She was with him all the time. Everybody else kind of viewed her as a problem. Remember, she was an interloper. Here comes a man who's getting a divorce, from one of the great families in the country, and here comes a girl with no show biz breeding, no qualifications. Having been divorced we had a lot of things in common, and we used to laugh about it. Helen never said anything about Kris. I never heard her say the word *Kris*. She was always there, and if he started talking about Kris, she would get up and make coffee."

Rick liked Venet's production of *California Bloodlines* by John Stewart, a 1969 album Venet recorded live to a two-track machine. They tried cutting some of Rick's album that way, but Rick had problems cutting satisfactory vocals live. They found the old echo chamber that Rick used to use in the studio on his Imperial sessions and put it back in action. As the sessions progressed, Rick became more interested in a pure rockabilly sound. "He was debating whether he should go totally rockabilly or just dip into it," said Venet. They talked about going to Nashville so the Jordanaires could overdub harmonies.

Rockabilly returned to vogue in pop music circles. A group of American expatriates living in England called the Stray Cats hit it big in 1982 with a sound that re-created the original fifties rockabilly, complete with stand-up bass and minimal drum kit. The Cats' lead vocalist, Brian Setzer, idolized Rick's old pal Eddie Cochran and eventually even portrayed the late rocker in the film *La Bamba*. Rockabilly-tinged records were a common product of the burgeoning new-wave movement, and although Rick didn't keep up on all the subterranean nuances of the scene, he was well aware of the Stray Cats.

Also aware of the sudden renewal of interest in rockabilly was Epic Records, which released a four-song, ten-inch edition of material from the Memphis sessions. But, for some unknown reasons, Epic felt the need for additional postproduction on the four songs. Producer Steve Buckingham overdubbed more guitars and added fake applause to the tracks, remixed the results, and put out what had been a straightforward rockabilly recording as a muddled mess. Rick was furious. "I've never seen him madder in his life," said one business associate. "It's a good thing Steve Buckingham wasn't there."

He got frustrated trying to record his second Capitol album. He recorded the John Hiatt song "Doll Hospital" over and over again, restlessly searching for the perfect take on the number, never quite satisfied with the results. He would show up at midnight for sessions scheduled to start at eight o'clock. And every few days, the sessions would be interrupted by out-of-town shows. "His schedule was such that if the dates came up, he was off," said Venet. Sometimes weeks would go by between recording sessions. Bills mounted up. And with an unfinished, unpromising album running far over budget, Capitol pulled the plug.

The label released a single from the sessions, "Give 'Em My Number," a song by Dave Loggins ("Please Come to Boston") that loped along in an easy, shuffling gait, to test the waters and see whether there was a responsive chord in the public breast for the work. Rick appeared on the syndicated TV show "Solid Gold" to lip-synch the single. But it sank like a stone in a lake, without so much as a ripple on the shore.

13
Big Train from Memphis

WITH A HEADLINE ENGAGEMENT SCHEDULED for the eighteen-thousand-seat Forum in Los Angeles, Rick agreed to an interview with the popular alternative newspaper the *Los Angeles Weekly* in October 1983. Reporter Bill Bentley arrived at the Mulholland house around six in the evening, but it wasn't dinnertime at the Nelson home. Freshly showered, Rick obviously had just gotten up from bed.

Rick went through his typical routine, although Bentley noticed Rick kept excusing himself to go to the bathroom, uncomplainingly trotting out some of the same tired stories he had been telling interviewers for years. He did show some genuine enthusiasm for his new band, just off the road from his first tour with the freshly formed group. Guitarist Bobby Neal still remained, but Rick had recruited a young rhythm section from the L.A. new wave scene and sounded somewhat excited about the new direction the band headed him into.

He also made a few vaguely caustic remarks about big record companies, the Capitol Records experience still sore in his mind. "I'm not going to jump into a deal with a major company unless they understand what I'm doing," he said. "It's easy to get sidetracked, because all of a sudden you have people up there who are attorneys or accountants telling you that you need more bass. When I started, the people who ran the companies were the people who had things they believed in musically. Now sometimes you find someone who doesn't want to take a stand because it may jeopardize their position. Before, the whole motivation of the owners was that they liked music. But it's got to get back to the music eventually. To my mind, if the record business is going to survive, it's got to start having much more to do with the music."

As he showed Bentley to the door at the end of the interview, Rick paused on his front step and surveyed his estate. "I don't know why I live here," he said wistfully. "It's much too big for me and I'm here all alone."

Except for Helen, Rick was alone. Tracy lived in her own apartment and was beginning a successful acting career. She picked up a plum role as Valley Girl Jennifer DeNuccio in "Square Pegs," a relatively intelligent sitcom that lasted one season beginning in the fall of 1982. She auditioned for the part during Christmas break from Bard College and left school after being cast. She also picked up a small role in the movie *Footloose* and appeared well on her way to establishing herself as the leading member of the fourth generation of Nelsons to go into show business. "My family is not a major part of my life," she told *TV Guide*. "My work is."

The twins still grudgingly lived with their mother and visited their father frequently. They had begun working in small local clubs as the rhythm section of a heavy-metal rock band initially called Strange Agents and later changed to the Nelsons. Sam never saw his father, as Kris kept the boy under close wraps at her new home in Brentwood or under the protective supervision of her parents. Few people came to visit the mansion on the hill, and not many people called. If he wasn't on the road, Rick rambled around the empty seven-bedroom house alone with Helen.

Things had not been going all that well with the band. Jay DeWitt White from the Stone Canyon Band rejoined for a few months in the summer of 1983, and he found the situation drastically different. "It had changed a lot," he said. "He always had girls, but to have Helen along, that in itself was uncharacteristic of Rick. He liked to go out and have a good time and party. But to spend all his time on the road with one girl was kind of weird. He was definitely a lot weirder. Something was wrong. His talent wasn't there. He wasn't singing very well, putting on weight.

"What makes everybody close to him in the situation angry was this guy McDonald kept it that way. He really screwed up his career as far as a lot of people are concerned. He was more interested in keeping him out working these dives and taking his fifteen, twenty percent. [McDonald] was never out there much. When he was, he took a band member's place on the airplane, and the band member had to ride in the truck. They were more interested in going out yahooing and partying than sounding good on a gig. That was kind of secondary. It bugged the shit out of me."

Rick's interest in a return to his rockabilly roots continued to grow, and Los Angeles at the time was a hotbed of rockabilly revivalists littered around the fringes of the new-wave scene. The Blasters managed some national recognition, and Rockin' Ronnie Weisner boosted the careers of aging, little-known old-timers like Ray Campi on his Rollin' Rock label. Club Lingerie in Hollywood hosted popular "Rockabilly Wednesdays." Rick first stumbled across this renaissance of California rockabilly in person when he caught James Intveld opening a show for him at a Long Beach club called the Rumbleseat Garage.

"The Stray Cats was the only thing he had heard of," said Intveld. "He didn't like the Blasters, I guess 'cause they didn't have that teen sound. It didn't sound like Elvis. I can't believe that Rick Nelson saw us play, because he's never watched an opening act."

Rick's road manager tipped him to the band and his cousin Willy Nelson knew about Intveld, but it was unlike Rick to get to a gig early for any reason. He must have liked what he saw. Intveld was backed by guitarist Jerry McGee, an old Hollywood hand who used to play in the house combo at the Sea Witch back in the fifties, belonged briefly to instrumentalists the Ventures, played on a couple of Rick's sessions in the sixties, and even coauthored a song, "Louisiana Belle," that appeared on one of Rick's final MCA singles.

In addition to McGee, Patrick Woodward handled the upright bass, and Intveld's younger brother, Ricky Intveld, played rockabilly drums. Rick offered jobs to Woodward and Ricky Intveld. Although the younger Intveld opted to remain with his brother, Woodward brought slap bass back into Rick's band for the first time since James Kirkland left almost twenty-five years before. The Intvelds recommended Rix Roberts of the King Bees on drums. Roberts, however, didn't last long, and within a couple of months, Ricky Intveld joined up.

His first date with the band, without any more than one brief rehearsal, was "Garden Party II" at Madison Square Garden in November, another rock & roll revival produced by Richard Nader that featured almost exactly the same bill as the original concert more than ten years before that Rick made famous in song. He had been doing a number of these package oldies shows in large auditoriums since going back to work for Nader the previous year, regardless of any reservations he so eloquently expressed in his song "Garden Party." His headline performance at the Forum the month before was part of a seven-city tour titled "Lovin' Feelings" and featured Rick topping a bill that also included the Righteous Brothers, Jerry Lee Lewis, the Association, and Little Anthony. *Los Angeles Times* reviewer Robert Hilburn noted the irony of Rick playing such a "Garden Party" and questioned the wisdom of Rick's closing the show.

"Nelson, who is not dynamic as a singer or performer, should never have agreed to follow the Righteous Brothers and, especially, Jerry Lee Lewis on stage. Without those high-powered attractions, the show might well have been a Slumber Party. . . . In his 40s now, Nelson keeps working at reconnecting with the pop charts, and he exhibited some gritty vocal touches on the Stones' 'Honky Tonk Women.' But much of the crowd began heading home when Nelson edged away from the early favorites."

The only act from the original concert that didn't play Garden Party II was Gary U.S. Bonds, whose recent hits produced by Bruce Springsteen, Bonds thought, elevated him beyond mere oldies status. Rick no longer held any such notions. He needed the work, and the big package shows paid far better than steak-and-lobster houses. "I felt much more comfortable about doing the revival shows in 1982 than I did back in the early '70s," Rick said. "The music had created a lot more interest over the past couple of years. Anyway, I'd had my hair cut and I looked right."

For the Madison Square Garden concert, he rehearsed with the Jordanaires, brought in for the occasion, and new band members drummer Ricky Intveld and pianist Gene Taylor of the Blasters briefly in New York. Rick performed, without any apparent irony, his song "Garden Party," and the audience accepted the song as just another hit. "They didn't take it as any kind of statement," said Nader.

Rick said he hardly felt any apprehension about the performance. "Only a little bit," he said, "because I knew that I had a band behind me that was every bit as good as anything that had come out of the '50s. The New York press built the whole thing up. They were calling it Rick Nelson's comeback. But I've been coming back all my life, so really it was nothing new to me."

He still dabbled inconsequentially in acting and joined a cast of other old familiar faces from TV shows of the past for a ridiculous piece of fluff called *High School U.S.A.* This television version of lightweight, summer-fun teen movies featured former cast members of "Leave It to Beaver," "The Mickey Mouse Club," "Batman," and others. Rick played the hapless but likable principal of the high school, and his mother played his secretary. "Who does he think I am?" Harriet said in her first scene. "His mother?"

At Christmas Rick gave Helen a diamond ring. They were not officially engaged but more along the lines of engaged to be engaged. She nevertheless began calling herself Rick's fiancée.

His money problems remained monumental. State and Federal tax agencies applied liens for more than $100,000 in back taxes in 1984, and even his old friend and former bodyguard Jack Ellena had to sue to collect $5,000 in unpaid fees for Matthew and Gunnar attending Ellena's summer camp. His lawyer filed suit to collect nearly $100,000 worth of unpaid attorney fees. Rick battled as many as a dozen lawsuits at once.

When he fell behind in his payments to her attorney, Kris sent the marshals out to the Mulholland house at least twice to try to serve him papers that would allow her to take his prized Pantera. Sheriff's deputies finally managed to wrench the beloved car loose, but Greg McDonald bailed out the vehicle the following day. She tried to garnish empty bank accounts and record contracts that would never pay him any money in her frantic efforts to tie up his funds and collect her full share.

In early 1984 a deal to sell the Mulholland house for $900,000 was completed. A wealthy fan agreed to purchase the house and lease it back to Rick, so he could continue to live in splendid isolation. Under the divorce terms, Kris would receive $100,000 of the proceeds and Rick $200,000, since he had assumed a greater proportion of the community debt they incurred during the marriage. Of course, the real-estate sale became entangled, and the money was far from immediately forthcoming.

Rick took practically any gig he could get, working incessantly, although he turned down an invitation to perform at the White House. From his youth he remembered Ronald Reagan the actor as a friend of his parents and found the proposition simply too weird to accept. He burned through keyboardists, platooning three different pianists over the year. Johnny Meeks, who used to play with Gene Vincent back in the fifties, took the chair for a week, and Jerry McGee, his old associate whom he saw playing with James Intveld, joined the band on guitar for a week when Bobby Neal had to go back home for his father's funeral. Rick did a summer tour of "sheds," as the open-air amphitheater circuit is called, for Richard Nader, with a package that included the Coasters, Bobby Vee, Lesley Gore, the Marvelettes, and the Drifters, as well as a sentimental stop at Tupelo, Mississippi, birthplace of Elvis Presley, where Rick was named honorary police chief.

He could be remarkably cavalier about showing up for concerts on time. A few were simply scrubbed shortly ahead of show time, resulting in angry promoters taking legal action. He flew to San Francisco on a chartered airplane, landing five hours ahead of his scheduled opening for a prestigious two-week run at the Fairmont Hotel's elegant supper club, the Venetian Room. Instead of leisurely checking into his suite at the hotel, he immediately secreted himself with Helen in a private room at Butler Aviation at the airport and only emerged in time to hurry to the hotel and get onstage fifteen minutes late. He canceled a planned sound check and stood up a couple of would-be interviewers but on opening night dawdled with one interviewer long enough in between shows to be a half-hour late for the second show.

Greg McDonald exerted enormous control over Rick's life. Many people believe he even held his power of attorney. Unlike most managers, his influence extended into Rick's personal finances, and between McDonald and Rick's accountants, Rick could remain blithely ignorant of the details of his financial picture. McDonald served as a kind of alter ego to Rick, playing black hat to Rick's white hat. The two became so enmeshed in carrying out his affairs, even insiders experienced difficulty discerning which one was the puppet and which one held the strings.

Obviously Rick wanted it that way. He couldn't have entered into such a symbiotic relationship with a more professional manager. With McDonald, Rick didn't have to voice opinions unless he wanted to and then McDonald would treat them as word of law. For the most part, apparently, Rick was content to let McDonald call the shots and turn the wheels, leaving him to simply play the part and speak the lines.

Of course, this was also how it had worked with his father, and Rick clearly was used to giving himself over to such a controlling influence. He told Oscar Arslanian, in a reflective moment, that he didn't feel things had been right since his father died, and certainly McDonald brought a steadying factor into Rick's life.

"Dad did everything for us," he told writer Edward Kiersh in 1985. "He was always there when you needed him. Things really changed after he died. Boy, they sure did. I know where I want to go now, though. I have a new direction. I just hope Dad was proud of what I accomplished. I think he was."

Rick didn't have a recording contract, and McDonald

couldn't scare up much interest in signing Rick. It was Rick's idea to rerecord an album of his old hits. He thought he could sing them better this time. "Actually, I kind of wanted to reverse things—to record something and have somebody want what we recorded," he said. "It's been the other way around for quite a while. It was kind of different for me to work that way." He and McDonald borrowed the money from a bank to underwrite the venture. This was a long way from the person who sang "if memories were all I sang, I'd rather drive a truck."

He decided that to try to recapture the most authentic sound possible, he would turn his back on modern recording technology. He found a studio in North Hollywood, outfitted by members of the surf-punk band the Unknowns and equipped with only three-track recording, an old-fashioned tube console, and tape echo. He began recutting versions of his classic songs, even going so far as to record some songs in mono, not stereo.

Meanwhile, MTV, the cable TV music outlet, picked up a concert Rick filmed the previous year, edited out the one new song in the batch, and began playing the number like it was a new record. "You Know What I Mean" was a rockabilly period piece written by veteran British rocker Mickey Jupp, barely known outside England, where he enjoyed a brief return to popularity on the independent new-wave label Stiff Records, and produced by Nick Lowe (Elvis Costello, the Pretenders, Graham Parker). Rick used his new rockabilly band, Woodward on slap bass and Taylor on piano, to cut a version of the song for a single, but nothing was turning out to his satisfaction. The sessions staggered through the months, sandwiched between road trips.

He played New Year's Eve with Jerry Lee Lewis at the Riviera Hotel in Las Vegas. James Burton now belonged to Jerry Lee's band, and he hadn't seen Rick in some time. When the double bill rolled into Los Angeles's Universal Amphitheater six weeks later, Rick had honed the rockabilly sound of the new band to near perfection. "We try to play the older material as authentically as we can," he told Todd Everett of the *Los Angeles Herald-Examiner*. "I'd tried to play the old songs many different ways, but they sound the best the way we did 'em in the first place. It's kind of nice to go back to the sound I started with."

Early in 1985 Rick contacted Jimmie Haskell to see whether his seasoned hand could make any sense out of the mess the sessions produced. "Ricky, with all his brilliance, mistakenly thought that to accomplish the original we should do it the way we recorded in the old days," Haskell said. "He had already laid down some of the tracks incorrectly. It would have been nicer if I'd been involved from the beginning. I considered it a challenge. Other people do things like games and crossword puzzles. I'm not interested in crossword puzzles, but I am interested in working on a track from a music engineering standpoint and making it come out right."

Haskell and engineer Lee Miller spent hours putting the tapes together while Rick toured. Haskell would add a piano part where it was missing from the original or try to correct the cowbell sound on "Hello Mary Lou" with tape equalization. Many of the tracks were recorded over. The Jordanaires added their trademark harmony vocals, re-creating the parts they sang on the original records. Rick wanted special attention paid to "You Know What I Mean," since it would be the album's sole new song and the single from the set and had been getting the MTV airplay. But Haskell didn't like the existing recording.

The band's schedule did not allow much time for a new recording, but Haskell booked a morning session for the day Rick and the musicians would be leaving on tour. The band ripped off a new instrumental track, leaving Rick about twenty minutes to record his vocal. He sang it twice and left for the airport. On his return, he listened to Haskell's mix, made some suggestions, and left town again. Haskell prepared another set of three different mixes, and when Rick came back again, he selected one of the mixes and the album was ready.

A double-record set of twenty-two songs was released in May by Silver Eagle Records, a Canadian firm that specialized in advertising on late-night television and selling through mail order. It may not have been a distinguished release, but *All My Best*, as the set was titled, actually sold in substantial quantities.

All My Best had the eerie disassociation of a colorized movie. Rick's vocals came from an older voice, but his phrasing remained nearly identical with the originals. The instrumental tracks followed the basic floor plan of the initial recordings, but the inevitable slight sonic differences sounded jarring in the context. Guitarist Neal mimicked the precise moves of Burton's solos, but the edge of abandon was missing, like tracings of a shadow. The work was scrupulous but pointless, except from a financial standpoint.

The album sold well enough over television, and McDonald was able to negotiate a regulation release through MCA Records, who trimmed the LP down to one record with sixteen songs. Rick, buoyed by what he considered the success of the recording experiment, returned to the studio with Haskell to continue recording fresh material for a future release.

He sought out more songs from Mickey Jupp. He invited guitarist Billy Zoom of new-wave rockers X up to the house to play him some originals. Bobby Neal convinced him to record the old Beatles song "One After 909." He cut an old Elvis number, "As Long as I Have You," and tried again on the Buddy Holly song he first did in Memphis, "True Love Ways." He reworked the Guy Mitchell hit "Singing the Blues." The sessions took place on the few days the band was off the road, catch as catch can, and moved along slowly as a result.

In May he bought a vintage 1944 DC-3 airplane for $118,000. No more hurrying to make commercial flights; Rick could sleep as late as he wanted and take off for the next show when he got to the airport. The plane formerly belonged to Jerry Lee Lewis. "If Jerry Lee won't fly it," murmured James Burton, "it must be pretty well unflyable." But Rick loved the plane. The antique aircraft suited his sense of aesthetics, even if it was considerably slower than jet travel.

Rick was getting tired of the relentless touring. He took another role in a pilot for a possible TV series, "Fathers and Sons," and actually hoped the series would work out so he could stay home and relax for a while. He kept trying out for these pilots, looking for something to develop. So far, nothing had. "I've done more pilots than a TWA stewardess," he told friends.

In July one of Rick's one-night escapades on the road caught up with him, when Georgeanne Crewe won a paternity judgment against him in a New Jersey court. Rick and Crewe had met four years earlier during an engagement at the Playboy Club in Grand Gorge, New York, where she and her sister ended up staying at the same hotel as Rick and the band. After the show, road manager Alan Bush invited the two sisters to join the band and meet Rick. She wound up spending the night in Rick's bed. "He wanted me to stay," Crewe said, "and the way I felt, I wasn't going to leave because I felt an attachment, an immediate attraction."

Another person present at the scene said that after Crewe fell asleep, Rick slipped into her sister's bed. A couple of months later, Crewe, thirty-seven years old and separated from her husband, discovered she was pregnant and went to Connecticut, where Rick was performing. Bush introduced her to Greg McDonald, who told her "Rick won't ever want to see that child" and threatened her with a restraining order if she tried to take her pleas directly to Rick. Her efforts to communicate with Rick were consistently foiled by McDonald. "I got so many stories from Greg McDonald," she said, "it made me dizzy."

She named her son Eric, after Rick, and when the child was six months old took the baby in her arms to one of his concerts and planted herself in the front row. "The whole time he was performing he was looking at Eric," she said. She contacted a lawyer and began proceedings. She lived on welfare for three years, caring for her young son, while the legal wheels ground slowly. Blood tests finally concluded with a ninety-nine percent certainty that Rick was the father, and even before the court issued a ruling, McDonald paid her $1,200 so she could move out of the welfare hotel into an apartment of her own.

In August 1985 she took her priest and went to another concert, where she finally spoke with Rick personally. "All the time we were talking he held my hand," she said, "so there was no animosity." Regular monthly payments of $400 in child support began arriving the next month.

Rick played a series of dates across the West Coast in August with Fats Domino, which was filmed at the Universal Amphitheater in Los Angeles for a TV special. The New Orleans rhythm & blues great had not performed in California for more than twenty years (music lore has it that he stayed out of California until the statute of limitations on an old paternity suit had run out) so the shows were rather historic. Rick brought the Jordanaires to boost his vocal sound, and the highlight of each show was when Fats would call Rick out for a duet on "I'm Walkin'." "I need to retire again soon," he said in his best avuncular tones, his beefy arm around Rick's slender shoulder. "Will you record another one of my songs?"

But the pinnacle of the year for Rick came on September 20, when he flew to Memphis to participate in a once-in-a-lifetime recording session, joining an all-star cast singing background vocals to Jerry Lee Lewis, Roy Orbison, Johnny Cash, and Rick's original inspiration, Carl Perkins, whom he had never met.

Producer Chips Moman made a lot of great records at his American Studio during the sixties, including the first Memphis sessions by Elvis Presley since he left Sun Records. Moman too fled Memphis for Nashville as the city's music scene dried up in the seventies, and his project with the four surviving Sun Records greats, *Class of '55*, was designed to celebrate his return to recording in Memphis. To cap the historic weeklong sessions, he planned a recording of the John Fogerty song "Big Train from Memphis," which would include a stellar supporting cast singing behind the four rock & roll originals. A TV special of the event was being shot, and local and national news media crowded the tiny studio on the climactic day.

Rick took the DC-3 and brought McDonald, Bobby Neal, Ricky Intveld, and Intveld's brother James. They flew through the night and landed early in the morning. Rick went to the hotel to clean up and relax, while everyone else headed straight to the studio. The band members walked into American Studio and could barely suppress a gasp at the sight of this Mount Rushmore of rock—Cash, Jerry Lee, Orbison, and Perkins—sitting in chairs in front of microphones in the center of the room.

The crowd at the studio slowly gathered. June Carter Cash arrived, followed shortly by the mother-daughter country singing sensations the Judds. Welsh rocker Dave Edmunds showed up. Paul Burlison, the guitarist with Johnny and Dorsey Burnette in the Rock and Roll Trio, was there. Sam Phillips, whose Sun Records label started it all, wandered around. John Fogerty flew in from California on last-minute notice to watch his song be recorded. "It was a roomful of reputations and myths," said Fogerty.

Virtually the last to arrive was Rick. "Rick walked in very

noticed," said Fogerty. "I watched Rick walk through all this confusion, attention, and excitement. What I perceived was a very shy man wanting to get out of the limelight any way he could. He looked great, was wearing all black. How come I'm wearing a stupid plaid shirt and he's looking cool? 'Cause I didn't think it out. And he was looking bad. He smiled that nervous smile and went away."

Fogerty followed along, walking into the adjacent room that had been made over into a kind of Elvis shrine with a statue of the singer. He found Rick alone, and as he walked up to say hello, Rick froze. A large mass of photographers and video cameramen had followed Fogerty into the room and crowded behind him to capture their greeting for posterity. Rick did not relax.

Rick shared a microphone with his idol, Carl Perkins, and Fogerty paired off with Jerry Lee Lewis. Rick, Perkins, and Dave Edmunds worked up a three-part harmony to use on the third verse. Fogerty found himself somewhat nervous to be alongside Jerry Lee. "The song idolizes Elvis," said Fogerty, "and I had always known that Jerry Lee had this rivalry. So here we're going to sing this song and the words are printed and they put me right next to Jerry Lee, waiting for this volcano to finally figure what these words are about. Roy told me later Jerry Lee went through the words about four times and finally he turned around and said, 'Damn, this is a pretty good song. . . . This could be a hit song.' He was looking at it like some obscure piece of material that came in the window."

"Rick was very nervous," said James Intveld. "He was totally intimidated to be in this room in Memphis with those guys who made the sound."

"If I just get to sweep out the place when it's over," Rick told producer Moman, "it will be worth the trip to Memphis."

The media circus prevailed, and even when the song was finally put down on tape, nobody had much opportunity to kick back and hang out. Rick did a few brief interviews in a trailer parked outside—"I've always been such a big fan of all these guys, I wouldn't have missed it for anything"—and quickly returned to the hotel. Fogerty flew out to rehearse in Indiana with John Cougar Mellencamp because they would be appearing together the following day at Farm Aid in Champaign, Illinois. Rick decided he would go too and invited some of the other people from the "Class of '55" to join him on the plane.

Jerry Lee declined. There was no way he would get on that plane again. Cash accepted but never showed. Cash's guitarist, Marty Stuart, did turn up at the airport, and as the plane rumbled down the runway on takeoff, the engines backfired noisily, spit fire, and died. The flight was canceled on the spot.

Marty Stuart and Rick were talking during the aborted take-off. "We were talking about Buddy Holly's glasses," Stuart said, "about how some farmer found the glasses after the crash. Rick was laughing, and he was talking about how the plane used to belong to Jerry Lee. But I was thinking about how rickety I felt on it."

Leaving the plane behind in Memphis for repairs, Rick and the band booked commercial flights home and went back to California, forgetting about Farm Aid.

"On the flight to Memphis," said Intveld, "it was like riding on a bad bus, real loud and shaking the whole time. The plane had broken down so many times before with my brother. They had to push the plane off a runway once after an emergency landing. The thing that I was pissed off about was that everybody already said, 'We don't like the plane, and we don't want to fly on the plane.' Greg McDonald didn't do anything about it. It's kind of a tricky thing between Rick Nelson and Greg McDonald. Rick Nelson never takes the blame for anything. Greg is always the bad guy, trying to save money. But it had been brought up time and time again about the plane. Nobody wanted to fly on the plane."

He said that his brother called up worried about the plane

on several occasions and that pianist Andy Chapin actually left the tour on a commercial flight one time, rather than take the DC-3. Chapin threatened to quit the band over the issue of the airplane. "Everybody hated it," said Intveld, "but nobody would really listen. It was brought up all the time. It was like the main thing everybody always talked about."

MCA released *All My Best* and the single of "You Know What I Mean" in August, and Rick dutifully performed the new record on TV's "Solid Gold" and "Motown Revue," hosted by Smokey Robinson, before leaving for another tour of Australia a week after coming back from Memphis. He did fourteen shows in slightly more than two weeks, appeared on a couple of Australian TV programs, and managed to do enough shopping that Helen had to buy an extra suitcase for the trip back home. While in Australia, Rick introduced his version of "One After 909," one of the earliest songs written by John Lennon and Paul McCartney but not released by the Beatles until a version was recorded for the group's final album, *Let It Be*. On his return, he started talking about buying a house in Australia and spending half the year down under in the near future.

In October the band flew into Lincoln, Nebraska, on a day off and left the plane with Duncan Aviation to repair an inoperative cabin heater and a hydraulic leak on one of the engines. A repairman checked the heater's ignition, fuel filter, and fuel pump. All seemed to be working. The air blower sounded noisy and didn't appear to be running fast enough. Duncan did not have a new motor in stock, so the repairman cleaned up the old one, lubricated the bearings, and reinstalled it. The pilot tried the heater out, and although the repairman didn't think it was putting out a lot of heat, the pilot said it was working better than it had been.

Rick, Helen, and the rest of the crew arrived in London on October 31 for an eighteen-day tour of the British Isles, culminating with two sold-out shows on November 17 at London's Royal Albert Hall. Rick topped a package that also included Bo

Diddley, Del Shannon, Bobby Vee, the Marvelettes, and Frankie Ford, put together by promoter Richard Nader, who dubbed the tour "The Regal Rock 'n Blues Reunion."

Many of the fans at the London shows turned up dressed in full fifties teddy-boy regalia. Nader used a rotating stage in the center of the hall, and both the matinee and evening shows sold out. "The guy at Albert Hall told me he had never seen that in the history of the hall," said Nader. A backstage argument almost led to blows between Nader and McDonald, so the tour was not without tension.

The new album neared completion, with nine finished tracks awaiting Rick's lead vocals. A record deal was in the works with MCA/Curb Records, and Rick found time to join a chorus supplying background vocals to "Dancing on the Ceiling" and "Se La" for the new Lionel Richie album and appear in a video for a new record by Apollonia, the sexy costar of the hit Prince movie *Purple Rain*.

He looked forward to slowing down after New Year's. He took only a few dates for 1986, talked about moving into a smaller house, cutting back his lifestyle, perhaps taking a TV series and staying home and off the road as much as he could. He was going to fire the band, which would save money. Bobby Neal would be quitting after the new year anyway. Neal's wife was tired of her husband staying away from home most of the year, philandering his way across the country with an itinerant band of rock & rollers on an endless series of one-night stands, leaving a wife and family at home. Rick talked to his old colleague John Beland about coming aboard again.

But he still needed money, and when Kris threatened him with legal action if he fell behind in his backbreaking alimony payments, Rick asked McDonald to arrange a brief tour between Christmas and New Year's to pick up some quick cash.

The dates started in Orlando, Florida, and on Saturday, December 28, around dusk, the plane landed in Guntersville,

Alabama (population seventy-two hundred), after experiencing trouble with one of the plane's engines on the way from Florida. The plane taxied to a stop at the end of the short thirty-five-hundred-foot runway, and Rick lowered the built-in stairway. "I looked around, and I couldn't see anybody," said Guntersville resident Iris Harris. "I couldn't believe Rick Nelson was coming to Guntersville and there was nobody there to welcome him. I sort of curtsied and opened my arms and said, 'Welcome to Guntersville.' "

Harris and her friend Bob Lock gave Rick and some of the party a lift into town. Rick's pilot, Brad Rank, told former Boeing engineer Lock about the vintage aircraft, saying the plane suffered from a balky primer system but a powerful cabin heater kept the temperature comfortable.

The band was booked for two nights at P.J.'s Alley, a nightclub owned by Rick's former band member Pat Upton. Despite a record twelve-dollar admission, the club sold out both nights, and Rick offered to play a third, unscheduled show on Monday night. Rick and Helen stayed in the Holiday Inn facing the man-made Lake Guntersville, which cost two dollars more than rooms overlooking the parking lot. On Monday afternoon, the couple visited with Upton, his wife, and their four children.

That evening the band noticed a strange odor during the show. "I thought there was a dead rat somewhere," said Upton. The show ended around midnight, Rick closing with a version of the Buddy Holly song "Rave On." Afterward, the source of the bad smell was located. A ten-foot boa constrictor belonging to Rick's children had crawled into his guitar amplifier for warmth during the Christmas break at home and froze to death in the unheated cargo bay on the plane flying east.

The next morning, band and crew gathered at the airport, expecting to take off around ten o'clock for Dallas, where Rick was scheduled to perform at a New Year's Eve show at the Park Suite Hotel. They boarded the plane and got off when one of the engines wouldn't start; repairs delayed departure. The weather front changed, as the band waited for a break in the clouds, playing Space Invaders, eating cheeseburgers and onion rings, and petting the airport cat. Around two o'clock in the afternoon, the DC-3 finally lifted off the runway on the 450-mile trip to Dallas's Love Field.

The flight went quietly. Rick and Helen curled up on opposite benches and slept in the rear of the cabin. The other band members either dozed or rested quietly under blankets. Bobby Neal joined copilot Ken Ferguson in the cockpit for a while, as pilot Rank ambled through the passenger cabin, talking with Pat Woodward about commercial flights from Dallas to Los Angeles, since Woodward had recently moved to Dallas and would be staying behind for a couple of weeks after the New Year's gig.

About three hours into the flight, Rick complained to Rank about being cold, and Rank told his copilot to turn on the heater. After a number of unsuccessful attempts to make the heater work from the cockpit, Rank went back into the aft of the cabin to try to make the heater work.

"He signaled for me to turn it on or he came up front and told me to turn it on or whatever," Ferguson later testified. "This happened several times. One of the times I refused to turn it on. I was getting nervous. I didn't think we should be messing with the heater en route. I had discussed this with him on previous flights. He turned it on again." Pat Woodward came into the cockpit. "There is smoke in the cabin," he told Ferguson.

Rank later said he went back to the cabin and noticed some smoke curling around where Rick and Helen were asleep. He went back to investigate the heater and found it cool to his touch. He nevertheless activated one of the built-in fire extinguishers and opened fresh-air inlets on his way back through the cabin. Woodward helped him. Rick and Helen woke up startled to see wisps of smoke filling the plane.

Ferguson was already on the radio, beginning communications with Fort Worth and changing the plane's direction to reroute it to Texarkana airport. Rank resumed his seat behind the controls, and the two began to make preparations for landing.

In less than a minute, the "little problem" Ferguson mentioned to the Fort Worth tower turned into catastrophe. Black smoke boiled into the cockpit. The control panel was no longer visible, and they were choking and gagging on the smoke. The front window was stained. Rank broke out his side window and leaned out so he could see. Ferguson broke out his, and the open window acted like a chimney, drawing flames around him. He stuck his body out the window, to close down the chimney effect, and burned his hand while reaching for the lever that controlled the flaps. They began looking for an open space to make an emergency landing. Texarkana was out of the question.

Smoke in the cabin was so thick that Rank could no longer see his copilot. He saw a highway but discarded the idea of trying a landing there because there were ditches and power lines on both sides. He found the Joneses' cow pasture and brought the airplane down on the field, clipping phone wires as he flew over Debbie Foster's house and made a nearly perfect three-point landing. It all happened so fast, nobody had time to react on anything more than instinct. Less than four minutes after first advising Fort Worth they were in difficulty, the plane rolled to a crashing halt in a patch of trees at the far side of the field. Rank climbed out his window. Inside the plane all he could see was flames and black smoke.

Ferguson tumbled head first out of his side and staggered away from the plane, afraid of an explosion. Badly burned and dazed by shock, he was sitting in the field when Rank ran up to him. "Don't say anything about the heater," Rank said. "Don't say anything about the heater."

14

Epilogue

MORE THAN A THOUSAND PEOPLE tried to crowd into the 275-seat Church of the Hills at Forest Lawn Memorial Park for the funeral service. Rick's death took over the front pages of the nation's newspapers on New Year's Day and struck the hearts of millions of people, many of whom had virtually forgotten about him. A piece of their youths went up in flames with Rick.

Mourners came from all over the country. His bachelor roommate, Charley Britt, now working as an anchorman on the local TV news in his hometown, Augusta, Georgia, made the trip. Crew and cast members of his father's TV show were well represented: Skip Young, Don DeFore, who played the next-door neighbor Thorny, assistant director Dick Bremerkamp, among others. Some remembered Rick had been at the church before, to film a 1959 dream sequence for the episode "Ricky Gets Married."

Songwriter Sharon Sheeley attended, and she managed to squeeze Marcia Borie, who introduced Ricky to Elvis, into the

chapel. Greg McDonald brought Elvis's aging manager, Colonel Tom Parker. The star-studded crowd included vocalist
Connie Francis; actress Angie Dickinson, who came with
David's first wife, June Blair; and actors Richard Dreyfuss, Rob
Lowe, and Martin Milner. Even Rick's ex-wife, Kris, attended,
although it was her threats that sent him off on the fatal trip
in the first place. "We were karmically connected," she said,
professing grief.

The flower-laden altar included a large spray of blue and
white carnations shaped like a guitar. Father Frank Parrish,
who had presided over Rick's wedding, opened the services
with a twenty-minute sermon. "I think of him in heaven playing his instrument," said the Jesuit priest, "while all the heavenly beings gather around him, just like the teenagers on
earth."

His daughter, Tracy, twenty-two, poised and dignified, recalled "Pop" for the crowd. "I remember his grace, his gentle-
ness," she said. "He was the kindest man you ever met. The
man had class. He was an artist. He was wise. And he loved ice
cream." The crowd chuckled. "Pop wouldn't want you to be
sad," she said. Tracy herself obviously inherited some of that
class.

Sam, eleven, read an American Indian poem. The Jordanaires sang the old spiritual "Peace in the Valley." But it was the
eighteen-year-old twins who wrung the tears out of mourners
with their a cappella version of his song "Easy to Be Free."
"There wasn't a dry eye in the place when they were done,"
said Sharon Sheeley.

David Nelson, who arrived at the chapel with grief-stricken
Harriet, read condolences from President Reagan and recalled
their father leading the family in singing the Lord's Prayer at
bedtime every night. He asked the congregation to join him in
a recitation of the prayer.

The services were held without Rick's remains, which were

held up in Texas with transportation problems. The bodies were so badly burned, identification had to be made through dental records. The plane continued to burn after it landed, until fire decimated the body of the aircraft virtually from tail to nose. A fire truck with special equipment pumped several complete loads of foam onto the blazing wreckage, finally extinguishing the inferno after two hours. It took almost ten hours for the wreck to cool down enough for the bodies to be removed.

The pilots managed a splendid emergency landing, better than most of their regulation runway landings, so it wasn't the crash that killed the victims. The coroner's verdict was death by thermal burns and smoke inhalation. All seven passengers burned to death, choking for air in the throat-clogging smoke.

Those horrifying final minutes can only be imagined, as the fire flared up and acrid, black smoke from the gasoline blaze poured into the cabin. As the plane made its rocky descent and flames licked the insides of the craft, the clock stood still and panic filled the final seconds of the lives of the seven passengers.

The bodies of road manager Clark Russell and Bobby Neal were located in the companionway between the cockpit and the cabin. Rick and Helen were found together a few feet behind, with Pat Woodward nearby. Andy Chapin and Ricky Intveld lay slightly forward of midcabin. They had all died, blinded and gagging in the oily smoke as the flames consumed their flesh.

Reports began to surface about the airplane. Pat Upton's wife told reporters her husband had urged the band not to use the forty-year-old craft on the fatal flight. "They were having trouble with the left engine," Lynn Upton said. "It wouldn't crank over. Everyone was concerned over this one engine. Pat asked that they stay and fly out of Huntsville [on a commercial flight]."

Bobby Neal's sister said the guitarist's wife begged him only five days before the crash not to fly on the plane because of the engine problems. "The plane wasn't safe," said Shirley Wood. "Rick knew it wasn't safe." The sister-in-law of keyboardist Andy Chapin reported that Chapin was afraid of the plane. "He didn't want to go on that airplane," said Laurel Barzie. "He complained and complained for months. He was going to quit the job because he didn't want to go on that plane."

Barzie also said that Chapin told her "that it was a bad plane. He didn't trust it. He always talked to my husband about it, that he didn't trust the airplane, that all the guys felt the same in the band."

The president of an air-charter company at the Salinas, California, airport reported an emergency landing the DC-3 had made the previous summer to repair an oil leak. "He landed and we supplied the pilot with a ladder and a wrench," said Robert McGregor of Air Trails. "He climbed up, fixed the leak, put some more oil in the crankcase and took off." He thought the plane stayed on the ground about a half hour.

Two weeks after the crash, the *Washington Post* dropped a bomb. Freebasing. "Federal officials are investigating the possibility that a form of cocaine use involving fire caused the New Year's Eve plane crash in Texas that killed rock 'n' roll star Rick Nelson and six others, sources close to the investigation said," the paper reported.

The preliminary toxicology reports leaked to the paper found traces of cocaine in Rick's body, and investigators apparently discovered further reason for suspicion in the large number of aerosol spray cans found in the wreckage, since they could be homemade torches to ignite freebase pipes. The *Post* even dragged out the allegations of drug abuse by Kris's lawyer found in the public record of the divorce case.

Freebasing cocaine involves removing impurities from the

drug with ether and other highly flammable solvents and then smoking the purified coke in a pipe. Comedian Richard Pryor reportedly suffered serious burns in a freebasing mishap. The grim thought that Rick Nelson may have burned himself out of the sky in some kind of bizarre drug-related accident caught the imagination of the press, and the story was trumpeted in headlines across the country.

Two separate tests showed traces of cocaine in samples of blood and urine taken from Rick's body, along with small amounts of alcohol, marijuana, and the painkiller Darvon. One drug expert called the amount of coke in Rick's system "substantial" but added it was impossible to tell how long before the accident he used the drugs. "Somewhere in the previous twelve hours he had used some cocaine," said Dr. Reese Jones of UC, Berkeley. "That's about all it says."

The preponderance of cocaine found in the urine specimen implied the buildup of a chronic user, and the relatively minor amount in his blood sample would indicate that Rick gave himself an eye-opener earlier in the day. Helen's blood was too coagulated by the heat of the fire to produce any effective test results. Cocaine also turned up in blood samples drawn from Andy Chapin and Patrick Woodward.

The probe moved away from the freebasing speculation almost immediately. No evidence was ever found to support such a hypothesis, but it sure made good grist for the mill of the press. No drug paraphernalia was discovered in fine-tooth comb searches of the wreckage. Not only does hair spray and furniture polish, used in cleaning the interior of the plane, come in aerosol cans, but so does guitar string lubricant. Nor was Rick's plane the first DC-3 to experience problems with gasoline-powered heaters.

By the time the depositions of the pilot and copilot were taken by the National Transportation Safety Board, within weeks of the crash, the investigation focused almost exclusively on the troublesome heater in the rear of the passenger cabin. The testimony was released to the press, but headlines about the heater starting the fire didn't make quite the splash the freebasing rumor did two months before.

The rumor would not die. Greg McDonald vehemently addressed the question. "Rick did not freebase," he said over and over to reporters seeking comments. Appearing on TV's "Good Morning America," David Nelson denied his brother even ever used cocaine, apparently oblivious to Rick's drug habits.

Even before Rick's will was located, Kris filed papers with the court anticipating his not having made a new will since the divorce. Finally, his lawyers submitted a copy of an original will he supposedly signed backstage at a Universal Amphitheater concert the previous August, after being unable to locate the original document among his effects. The court accepted the two-page will, which named David Nelson as executor, even though David still holds suspicions about the authenticity of the document.

Rick left his estate equally divided among his four children, specifically not endowing his mother ("she is taken care of and comfortable at this time") and his fiancée Helen ("those are our wishes") and disinheriting Eric Crewe, whose paternity he disputed from the grave. He turned over control of his show business properties to Greg McDonald.

Among the first in a flurry of petitions filed with the estate by Kris was a request for the court to restrain McDonald from contact with Matthew and Gunnar. She claimed McDonald was telling the twins everything now belonged to them. "Because of their age, and the notoriety of their father, along with the undue influence of Mr. McDonald, Matthew and Gunnar are not acting responsibly," her lawyer wrote in her behalf. "I am greatly concerned that Mr. McDonald is making every effort to influence my children and is advising them improperly. If someone other than Mr. McDonald is not appointed to administer this estate properly, I sincerely believe the estate will be so depleted as to rob heirs at law of their rightful entitlements."

Clearly there was no love lost between Kris and McDonald.

As for the dollar value of the estate, Rick died in debt somewhere in the neighborhood of $1 million. Creditors scrambled to get the court to approve their bills. The court rejected more than a million dollars' worth of claims filed by Kris in the first six months after the crash. Wrongful death suits stemming from the crash further muddied the financial waters. Bit by bit, the court doled out payments to other creditors, a tangled financial mess that would require years to straighten out.

In the final year of his life, Rick earned a gross income of more than $700,000, but after expenses, commissions, alimony, and other costs, he ended up with a net income around $43,000—not a lot of money for a headline entertainer working more than two hundred dates.

A handful of benefits for families of the crash victims were held in Los Angeles during the summer. The Blasters, Lone Justice, and X, three top new-wave bands, played the Club Lingerie, and John Denver showed up at a similar show at the Palomino, the North Hollywood country-music club where Rick made so many appearances during the last ten years of his life.

But the most sentimental reunion took place at the Beverly Theater, where Mick Fleetwood's Zoo, Dave Mason, Gary Busey, Jack Mack and the Heart Attack, Tommy Tutone, Leon Redbone, and others appeared. Hosted by comic Kip Addotta, the four-hour show featured an array of alumni from Rick's bands. Dennis Sarokin acted as the evening's musical coordinator. Randy Meisner sang a couple of Eagles songs. Richie Haywood sat in on drums. Steel guitarist Tom Brumley was there. James Intveld, whose brother died in the crash, sang. And the free-for-all finale was a rousing "Believe What You

Say," led by Billy Burnette, whose father and uncle wrote the song for Ricky.

Epic Records finally released an album of the Memphis sessions but not before sending Nashville producer Steve Buckingham back into the studio to overdub new instrumentation and destroy the original informality of the unreleased album. If Rick was furious over what Buckingham did to the four songs he reworked for the 1981 four-song release from the same sessions, he would have gone through the roof at the album version. John Beland practically did.

"What CBS did on that album," he said, "was exactly what Rick hated about Nashville. CBS wasn't even aware of the tapes until I called them. They took those tracks after the artist died and overdubbed them. When we cut *Memphis*, we wanted a rockabilly album, not a country album. It was totally against Rick's philosophy. I wrote the liner notes, and when I realized what they had done, I withdrew them. After the initial press, the album died a natural death.

"I don't want to say CBS cashed in, but they rushed it out after he died," Beland said.

A few weeks more than a year after his death, Rick Nelson was inducted into the Rock & Roll Hall of Fame before a banquet at the Waldorf-Astoria Hotel in New York attended by a multitude of his peers in the music business and fat-cat record company executives. He was one of the fifteen named in the hall's second installation. John Fogerty made the presentation, and Tracy and the twins accepted the award. He probably would not have been selected if he hadn't died. Many of the voters who picked Rick along with Bill Haley, Jackie Wilson, Aretha Franklin, Bo Diddley, Muddy Waters, Roy Orbison, Carl Perkins, Eddie Cochran, and the others had all but forgotten about him when the gruesome headlines refreshed their memories a year before.

In May 1987 the National Transportation Safety Board issued

their report on the plane crash, pointing a firm finger, without coming to any concrete resolution, to the faulty heater as the source of the fire that brought the craft down. Examination showed a fuel filter slipped loose from its mounting bracket, a potential cause of fire.

Although the board was unable to reconcile differences in the accounts of pilot Rank and copilot Ferguson, the report did criticize Rank for failing to follow the in-flight checklist when smoke was detected; for opening the fresh-air vents, which should have remained closed; for failing to direct passengers to use supplemental oxygen; and for not attempting to fight the fire with a hand-held cockpit fire extinguisher.

The board said that, although proper procedures might not have prevented the crash, "they would have enhanced the potential for survival of the passengers."

Peter Garrison, writing about the report in *Flying* magazine, could be even more direct. "Opening the cockpit windows on the DC-3," he wrote, "was most likely responsible for the cockpit filling rapidly with smoke. Ventilating the fuselage probably made conditions in the passenger cabin worse.

"Inflight fire is terrifying but uncommon. When it occurs, there is little time to take action. Since it's difficult to think clearly in a cockpit full of smoke, pilots must consider their reactions to a fire in advance. The steps outlined in the emergency procedures section of the flight manual should be memorized. There is valuable insight and experience contained in actions that may appear counterintuitive, such as closing the air vents when smoke is detected.

"Above all, time is of the essence. At the first suspicion of fire or smoke the pilot should begin a descent before doing anything else. If fire breaks out, every second will count. If it turns out to be a false alarm, he can console himself with the reflection that regaining lost altitude is a minor inconvenience compared with being burned alive."

While the federal government investigation was concluded, the wrongful death suits continued, as more scrupulous interrogations revealed even more details. Nobody ever mentioned freebasing after the first horrific news flash, but that report lingers in the public mind despite a complete and utter lack of evidence to support the wild hypothesis. In fact, in January 1990, the insurance company representing Duncan Aviation, who allegedly repaired the malfunctioning heater two months prior to the crash, settled the case as it was being presented to a Los Angeles superior court, spreading $4.5 million among ten plaintiffs.

The same month the board released its report, Kris entered a Los Angeles drug rehabilitation clinic called New Beginnings. She first began attending meetings of Alcoholics Anonymous in 1983, but a dependency on what she claimed was diet medicine left her a shambles. Her brother, Mark Harmon, now a successful TV actor who got his start on "Ozzie's Girls," and his wife, Pam Dawber, costar of TV's "Mork & Mindy," ran into Kris while shopping on Santa Monica's elegant Montana Avenue. "She was mumbling and stumbling and bumping into things," said Dawber. "She was obviously blasted, stoned out of her mind."

Mark talked Kris into checking into the hospital drug-treatment program, assuring her he would take care of her son Sam.

"What Pam and Mark saw," Kris said, "was an extremely exhausted individual. I'd had a relationship go bad—a good long-term relationship—and I hadn't slept for four nights. Also, I'd been going to a diet clinic because I was up to 142 pounds and I wanted to be thin for Tracy's wedding. They give you liquid stuff, powdered stuff and some pills. I still don't know what it all was because it was not labeled. I honestly didn't know it was making me crazy. My kids noticed it. So did my friends. But to my way of thinking, I wasn't abusing drugs. I was very innocent."

Recovering addicts are familiar with the workings of denial. It is a powerful impulse to escape responsibility. Few people go into treatment programs admitting the full scope of their problems. They are often sent there by family and friends or other external pressures. Many emerge with their denial fully or at least partly intact. Recovery is a process, not an event. Strong-willed, egocentric individuals often find it difficult to surrender to the humility necessary to recovery.

Kris's family participated in the family sessions at the clinic, although brother Mark bolted out of one session, according to Kris, when the therapist asked him to give his sister a hug. They eventually stopped coming altogether. Mark found his nephew Sam alarmingly fragile and withdrawn. The thirteen-year-old grew up barely knowing his father, receiving scant attention from his mother, and was left extensively in the care of housekeepers, his sister, aunt, and grandmother. Mark determined drastic action was necessary.

The day she prepared to leave New Beginnings, Kris was served with a subpoena summoning her to court in two hours for a custody hearing involving her son.

She got the hearing postponed until three days after her oldest child's wedding on July 25. Tracy married actor Billy Moses, star on the prime-time soap opera "Falcon Crest," in the old Wrigley mansion on Catalina Island before two hundred guests, ferried to the ceremony on two chartered yachts. Relations between Tracy and her mother were strained, and the impending custody case left a cloud over the family's celebration. Tracy and her husband departed immediately on a Hawaiian honeymoon.

At the hearing, Mark Harmon won temporary custody of Sam, and Kris was ordered to stay two hundred yards away from her brother's home and anywhere his wife was working. "No problem," she sneered.

The public battle of the renowned family was a heyday for the press. Kris arrived dressed well and calm and pleasant.

Her brother showed up in an open-neck shirt and baggy corduroys, scowling and icily ignoring reporters. Sam wore sneakers and a baseball cap, his shirt untucked.

Harmon's major witness, a psychiatrist he hired for a $1,800-a-day fee, testified that Sam was aware of his mother's drug problem and described her in interviews as depressive and suffering from severe mood swings. He said Sam depicted his mother as a powerful person who often isolated him from his siblings and other relatives. Sam drew the doctor a picture of his mother as a dragon and told him of a dream in which he was reunited with his father in an airplane. Under cross-examination, the psychiatrist admitted he had never interviewed Kris, outside of a few phone calls, and didn't speak with the psychiatrist who had been treating Sam since his father's death.

The trial came to a sudden end on the third day with the cross-examination of Harmon's wife, Pam Dawber. Kris's lawyers asked Dawber if she had ever used cocaine.

"No," snapped Dawber.

"With Robin Williams?" he asked.

"Absolutely not," she said firmly.

"With actor Robert Hays?" he asked.

"No," she said.

"With actor Gregory Harrison?" he asked.

"Never," she said, flustered.

The list went on. Finally, he took a harsh, almost sarcastic tone with the witness.

"Are you saying," he said, "that if I brought these people into court and they said you'd done coke with them, you'd say they were lying?"

"Absolutely," she said shakily. But Kris's lawyer had made his point. He ended his cross-examination, and court was recessed for the day.

The next morning, before the session began, Harmon ran up the white flag. "This is an unconditional surrender," gloated

Kris's lawyer. "I don't think Pam Dawber wanted to get more deeply involved. She has a successful career."

The custody case may have ended, with Sam returned to Kris's care and upbringing, but Harmon retained attorneys to watch over her guardianship. David Nelson said the court ordered Kris to pay back some $10,000 she spent out of Sam's trust fund, and while Kris laughed on TV under questioning by Geraldo Rivera that she didn't hold any resentments toward Mark one good punch wouldn't solve, the rift in the Harmon family obviously runs deep and rancorous.

Neither the twins nor Tracy stayed close to their mother, although the twins lived with her off and on. They continued to pursue their heavy-metal rock ambitions and signed to record an album with Geffen Records in 1988. When they finally moved out of their mother's house, they rented a one-bedroom apartment with one bed, which, presumably, they shared. Tracy continued to experience success in the acting field, picking up roles in movies like *Down and Out in Beverly Hills* and TV shows like the "Father Dowling" series in which she appeared as a regular.

Harriet Nelson lives alone in the family's Laguna Beach house. She sold the famous Camino Palmero home after Ozzie died, and the new owner installed a brass plaque on a brick fence pillar celebrating "The Nelson Home" as "the most televised house in America." David Nelson produced and directed commercials for a mammoth advertising agency run by Dennis Hoyt, a successful ad man who once played bit parts on "The Adventures of Ozzie and Harriet."

In 1987 he directed a special about Rick called *A Brother Remembers* for the Disney channel on cable TV, where the old TV series aired nightly. Producer Phil Savenick asked David if he could look through Rick's effects during research for the show. David took Savenick to a self-storage operation near the Los Angeles airport.

"I was looking for Rosebud," said Savenick. The small stall

was crowded with a lifetime's worth of accumulation, junk and treasures of all sorts. Ozzie's old four-string guitar was there, along with a lot of Rick's old instruments. Tucked away in the corner was a huge frame.

As a child, Rick hung on to his baby blanket longer than most children, and when he was married, his mother presented the tattered cloth to his wife. Kris framed the baby blanket.

"I found Rosebud," said Savenick.

Discography

SINGLES

I'm Walkin'/A Teenager's Romance (Verve 10047)

You're My One and Only Love/Honey Rock (instr.) (Verve 10070)

Be-Bop Baby/Have I Told You Lately That I Love You (Imperial 5463)

Stood Up/Waitin' in School (Imperial 5483)

My Bucket's Got a Hole in It/Believe What You Say (Imperial 5503)

Poor Little Fool/Don't Leave Me This Way (Imperial 5528)

I Got a Feeling/Lonesome Town (Imperial 5545)

Never Be Anyone Else But You/It's Late (Imperial 5565)

Just a Little Too Much/Sweeter Than You (Imperial 5595)

I Wanna Be Loved/Mighty Good (Imperial 5614)

Young Emotions/Right by My Side (Imperial 5663)

Yes Sir, That's My Baby/I'm Not Afraid (Imperial 5685)

You Are the Only One/Milk Cow Blues (Imperial 5707)

Travelin' Man/Hello Mary Lou (Imperial 5741)

A Wonder Like You/Everlovin' (Imperial 5770)

Young World/Summertime (Imperial 5805)

Teen Age Idol/I've Got My Eyes on You (Imperial 5864)

It's Up to You/I Need You (Imperial 5901)

I'm in Love Again/That's All (Imperial 5910)

I Got a Woman/You Don't Love Me Anymore (Decca 31475)

If You Can't Rock Me/Old Enough to Love (Imperial 5935)

Gypsy Woman/String Along (Decca 31495)

A Long Vacation/Mad Mad World (Imperial 5958)

There's Not a Minute/Time After Time (Imperial 5985)

Fools Rush In/Down Home (Decca 31533)

Today's Teardrops/Thank You Darlin' (Imperial 66004)

For You/That's All She Wrote (Decca 31574)

Congratulations/One Minute to One (Imperial 66017)

The Very Thought of You/I Wonder (If Your Love Will Ever Belong to Me) (Decca 31612)

Everybody But Me/Lucky Star (Imperial 66039)

There's Nothing I Can Say/Lonely Corner (Decca 31656)

A Happy Guy/Don't Breathe a Word (Decca 31703)

Mean Old World/When the Chips Are Down (Decca 31756)

Come Out Dancin'/Yesterday's Love (Decca 31800)

Love and Kisses/Say You Love Me (Decca 31845)

Fire Breathin' Dragon/Your Kind of Lovin' (Decca 31900)

Louisiana Man/You Just Can't Quit (Decca 31956)

Alone/Things You Gave Me (Decca 32026)

They Don't Give Medals . . ./Take a Broken Heart (Decca 32055)

Take a City Bride/I'm Called Lonely (Decca 32120)

Suzanne on a Sunday Morning/Moonshine (Decca 32176)

Dream Weaver/Baby Close Its Eyes (Decca 32222)

Don't Blame It on Your Wife/Promenade in Green (Decca 32284)

Don't Make Promises/Barefoot Boy (Decca 32298)

She Belongs to Me/Promises (Decca 32550)

Easy to Be Free/Come on In (Decca 32635)

I Shall Be Released/If You've Got to Go, Go Now (Decca 32676)

Look at Mary/We Got Such a Long Way to Go (Decca 32711)

How Long/Down Along the Bayou Country (Decca 32739)
Life/California (Decca 32779)
Thank You Lord/Sing Me a Song (Decca 32860)
Love Minus Zero/No Limit/Gypsy Pilot (Decca 32906)
Garden Party/So Long Mama (Decca 32980)
Palace Guard/A Flower Opens Gently By (MCA 40001)
Lifestream/Evil Woman Child (MCA 40130)
Windfall/Legacy (MCA 40187)
One Night Stand/Lifestream (MCA 40214)
Try (Try to Fall in Love)/Louisiana Belle (MCA 40392)
Rock and Roll Lady/Fade Away (MCA 40458)
You Can't Dance/It's Another Day (Epic 850458)
Gimme a Little Sign/Something You Can't Buy (Epic 850501)
Dream Lover/That Ain't the Way Loves Supposed to Be (Epic
   850674)
It Hasn't Happened Yet/Call It What You Want (Capitol 4974)
Believe What You Say/The Loser Babe Is You (Capitol 4988)
Give 'Em My Number/No Fair Falling in Love (Capitol 5178)
You Know What I Mean/Don't Leave Me This Way (MCA 52781)

ALBUMS

Ricky (Imperial 9048) 1957

Am I Blue, Baby I'm Sorry, Boppin' the Blues, Your True Love,
True Love, Be-Bop Baby, Have I Told You Lately That I Love
You, Honeycomb, I'm Confessin', Teenage Doll, Whole Lotta
Shakin' Goin' On, If You Can't Rock Me

Ricky Nelson (Imperial 9050) 1958

Shirley Lee, Someday, Good Rockin' Tonight, I'm Feeling Sorry,
Down the Line, Unchained Melody, I'm in Love Again, Don't
Leave Me This Way, My Babe, I'll Walk Alone, There Goes My
Baby, Poor Little Fool

Ricky Sings Again (Imperial 9061) 1959

Believe What You Say, Be True to Me, I Can't Help It, It's All in the Game, It's Late, Lonesome Town, Never Be Anyone Else But You, Old Enough to Love, One of These Mornings, Restless Kid, Trying to Get to You, You Tear Me Up

Songs by Ricky (Imperial 9082) 1959

A Long Vacation, Blood from a Stone, Don't Leave Me, Half-breed, I've Been Thinkin', Just a Little Too Much, You're So Fine, One Minute to One, So Long, Sweeter Than You, That's All, You'll Never Know What You're Missing

More Songs by Ricky (Imperial 9122) 1960

I'm Not Afraid, Baby Won't You Please Come Home, Here I Go Again, If I Knew I'd Find You, Make Believe, Ain't Nothing But Love, Time After Time, When Your Lover Has Gone, Proving My Love, Hey Pretty Baby, I'm All Through with You, Again

Rick Is 21 (Imperial 9152) 1961

My One Desire, That Warm Summer Night, Break My Chain, Travelin' Man, Hello Mary Lou, Do You Know What It Means to Miss New Orleans, Lucky Star, Oh Yeah, I'm in Love, Everybody But Me, Sure Fire Bet, Stars Fell on Alabama

Album Seven by Rick (Imperial 9167) 1962

Summertime, Congratulations, Baby You Don't Know, I Can't Stop Loving You, Excuse Me Baby, History of Love, Today's Teardrops, Mad Mad World, Thank You Darlin', Poor Loser, Stop Sneakin' Around, There's Not a Minute

Best Sellers by Rick Nelson (Imperial 9218) 1962

Baby I'm Sorry, Be-Bop Baby, Believe What You Say, Have I Told You Lately That I Love You, I'm in Love Again, Just a Little Too Much, Waitin' in School, Lonesome Town, Poor Little Fool, Stood Up, Poor Loser, That's All

It's Up to You (Imperial 9223) 1962

Again, Baby Won't You Please Come Home, Boppin' the Blues, Break My Chain, Halfbreed, I'd Climb the Highest Mountain, If You Can't Rock Me, It's Up to You, Shirley Lee, Stars Fell on Alabama, Tryin' to Get to You, I Need You

Million Sellers by Rick Nelson (Imperial 9232) 1963

Hello Mary Lou, I'm Not Afraid, It's Late, I Wanna Be Loved, Milk Cow Blues, My One Desire, Never Be Anyone Else But You, Right by My Side, Travelin' Man, Yes Sir, That's My Baby, You Are the Only One, Young Emotions

A Long Vacation (Imperial 9244) 1963

A Long Vacation, Baby Won't You Please Come Home, Excuse Me Baby, Honeycomb, I Can't Stop Loving You, I'll Walk Alone, I'm Confessin', It's All in the Game, Mad Mad World, Someday, Stars Fell on Alabama, Unchained Melody

Rick Nelson Sings for You (Imperial 9251) 1963

Be True to Me, Congratulations, Don't Leave Me, Excuse Me Baby, I Can't Help It, I'll Make Believe, I'm All Through with You, Lucky Star, One of These Mornings, Thank You Darlin', There Goes My Baby, Today's Teardrops

For Your Sweet Love (Decca 4419) 1963

For Your Sweet Love, Gypsy Woman, You Don't Love Me Anymore, Everytime I See You Smiling, Pick Up the Pieces, String Along, One Boy Too Late, Everytime I Think About You, Let's Talk the Whole Thing Over, I Got a Woman, What Comes Next, I Will Follow You

Rick Nelson Sings "For You" (Decca 4479) 1963

For You, Fools Rush In, Down Home, That Same Old Feeling, You're Free to Go, I Rise, I Fall, That's All She Wrote, A Legend in My Time, Just Take a Moment, Hello Mister Happiness, Hey There Little Miss Tease, The Nearness of You

The Very Thought of You (Decca 4559) 1964

My Old Flame, Just a Little Bit Sweet, The Loneliest Sound, You'll Never Fall in Love Again, The Very Thought of You, I Don't Wanna Love You, I'll Get You Yet, I Wonder, Be My Love, I Love You More Than You Know, Love Is the Sweetest Thing, Dinah

Spotlight on Rick (Decca 4608) 1964

I'm a Fool, I Tried, I'm Talking About You, Yesterday's Love, A Happy Guy, From a Distance, Stop Look Listen, Don't Breathe a Word, That's Why I Love You Like I Do, In My Dreams, Just Relax, Live and Learn

Best Always (Decca 4660) 1965

I'm Not Ready for You Yet, You Don't Know Me, Ladies' Choice, Lonely Corner, Only the Young, Mean Old World, I Know a Place, Since I Don't Have You, It's Beginning to Hurt, My Blue Heaven, How Does It Go, When the Chips Are Down

Love and Kisses (Decca 4678) 1965

Love and Kisses, I Catch Myself Crying, Love Is Where You Find It, Try to Remember, Our Own Funny Way, Liz, Say You Love Me, More, Raincoat in the River, Come Out Dancin', I Should Have Loved You More, I Paid for Loving You

Bright Lights and Country Music (Decca 4779) 1966

Truck Drivin' Man, You Just Can't Quit, Louisiana Man, Welcome to My World, Kentucky Means Paradise, Here I Am, Bright Lights and Country Music, Hello Walls, No Vacancy, I'm a Fool to Care, Congratulations, Night Train to Memphis

On the Flip Side (Decca 4836) 1966

It Doesn't Matter Anymore, They Don't Give Medals, Take a Broken Heart, Try to See It My Way (with Joannie Sommers), plus six other cuts.

Country Fever (Decca 4827) 1967

Take a City Bride, Funny How Time Slips Away, The Bridge Washed Out, Alone, Big Chief Buffalo Nickel, Mystery Train, Things You Gave Me, Take These Chains from My Heart, Lonesome Whistle Blow, Walkin' Down the Line, You Win Again, Salty Dog

Another Side of Rick (Decca 4944) 1968

Dream Weaver, Marshmallow Skies, Don't Blame It on Your Wife, Reason to Believe, Suzanne on a Sunday Morning, Baby Close Its Eyes, Barefoot Boy, Don't Make Promises, Promenade in Green, Georgia on My Mind, Daydream, I Wonder If Louise Is Home

Perspective (Decca 5014) 1968

Hello to the Wind, I Think It's Gonna Rain Today, Love Story, Stop by My Window, The Lady Stayed with Me, Three Day Eternity, Wait 'Til Next Year, When the Sun Shines Its Face on Me, So Long Dad, Without Her, For Emily Wherever I May Find Her

Rick Nelson in Concert (Decca 5162) 1970

Come on In, Hello Mary Lou, Violets of Dawn, Who Cares About Tomorrow/Promises, She Belongs to Me, If You Gotta Go, Go Now, I'm Walkin', Red Balloon, Louisiana Man, Believe What You Say, Easy to Be Free, I Shall Be Released

Rick Sings Nelson (Decca 5236) 1970

We've Got Such a Long Way to Go, California, Anytime, Down Along the Bayou Country, Sweet Mary, Look at Mary, The Reason Why, Mr. Dolphin, How Long, My Woman

Rudy the Fifth (Decca 5297) 1972

This Train, Just Like a Woman, Sing Me a Song, The Last Time Around, Song for Kristin, Honky Tonk Women, Feel So Good, Life, Thank You Lord, Love Minus Zero/No Limit, Gypsy Pilot

Garden Party (Decca 5391) 1972

Let It Bring You Along, Garden Party, So Long Mama, I Wanna Be with You, Are You Really Real?, I'm Talking About You, Nighttime Lady, A Flower Opens Gently By, Don't Let Your Good-bye Stand, Palace Guard

Windfall (MCA 383) 1974

Legacy, Someone to Love, How Many Times, Evil Woman Child, Don't Leave Me Here, Wild Nights in Tulsa, Lifestream, One Night Stand, I Don't Want to Be Lonely Tonight, Windfall

Intakes (Epic 34420) 1977

If You Can't Dance, One × One, I Wanna Move with You, It's Another Day, Wings, Five Minutes More, Change Your Mind, Something You Can't Buy, Gimme a Little Sign, Stay Young

Playing to Win (Capitol 12109) 1981

Almost Saturday Night, Believe What You Say, Little Miss American Dream, The Loser Babe Is You, Back to Schooldays, It Hasn't Happened Yet, Call It What You Want, I Can't Take It No More, Don't Look at Me, Do the Best You Can

All My Best (Silver Eagle Records 1035) 1985

Travelin' Man, Hello Mary Lou, Poor Little Fool, Stood Up, It's Late, You Know What I Mean, Young World, Lonesome Town, You Are the Only One, Just a Little Too Much, Believe What You Say, It's Up to You, Waitin' in School, Never Be Anyone Else But You, Don't Leave Me This Way, I Got a Feeling, Fools Rush In, Teen Age Idol, I'm Walkin', Mighty Good, Sweeter Than You, Garden Party

Rick Nelson Memphis Sessions (Epic 40388) 1985

That's Alright Mama, It's All Over Now, Dream Lover, Rave On, Sleep Tight Goodnight Man, Almost Saturday Night, Lay Back in the Arms of Someone, Stuck in the Middle with You, Send Me Somebody to Love, True Love Ways

Live 1983-1985 (Rhino) 1988

Stood Up, Waitin' in School, I Got a Feeling, Travelin' Man, Hello Mary Lou, Garden Party, You Know What I Mean, That's All Right, Believe What You Say, Milk Cow Blues Boogie, Never Be Anyone Else But You, Fools Rush In, It's Up to You, Poor Little Fool, It's Late, Honky Tonk Women, My Bucket's Got a Hole in It, Boppin' the Blues, Lonesome Town.

Bibliography

BOOKS

Baggelaar, Kristin, and Donald Milton. *The Folk Music Encyclopaedia.* London: Omnibus Press, 1977.

Blumenthal, John. *Hollywood High: History of America's Most Famous Public School.* New York: Ballantine Books, 1988.

Brooks, Tim, and Earle Marsh. *The Complete Directory to Prime Time Network TV Shows 1946–Present.* New York: Ballantine Books, 1981.

Cullen, Lee. *All Shook Up: Elvis Day-by-Day 1954–1977.* Ann Arbor, MI: Pierian Press, 1985.

Flynn, Errol. *My Wicked, Wicked Ways.* New York: G. P. Putnam's Sons, 1959.

Fowler, Lana Nelson, compiler. *Willie Nelson Family Album.* Amarillo, TX: H. M. Poirot and Co., 1980.

Gentry, Linell. *A History and Encyclopedia of Country, Western, and Gospel Music.* Nashville, TN: McQuiddy Press, 1961.

Goldman, Albert. *Elvis.* New York: McGraw-Hill, 1981.

Green, Abel, and Joe Laurie, Jr. *Show Biz: From Vaude to Video.* New York: Henry Holt and Co., 1951.

Harmon, Lt. Tom. *Pilots Also Pray.* New York: Thomas Crowell, 1944.

Higham, Charles. *Errol Flynn: The Untold Story.* New York: Doubleday, 1980.

Hill, Doug, and Jeff Weingrad. *Saturday Night: A Backstage History of Saturday Night Live.* New York: Beech Tree Books, 1986.

Horstman, Dorothy. *Sing Your Heart Out, Country Boys.* Nashville, TN: Country Music Foundation, 1975.

Hounsome, Terry. *New Rock Record.* New York: Facts on File, 1983.

Katz, Ephraim. *The Film Encyclopedia.* New York: Thomas Crowell, 1979.

Kiersh, Edward. *Where Are You Now, Bo Diddley?* New York: Doubleday, 1986.

Kinkle, Roger D. *The Complete Encyclopedia of Popular Music and Jazz 1900–1950.* New York: Arlington House, 1974.

Lazell, Barry, ed. *Rock Movers and Shakers.* New York: Billboard Publications, 1989.

Lowe, Leslie. *Directory of Popular Music.* Worcestershire, England: Peterson Publishing, 1975.

Mast, Gerald. *Howard Hawks, Storyteller.* New York: Oxford University Press, 1982.

McGregor, Craig, ed. *Bob Dylan: A Retrospective.* New York: William Morrow, 1972.

Nelson, Ozzie. *Ozzie.* New York: Prentice-Hall, 1973.

Nite, Norm N. *Rock On, Volume 2.* New York: Harper & Row, 1978.

Pareles, Jon, and Patricia Romanowski, ed. *The Rolling Stone Encyclopedia of Rock and Roll.* New York: Rolling Stone Press/Summit Books, 1983.

Poague, Leland A. *Howard Hawks.* Boston: Twayne Publishers, 1982.

Presley, Priscilla Beaulieu, and Sandra Harmon. *Elvis and Me.* New York: G. P. Putnam's Sons, 1985.

Rohde, H. Kandy. *The Gold of Rock and Roll 1955–1967.* New York: Arbor House, 1970.

Rolling Stone, Editors of. *Record Review II.* New York: Pocket Books, 1974.

Simon, George T. *The Big Bands.* New York: Collier Books, 1973.

Smith, Joe. *Off the Record: An Oral History of Popular Music.* New York: Warner Books, 1988.

Stafford, John, and Iain Young. *The Ricky Nelson Story.* Folkestone, England: Finbarr International, 1988.

Stambler, Irwin, and Grelun Landon. *The Encyclopedia of Folk, Country and Western.* New York: St. Martin's Press, 1983.

Stambler, Irwin. *The Encyclopedia of Pop, Rock, and Soul.* New York: St. Martin's Press, 1989.

Tobler, John, and Stuart Grundy. *The Guitar Greats.* New York: St. Martin's Press, 1984.

Walker, Stanley. *The Night Club Era.* New York: Frederick A. Stokes Co., 1933.

Whitburn, Joel. *Top Pop Albums 1955–1985.* Menomonee Falls, WI: Record Research, 1985.

Whitburn, Joel. *Top Pop Records 1955–1972.* Menomonee Falls, WI: Record Research, 1973.

Wood, Robin. *Howard Hawks.* London, England: BFI Publishing, 1981.

Worth, Fred L., and Steve D. Tamerius. *All About Elvis.* New York: Bantam Books, 1981.

Worth, Fred L., and Steve D. Tamerius. *Elvis: His Life from A to Z.* Chicago: Contemporary Books, 1988.

ARTICLES

Ames, Walter. "Ricky Nelson, Going Back to TV, Stays Funny Being Natural." *Los Angeles Times*, September 13, 1953.

Anderluh, Deborah. "A Tearful Farewell to Rick Nelson." *Los Angeles Herald-Examiner*, January 7, 1986.

Baessler, Paul. "Sand, Sea and Lip-Sync for Next 7 Weeks on Channel 7." *Los Angeles Herald-Examiner*, July 27, 1967.

Bangs, Lester. "Rick Nelson in Concert." *Rolling Stone*, April 1970.

Bentley, Bill. "The Irrepressible Ricky." *Los Angeles Weekly*, October 21, 1983.

Borie, Marcia. "Dave and Rick Nelson in Dave's New Home." *Photoplay*, March 1959.

Carmack, Michael. "Rick Nelson: Throwing off the Malt Shop Image." *Los Angeles Herald-Examiner*, April 15, 1973.

Carroll, Harrison. "Rock, Roll Girl Star Wed." *Los Angeles Herald-Examiner*, February 25, 1959.

Coleman, Stuart. Interview on BBC radio. November 1985.

Considine, Shaun. "Wow, Has Little Ricky Changed." *New York Times*, January 23, 1972.

Cromelin, Richard. "Rick Nelson Stars Anew." *Los Angeles Times*, January 25, 1981.

Dahl, Walter. "Ricky Is Leaving Home." *Motion Picture*, April 1959.

Darrach, Brad. "Life After Ozzie and Harriet." *People*, September 7, 1987.

Davidson, Sara. "The Happy, Happy, Happy Nelsons." *Esquire*, June 1971.

Demaret, Kent. "Rick Nelson 1940–1985." *People*, January 20, 1986.

Dickerson, Jim. "The Sun Session, Together Again in Memphis." *Nine-O-One Network*, 1986.

Dodds, Harry. "Ricky Nelson, The Story of a Teenage Idol," parts 1–3. *Now Dig This*, 1986.

Everett, Todd. "Eclectic Concert at the Beverly." *Los Angeles Herald-Examiner*, July 2, 1986.

Everett, Todd. "It's Nice to Go Back to a Sound I Started With." *Los Angeles Herald-Examiner*, February 15, 1985.

Everett, Todd. "Rick Nelson, You're Not a Kid Anymore!" *Phonograph Record*, 1972.

Garrison, Peter. "Falling Stars." *Flying*, February 1987.

George, Wally. "Old Pros Watch Ricky Nelson Tackle First Western." *Los Angeles Times*, June 8, 1958.

Goodwin, Betty. "Tracy Nelson Gets Revenge." *TV Guide*, May 21, 1983.

Hackford, Taylor, director. *Rick at the Fair*. Transcript of interview from unreleased TV documentary, Monroe, Louisiana, 1977.

Harford, Margaret. "Listenable 'Sound of Music.' " *Los Angeles Times*, August 4, 1966.

Harford, Margaret. "*Love and Kisses* Is Wholesome Stuff." *Los Angeles Times*, October 1, 1965.

Harford, Margaret. "Mike Failure in 'Succeed.' " *Los Angeles Times*, July 21, 1966.

Harford, Margaret. "Raitt and *Carousel* Jackpot." *Los Angeles Times*, May 12, 1966.

Hartley, Jeff. "Ricky and the Postman's Daughter." *Motion Picture*, May 1958.

Hilburn, Robert. "Nelson Searching for Own Style." *Los Angeles Times*, September 10, 1970.

Hilburn, Robert. "Oldies Take the Stage at Nostalgic 'Forum Party.' " *Los Angeles Times*, October 24, 1983.

Hilburn, Robert. "Rick Nelson at Musical Crossroads." *Los Angeles Times*, October 17, 1972.

Hilburn, Robert. "Rick Nelson at Nightclub." *Los Angeles Times*, October 31, 1969.

Hilburn, Robert. "Rick Nelson in Country Music Bow." *Los Angeles Times*, June 13, 1967.

Hopkins, Jerry. "Records." *Rolling Stone*, April 1969.

Hopper, Hedda. "Ricky Nelson Can't Be All Shook Up Over Fame at 18." *Los Angeles Times*, October 5, 1958.

Hopper, Hedda. "Ricky Nelson to Do Film with John Wayne." *Los Angeles Times*, April 26, 1958.

Johnson, Bob. "What Makes Ricky Tick?" *TV Guide*, December 28, 1957.

Kemnitz, Robert. "No 'Labels' for Rick Nelson." *Los Angeles Herald-Examiner*, August 15, 1975.

King, Susan. "Keeping Up with the Nelsons." *Los Angeles Herald-Examiner*, July 12, 1987.

Lieberman, Frank. "Homeward Comes 'Little Ricky.' " *Los Angeles Herald-Examiner*, September 19, 1971.

Lieberman, Frank. "Years Change Rick Nelson." *Los Angeles Herald-Examiner*, October 26, 1969.

Ludwin, Rick. "An Historical Study of 'The Adventures of Ozzie and Harriet' Television Program: 1952–1966." UCLA term paper, May 26, 1971.

McGraw, Carol. "Rick Nelson Eulogized as Humorous and Sensitive." *Los Angeles Times*, January 7, 1986.

Morrison, Hobe. "*Love and Kisses* Trite, Corny Comedy." *San Francisco Chronicle*, December 20, 1962.

Muir, Florabel. "Almost Too Good to Be True." Unknown 1940s movie magazine.

National Transportation Safety Board. Report on air crash, 1987.

Nelson, Harriet, and Stanley Gordon. "The Men in My Life." *Look*, November 11, 1958.

Nelson, Ozzie. "The Girl That I Married." Unknown 1940s movie magazine.

Nelson, Rick. "International Commemorative Society: A Travelin' Man." 1986.

Nelson, Rick, as told to Marcia Borie. "Luck: Everything Happens to Me." *Photoplay*, May 1958.

Pagano, Penny. "Probe Discounts Drugs as Cause of Air Crash That Killed Rick Nelson." *Los Angeles Times*, May 29, 1987.

Parsons, Louella. "Rick Nelson to Marry Tom Harmon's Daughter." *Los Angeles Herald-Examiner*, December 26, 1962.

Pierce, Michael. "James Burton." *Guitar Player*, March 1972.

Pryor, Thomas M. "Ozzie and Harriet: Life with the Nelsons Is Now on Video." *New York Times*, November 23, 1952.

Scheuer, Phillip K. "*Rio Bravo* Scores as Folksy Western." *Los Angeles Times*, March 19, 1959.

Scott, John L. "*The Wackiest Ship* Sails on 22 Screens." *Los Angeles Times*, February 16, 1961.

Selvin, Joel. "Domino Reclaims His Rock Throne." *San Francisco Chronicle*, August 20, 1985.

Selvin, Joel. "44 and Still Rocking." *San Francisco Chronicle*, May 31, 1984.

Selvin, Joel. "Rick's Place at the Sahara." *San Francisco Chronicle*, October 8, 1978.

Shanley, J. P. "Ozzie Nelson—Practical Parent." *New York Times*, June 8, 1957.

Smith, Cecil. "Breaks in Routine Will Feature Musical Show, Kovacs with Top World Magicians." *Los Angeles Times*, May 26, 1957.

Smith, Cecil. "From Superteen to Supersick Role." *Los Angeles Times*, January 27, 1972.

Smith, Cecil. "Rick Nelson Plays Unlikely Role Tonight in *Business.*" *Los Angeles Times*, July 19, 1966.

Snyder, Camilla. "Only an Acre, But to the Rick Nelsons It's a Farm." *New York Times*, August 29, 1973.

Stull, Christopher. "Ozzie Nelson and Company Keep the Customers Happy." *San Francisco Chronicle*, June 18, 1942.

Stump, Al. "Meet Hollywood's Most Exciting Family." *American*, October 1955.

Tepper, Ron. "Young Ricky Nelson Eyes Fling as Bullfighter." *Los Angeles Times*, April 12, 1959.

Terry, Clifford. "You Were Expecting Maybe Some Teenage Heart Throb?" *Chicago Tribune Magazine*, May 2, 1971.

Thomas, Bob. "At 18, Ricky Nelson Earns $400,000 a Year." *Los Angeles Herald-Examiner*, February 3, 1958.

Torres, Ben Fong. "Rick Nelson: Travelin' Man." *San Francisco Chronicle*, June 3, 1984.

Tuber, Keith. "Rick Nelson Still Riding Rock 'n' Roll Roller Coaster." *Los Angeles Herald-Examiner*, January 2, 1981.

Wasserman, John L. "The Plans of a Serious Young Man." *San Francisco Chronicle*, November 7, 1966.

Wesley, Bret. "The Kind of Girls Dave and Ricky Date." *Movie World*, November 1959.

Index

Acuff, Roy, 165
"Adam 12," 218
Adams, Nick, 83
"Adventures of Ozzie and
    Harriet," 6
  beginning as TV show, 41
  debut of Ricky and David,
        32–33, 34
  early shows, 41–42, 46–47
  end of show, 161–62
  radio show, 30–41
  rock & roll, effects on show,
        85–86, 104, 107, 128
  salaries, 35, 42
  wives of David/Rick on show,
        150–51, 159
Album Seven by Rick, 146
Alexander, J.W., 126
Alexenburg, Ron, 225
All My Best, 276, 282
Allen, Dick, 118
"Almost Saturday Night," 243, 253
"Alone," 170
"Am I Blue," 76

"American Music Awards," 230
American Studio, 279
Andersen, Eric, 182, 185, 187
Anka, Paul, 89
Another Side of Rick, 173
"Anytime," 193
Apollonia, 283
Arslanian, Oscar, 253, 273
Artists Helping UNICEF, 216
"As Long as I Have You," 276

"Baby Keep Cuddlin' Me," 107
Bacharach, Burt, 155
"Back to Schooldays," 253
Back to Vienna, 235
Backus, Jim, 40, 46
Baker, LaVern, 88
"Bakers' Broadcast, The," 20
"Ballerina, The," 153
Bancroft Junior High, 43, 47
Barbizon Plaza Hotel, 16
Bard College, 173, 267
Basin Street West, 192
Baxter, Jeff "Skunk," 234

"Be True to Me," 109
"Be-Bop Baby," 75, 80, 85, 86
Beach Boys, 163
Beal, Bobby, 283, 285
Beatles, 157
Beland, John, 232, 235, 240, 250,
    251, 294
"Believe What You Say," 87, 88,
    109, 253, 293-94
Belland, Bruce, 47, 54, 68, 71, 81,
    129, 134
Bellson, Louis, 39
Bentley, Bill, 53, 266, 267
Bernard, Tommy, 32
Best Always, 162
Beverly Theater, 293
Big Bands, The (Simon), 18
"Big Chief Buffalo Nickel," 166
Big Circus, The, 94
Birdcage Theater, 70
Blackhawk Restaurant, 25
Blair, Henry, 32
Blair, June (David's wife), 133-34,
    149-50
Blair, Streeter, 152, 153
Blasters, 268, 269
Blonde Sinner, The, 17
Bogart, Humphrey, 26
Boone, Pat, 118
"Boppin' the Blues," 76
Borie, Marcia, 287
Bottom Line, 217
"Bound to Fall," 181
Boylan, John, 172-76, 181-84, 197
Boylan, Terry, 173, 174
"Boys Land in Jail, The," 86
Bright Lights and Country Music,
    164
British invasion, rock & roll, 157,
    163, 172
Britt, Charley, 134-35, 141-44, 147,
    149, 151, 168, 185-86

Brother Remembers, A, 18, 299
Bruce, Denny, 174
Brumley, Jack, 223, 232
Brumley, Tom, 183, 220, 233, 243,
    293
Bryant, Anita, 124
Buckingham, Steve, 264-65, 294
Budny, Zeke, 97, 129
Burgess, Dave, 125, 145, 146
Burgess, Sonny, 87
Burlison, Paul, 279
Burnette, Billy, 294
Burnette, Dorsey, 78-79, 87, 109,
    164
Burnette, Johnny, 78-79, 87, 156,
    162-63
Burnette, Rocky, 248-49
Burton, James, 7, 76-77, 80, 97, 99,
    110, 163-64, 173, 203, 233, 274
Bush, Alan, 252, 277
Byrds, 163
Byrne, Joe, 63, 66, 85, 93, 113, 120,
    149, 165, 190

Caballero, Candy, 149
Cady, Frank, 46
"California," 193, 195
California Collegians, 17
"Call It What You Want," 254
Cameron, Paul, 99
Camino Palermo, 28, 34, 35
Campbell, Bruce, 55
Campbell, Glen, 125, 165, 189, 203
Canal Zone, 27
Canyon, 209
Capehart, Jerry, 105, 111
Capitol Records, 246, 249, 252-53,
    262-63, 266
Capitol Theatre Corps de Ballet,
    17
Carnall, Lorrie Collins, 81-84, 114,
    228

Carnall, Stu, 84, 228
Carnegie Hall, 210, 211
Carousel, 165
Carson, Johnny, 216
Casa Mañana, 24, 27
Casa Vega, 259
Cash, Johnny, 108, 189–90, 204, 279
Cash, June Carter, 279
Cetera, Tim, 192
Challenge Records, 126
Chapin, Andy, 282, 289
Chasen's, 36
Chess Records, 63
Chudd, Lew, 73–74, 77, 85, 89, 102, 107, 126, 146, 155, 156, 157, 194
"Cindy," 108
Circle Star Theater, 170
Class of '55, 279–81
Claypool Hotel, 20
Cochran, Eddie, 105–6, 111, 129–30, 264
Cocoanut Grove, 21
Cocoanut Grove, 23
Cole, Jerry, 156, 176
Collins, Lorrie. *See* Carnall, Lorrie Collins
Columby, Bobby, 243
"Come On In," 188
Cooke, Sam, 126
Correll, Charlie, 36
Country Fever, 170
Crewe, Eric, 278, 292
Crewe, Georgeanne, 277–78
Croft, Mary Jane, 32, 46
Crosby, Bing, 31–32, 33
Crosby, Lindsay, 32
Curtis, Sonny, 160

"Dancing on the Ceiling," 283
Dant, Charles "Bud", 155

Darin, Bobby, 123, 171
Davenport, Bill, 40
David, Hal, 169
"David Has a Date with Miss Universe," 86
"David and the Hot Dog Stand," 52
Davidson, Sara, 9
Davis, Joel, 32
Davis, John, 250
Dawber, Pam, 296, 298
de Cordova, Fred, 41
Decca Records, 146, 154–56, 171, 181–82, 184, 202, 215
DeFore, Don, 46
Dempkitch, Mitch, 118
Dooilu Culver Studioo, 160
"Dick Clark's Live Wednesday," 241
DiMucci, Dion, 142
Dinah Shore show, 220
Dr. John, 234
"Doll Hospital," 265
Domino, Fats, 278
Don the Beachcomber's, 36
"Don Kirshner's Rock Concert," 215–16
"Don't Leave Me This Way," 164
Drake Hotel, 24
"Dream Lover," 240, 243
Duncan, Danny, 17
Dylan, Bob, 7, 9, 106, 163, 183, 194

Eagles, 197, 208, 213, 215
Eastman Kodak commercials, 119
"Easy to Be Free," 187, 193
Easy to Be Free (documentary), 206
"Ed Sullivan Show," 163
Edmunds, Dave, 279, 280
Eiler, Barbara, 34
Ellena, Jack, 99, 144, 149, 160, 271

Elskers, 48, 54

Emmons, Buddy, 182

Epic Records, 224–25, 229, 233, 235, 244, 247, 264, 294

Eric Music, 102

Everett, Todd, 275

"Everlovin'," 145

Everly Brothers, 88–89, 111, 156

"Every Day I Have to Cry Some," 235

"Evil Woman Child," 215

Fabian, 203

Farm Aid, 281

Farrow, Mia, 140

"Fathers and Sons," 277

Faunce, Johnny, 31–32

"Feel So Good," 194

Ferguson, Ken, 285–86

"Fire Breathin' Dragon," 163

Fisher, Ham, 12

"Fixing Up the Fraternity House," 86

Flying Viennas, 95

Flynn, Errol, 245–46

Flynn, Joe, 128

Fogerty, John, 8–9, 247–48, 279, 294

Fol-de-Rol, 205

Foladare, Maury, 31, 76, 86, 99, 120

Follow the Fleet, 22

"Fools Rush In," 156

Footloose, 267

"For You," 157

For Your Sweet Love, 155

Forum, 269

Four Preps, 47, 68–72

Fowley, Kim, 112–13

Franson, Wally, 224

Free, Blonde and Twenty-One, 137

Frey, Glenn, 197

Frio, Rich, 202, 208

Frost, Richie, 98, 165

Fuller, Jerry, 125–26, 128, 145, 146, 219–20

Gaba, Marianne, 72–73

Gallup, Cliff, 7

"Game Room, The," 162

Garden Party, 208–10

"Garden Party," 201–3, 204, 205, 208, 215

Garden Party I tour, 198–201

Garden Party II tour, 269–70

Gardner Street School, 36

Garf, Gene, 102–3, 155

Garr, Teri, 153

Garrett, Snuff, 155

Garrison, Peter, 295

Geller, Gregg, 224

General Service Studios, 47, 160

Gentry, Bobbie, 190

"Georgia on My Mind," 174

"Get It Together," 190

"Gettin' It On," 235

"Gimme a Little Sign," 230

"Girl I Married, The," 13

"Give 'Em My Number," 265

Glaub, Bob, 234

Glen Island Casino, 16, 19

"Gloomy Sunday," 103

"Glory Train," 125

Goemans, Gretchen, 149

Golasinski, Chester, 258–59

Golden Gate Theater, 29

Goldner, George, 63

Gomez, Vincente, 97

"Good Morning America," 256

Goodrich, Gail, 237

"Goody Goody," 107

Gordon, Gale, 40

Grand Ole Opry, 204

Granz, Norman, 64

Gray, Glen, 157
Guedel, John, 29
"Gypsy Pilot," 194
"Gypsy Woman," 156

Haffner, Mike, 117
Halsey, Jim, 238
Hamblen, Stuart, 246
"Hand for Sonny Blue, A," 229
"Happy, Happy, Happy Nelsons,
    The" (Davidson), 9
Hardin, Glen D., 166
Hardin, Tim, 187
"Hardy Boys Mysteries, The," 229
Harmon, Elyse, 137, 138, 223
Harmon, Kelly, 140, 147
Harmon, Kristin. *See* Nelson,
    Kristin
Harmon, Mark, 140, 214, 296
Harmon of Michigan, 137
Harmon, Tom, 136–39
Harmony, Dottie, 110, 113
Harper, Connie, 76, 128, 147, 170
Harris, Iris, 284
Harrison, George, 207
Harwood, Charlie, 250, 251
Haskell, Jimmie, 74, 77, 101, 107,
    127, 165, 173, 248, 275
"Have I Told You Lately That I
    Love You," 75
Hawkins, Jimmy, 129
Hawks, Howard, 92, 108
Hawn, Goldie, 168
Haywood, Richie, 216, 293
Heir to the Hoorah, The, 17
"Hello Mary Lou," 127, 145
"Hello Walls," 165
"Hello to the Wind (Bonjour le
    Vent)," 175
Henley, Don, 197
Here Come the Nelsons, 40–41
Hesse, Paul, 138

Hiatt, John, 253, 265
Hickman, Dwayne, 52
High School U.S.A., 271
Hillburn, Robert, 166, 193
Hilliard, Harriet. *See* Nelson,
    Harriet
Hilliard, Hazel (Harriet's mother),
    16, 17, 36
Hilliard Music, 102
Hilliard, Roy E. (Harriet's father),
    16, 17
Holly, Buddy, 111, 156, 281
Hollywood Boulevard, 218
Hollywood High School, 43, 47–48,
    53
"Honey Rock," 73
"Honky Tonk Women," 194, 201
Hopper, Dennis, 115
Hotel Paramount Grill, 19
Houston Astrodome, 210, 211
"How Long," 193
*How to Succeed in Business
    Without Really Trying*, 166–68,
    170
Hoyt, Dennis, 299
Hudson, Rock, 40
Hughes market, 259
Humphreys, Holly, 18, 23
Huston, Yvonne O'Connor, 218,
    228

"I Can't Help It," 109
"I Don't Want to Be Lonely
    Tonight," 213
"I Got a Feeling," 105, 106
"I Got a Woman," 155
"I Heard That Lonesome Whistle
    Blow," 166
"I Wanna Be Loved," 123
"I Wanna Move with You," 229
Ianerelli, Jack, 99
"If You Can't Rock Me," 156

"I'm Called Lonely," 170
"I'm a Fool," 162
"I'm Looking for a Guy Who Plays
    Alto and Baritone and
    Doubles on Clarinet and
    Wears a Size 37 Suit," 25
"I'm in Love Again," 155
"I'm Not Afraid," 124
"I'm Talking About You," 162
"I'm Walkin'," 64–67
Imperial Records, 63, 73–74, 87
Indian Creek Club, 16
Intakes, 229, 230, 233
Intveld, James, 268, 272, 279, 293
Intveld, Ricky, 270, 279, 289
"Invitation to Dinner," 34
"It Hasn't Happened Yet," 253
"It's All in the Game," 109
"It's All Over Now," 243
"It's Another Day," 230
"It's Late," 109
"It's Up to You," 146, 232

Jagger, Mick, 194
"Jersey City's Honey Boy," 13
Johnson, Ray, 155
Jordanaires, 87, 109, 270, 278, 288
Judds, 279
Jupp, Mickey, 274, 276
"Just Because," 83
"Just Like a Woman," 194

Kaempfert, Bert, 182
Kapp, Jack, 16
"Kappa Sig Party, The," 51
Kellerman, Sally, 47
Kelley, Don, 128
Kemp, Allen, 179, 184, 190, 193,
    199, 207
Kennedy, Jackie, 170
Kershaw, Doug, 187, 189
Kessel, Barney, 64, 65

"Kid in the Three-Cornered Pants,
    The," 24
Kiersh, Edward, 273
Kindberg, Karl, 129, 149
Kirkland, James, 76–77, 110, 269
Kleinow, Sneaky Pete, 180
Knight, Baker, 105, 106, 109, 115,
    123, 125, 128, 146, 213, 229
Knott's Berry Farm, 70, 215
Knox, Elyse. *See* Harmon, Elyse
Knox, Frank, 137
Kooper, Al, 233–36
Koppelman, Charles, 171–72, 173

La Creation, 185
Laboe, Art, 68
Lahr, Bert, 17
Larden, Dennis, 215
Larson, Glen, 88, 205, 229
"Last Time Around, The," 195
Latin Quarter, 177
"Lay Back in the Arms of
    Someone," 243
Leiber, Jerry, 155
Lemmon, Jack, 120, 122
Leonard, Sheldon, 40
Letterman, David, 256
Lewis, Jerry Lee, 111, 274, 277,
    279, 280, 281
Lexington Hotel, 21
Lichine, David, 185
"Life," 193, 195
Life magazine, 107, 139
Life of the Party, The, 23
"Lifestream," 215
Lime, Yvonne, 114
Linkletter, Art, 29, 36
Lloyd, Shirley, 22
Lock, Bob, 284
Loggins, Dave, 265
"Lonely Corner," 162
"Lonesome Town," 9, 105, 106–7, 109

Los Angeles Weekly, 266
"Loser Babe Is You, The," 254
"Louisiana Belle," 219
"Louisiana Man," 189
"Love Boat, The," 241
Love and Kisses (movie), 158–61, 163
"Love Minus Zero/No Limit," 194, 207
"Lovin' Feelings" tour, 269–70
Lowe, Nick, 274
"Lucky Star," 145
Luman, Bob, 76
Lyn-Lou Studios, 239–40

MacMurray, Fred, 17, 36
MacNutt, Hazel. *See* Hilliard, Hazel
Madison Square Garden, 198–201, 269
"Malibu U," 171, 172
Mama Cass, 190
"Mama You Been on My Mind," 235
Maphis, Joe, 80, 81
Marshall, Frank, 64
Master Recorders, 65, 76
Matz, Peter, 169
MCA Records, 202, 221, 276, 282
McCartney, Paul, 207, 230, 262–63
"McCloud," 205
McCord, Kent, 118, 154, 195, 218, 261
McDonald, Greg, 10–11, 223–24, 226–28, 230, 231, 238, 251, 259, 268, 273
McDonald, Michael, 234
McGee, Jerry, 219, 269, 272
McGee, Mickey, 250, 251
McManus, Luis, 96
McWhirter, Cynthia, 149
McWhirter, Kent, 118, 149

"Mean Old World," 163
Meeks, Johnny, 272
Meet Boston Blackie, 27
Meisner, Randy, 178–80, 191–92, 193–94, 197, 213, 293
Mellor, William, 42–43
Memphis, 294
"Midnight Special," 216, 241, 256
"Mike Douglas Show," 170
"Milk Cow Blues," 124
Miller, Lee, 275
Moman, Chips, 279
Moon, Keith, 218–19
Moore, Scotty, 7
"More," 163
More Songs by Ricky, 124
Morse, Carol, 86
"Motown Revue," 282
"Mr. Dolphin," 193
Mrs. Wiggs of the Cabbage Patch, 17
MTV, 274, 275
Murphy, Richard, 120–22
Murray, Feg, 23
Murray, Ken, 17
"Musical Appreciation," 62
"My Babe," 103
"My Bucket's Got a Hole in It," 87
"My One Desire," 145
"My Rifle, My Pony and Me," 108
"My Uncle," 168
"Mystery Train," 171, 220

Nader, Richard, 198–99, 261, 269, 272, 283
Nashville Skyline, 183
Neal, Bobby, 243, 250, 266, 272, 279, 289
Nelson, Alfred (Ozzie's brother), 13, 14, 202
Nelson, Danny (David's son), 149
Nelson, David, 160
    athletic excellence of, 43, 47

birth of, 22
childhood of, 24, 27, 35, 36–39
college education, 51, 52, 119
as director, 206–7, 299
effect of Rick's death on, 9–10
films of, 85, 94
friction with Ozzie, 154
lives with Rick, 114
marries June Blair, 133
marries Yvonne O'Connor
    Huston, 218
musical tastes of, 62
on Nelson family, 206
personality of, 37, 47–48
sibling rivalry and, 38–39, 41,
    116
as trapeze artist, 94–96, 121, 133
Nelson, Don (Ozzie's brother), 15,
    26, 30, 34, 40, 98, 124
Nelson, Eric Hilliard. *See* Nelson,
    Rick
Nelson, Ethel (Ozzie's mother), 13,
    14, 15, 26
Nelson, George (Ozzie's father),
    16–18
Nelson, Gunnar Eric (Rick's son),
    173, 238
  rock career of, 267, 299
Nelson, Harriet, 299
  early career, 16–18
  family background, 16–17
  films of, 21–23, 27, 29
  marries Ozzie, 21
  and Ozzie's band, 12, 18, 19–21,
      22, 24, 28
  personality of, 6
Nelson, June (David's wife), 133,
    149
Nelson, Kris
  alcoholism/drug use, 237, 250,
      258, 262
  ballet and, 153, 185–86

childhood of, 139–140
custody dispute with Mark
    Harmon, 296–99
divorce/alimony and Rick, 230,
    252, 256–60, 263, 271–72
extra-marital affairs, 184–85,
    237
family background, 136–41
involvement in Rick's career,
    174–75, 222
marries Rick, 149–50
as painter, 153, 170, 184, 214,
    218
personality of, 184, 185, 191–92,
    214–15, 222, 236–37
rehabilitation of, 296–97
spending habits, 190–91, 238
stage career, 165–66, 169
on TV show, 150–51, 153–54
Nelson, Matthew Gray (Rick's son),
    173, 238
  rock career of, 267, 299
Nelson, Ozzie
  as bandleader, 12, 15–16, 18–30
  control of publicity, 131–32
  death of, 217–18
  family background, 13–15
  financial manager role, 102
  marries Harriet, 21
  meets Harriet, 12–13, 18
  perfectionism of, 42–43, 44, 75
  personality of, 6, 10, 15, 19, 35,
      37, 104–5, 158
  Rick's musical career and,
      101–5, 109, 124, 128, 187
  work after show ended, 168–69
Nelson, Rick
  on acting (age 13), 44–45
  asthma and, 37
  Australian tours, 261–62, 282
  birth of, 25
  Bob Dylan, influence of, 183

bodybuilding and, 152
British tours, 207, 282–83
bullfighting and, 96–97
childhood of, 35, 36–39
children of, 151, 173, 217
commercial/bubblegum type
  recordings, 124, 125, 155–56
country sound, 164–66, 170–71,
  185, 188, 215, 239, 247
dates Kris Harmon, 141, 147–48
DC-3 airplane, condition of, 277,
  281–82, 284, 289–90
death/airplane disaster, 1–4,
  285–86, 288–92, 295–96
discography of, 301–9
drug use in early career,
  113–14, 174, 185
drug use in later career, 237,
  240, 250, 257, 261, 263–64,
  266
early recordings, 73–80, 85,
  87–88
education/schooling and,
  53–54, 85
Elvis/Rick football game, 117–18
Errol Flynn mansion and,
  245–46, 255, 258– 59, 260,
  267, 272
estate of, 292–93
fairground performances, 211,
  215, 239
Far East tour, 165
fear of flying, 176, 191
films of, 45–46, 91–94, 119, 120,
  122–23, 186
financial difficulties, 224, 227,
  251–52, 259–60, 271, 283
first live appearances, 68–72
first record, 64–68
first sexual experience, 50–51
first Troubador appearance,
  178–81

freebasing and crash rumors,
  290–92
Greg McDonald and, 223–24,
  226–28, 273–74
Helen Blair and, 260–61, 263–64,
  267, 271
hippie image, 174–76, 181, 185,
  195–96, 200
home at the Farm, 213–14
karate and, 142–43
Las Vegas show, 228, 232, 233,
  236
last tour, 283–84
life as teen idol, 98–100, 107–8,
  120, 124, 144
lives with Charley Britt, 134,
  141–44
lives with David, 114
at Madison Square Garden,
  198–201, 269–71
married life, early, 151
marries Kris Harmon, 149–50
meet Elvis, 84–85, 111
memorial service for, 287–88
music, importance of, 7, 11, 39,
  62–63, 82, 97–98, 142,
  203–4, 219
musical accomplishments, 7–9,
  76, 80, 87, 109– 10, 127–28
oldies shows, 198–201, 261,
  269–70, 272, 282–83
other TV appearances, 171, 172,
  204, 205, 215–16, 220, 229,
  241, 256, 265, 271, 277
paternity case, 277–78, 292
personality of, 4, 5, 10–11, 37,
  38, 44, 101, 112, 113, 130,
  207–8, 212, 225– 26
professional abyss, periods of,
  159–60, 162–63, 172–73,
  175, 176–77, 219–22,
  229–31, 233, 268

rebellious period of, 54–57
rejects commercial ventures,
    227
revitalization of career, 181–98
rockabilly and, 226, 243, 248,
    264, 268– 69, 274–75
romantic involvements,
    pre-marriage, 81– 84, 86,
    114–16, 135, 141
sexual exploits on road, 184–85,
    256, 277
sibling rivalry and, 38–39, 41,
    116
songwriting of, 164–65, 187–88,
    192–93, 194–95, 201, 203,
    230, 254
and Stone Canyon Band,
    178–209
tennis achievements, 55–56
theater work, 166–68, 169–70
trust fund of, 138
TV image of, 7–8
Nelson, Sam Hilliard (Rick's son),
    217, 255, 267
    custody dispute and, 296–99
Nelson, Tracy Kristine (Rick's
    daughter), 254–55
    acting career, 171, 267, 299
Nelson, Willie, 165
Nelson, Willy (Rick's cousin), 202,
    209
the Nelsons, 267
"Never Be Anyone Else But You,"
    109
New Beginnings, 296–97
"New Delhi Freight Train," 235
New Faces of 1937, 23
Newton-John, Olivia, 207
Nichols, Junior, 166
Nielson, Norma Jean, 47
"Night Train to Memphis," 165
Nimoy, Leonard, 168

Nitzche, Jack, 173–74, 249–50
Nugent, Luci Baines, 214

"O.K. Crackerby," 206
Ocean Way Studios, 263
"Oh, Brother," 168
O'Keefe, Johnny, 262
O'Keefe, Vicki, 262
"Old Enough to Love," 109, 156
"Old Grey Whistle Test, The," 207
Olsen, Keith, 225–26
"On Dreams Alone," 220
On the Flip Side, 169
"One After 909," 276, 282
"One Night Stand," 212, 216, 218
"One of These Mornings," 109
Orbison, Roy, 156, 279
Orr, Ethel. *See* Nelson, Ethel
Osborn, Joe, 110, 126, 164, 203
Over-the-Hill Gang, The, 186
"Owen Marshall, Counselor at
    Law," 204
"Ozzie's Girls," 205, 296

P.J.'s Alley, 284
"Palace Guard," 209
Palace Hotel, 27
Palace Theater, 17
Palmer, Earl, 65
Palomar Ballroom, 23
Palomino Club, 219
Paramount Theater, 22
Park Suite Hotel, 284
Parker, Colonel Tom, 223
Parker, Graham, 253
Peake, Dan, 172
Pelham Heath Inn, 16
Penner, Joe, 20
"People Are Funny," 29
Peppin, Leo, 43
Perkins, Carl, 61, 76, 279, 280
Perspective, 175
Petit, Leslie, 114–16

"Petrocelli," 216
Petty, Dorothy, 116
Peyton Place, 85
Phillips, Sam, 8, 62, 279
"Picture in Rick's Notebook, A," 86
Pitney, Gene, 127, 145, 146
Playboy Club, 277
Playing to Win, 253–54
Plumstead, Wally, 52–53
Poco, 177, 179
"Poor Little Fool," 90, 91
Portrait of a Legend, 255–56
Poynton, Dorothy, 39
Presley, Elvis, 7, 61, 98, 111, 117–18, 156, 189, 223, 259
Presley, Priscilla, 189
Preston, Don, 233

Randolf, Joe, 46
Randolph, Clara, 32, 46
Rank, Brad, 284–86
"Reason Why, The," 193
Record Plant, 235
Red Skelton radio show, 27–28, 29
Reeves, Jim, 110, 165
Reeves, Sheila, 149
"Regal Rock 'n Blues Reunion" tour, 283
Remarkable Mr. Pennypacker, The, 85
"Restless Kid," 108–9
Richard, Cliff, 207
"Rick at the Fair," 239
Rick is 21, 145
Rick Nelson in Concert, 187–89
Rick Sings Nelson, 192, 194–95
Ricky, 76
"Ricky Gets Married," 287
Ricky Nelson, 89
Ricky Nelson Sings "For You," 157
Ricky Nelson Sings for You, 157
Ricky Sings Again, 109, 124

Ricky Sings Spirituals, 124
"Ricky's Big Night," 86
Ridgefield Park, New Jersey, 13–14
Rio Bravo, 91–94, 96, 97, 108, 129
Ripley, Robert, 20
Ritz Tower, 16
Riviera Hotel, 274
Riverside Theater, 25
Roberts, Rix, 269
Robyn, Bunny, 64–65, 80, 101, 152, 155
Rock & Roll Hall of Fame, 8, 294
Rock & Roll Revival, 198–201
"Rock and Roll Lady," 220
Rockabilly Renaissance, 243
Rockford, Mickey, 146
"Rockin' All Over the World," 243
Rolling Stone, 181, 188, 192, 215
Rolling Stones, 163
Rondell, Ronnie, 41
Ronstadt, Linda, 197
Rooks, 54
Rosenberg, Aaron, 40
Roxy, 232, 256
Royal Albert Hall, 207, 282–83
Rubin, Dan, 171–72, 173
Rudy the Fifth, 194–95
Rumbleseat Garage, 268
Russell, Clark, 289
Russell, Leon, 155, 216
Russell, Lynn, 166
Rutgers University, 15
Ryan, Tim, 230

Sahara Tahoe, 228
St. Agnes Academy, 17
Salerno, Charlene, 53
San Diego County Fair, 171
Sandrich, Mark, 21
Sari Heller Gallery, 170
Sarokin, Dennis, 210–12, 229, 230–32, 293

"Saturday Night Live," 241–43
Savenick, Phil, 299–300
Schroeder, Aaron, 127
Scrivner's Drive-In, 68
"Se La," 283
Setzer, Brian, 264
Shanahan, Patrick, 179
"She Belongs to Me," 182, 184
Sheeley, Mary Jo, 88, 110
Sheeley, Sharon, 88, 105–6, 110–12, 114, 116, 129–30, 287
Shiloh, 240
"Shindig," 163, 164, 202
"Shirley Lee," 103
"Shivaree," 153
Shrine Auditorium, 166
Silver Eagle Records, 276
Simon, George, 18
"Singing the Blues," 276
Smith, Vern, 46
Snyder, Peggy Lou. *See* Nelson, Harriet
Snyder, Tom, 256
"So Long," 124
"Solid Gold," 256, 265, 282
"Something You Can't Buy," 230
Sommers, Joannie, 169
Songs by Ricky, 124, 155
Sound of Music, The, 169
Spector, Phil, 155, 249
Spotlight on Rick, 162
"Square Pegs," 267
Stacy, Jim, 118, 129
"Stars Fell on Alabama," 145
"Stay Young," 229
Steel Pier, 100, 143
Steinberg, Billy, 250
Sterling, Tisha, 140
Stevens, Rose Anne, 24, 25
Stevenson, Venetia, 114
Stewart, Forrest, 56, 58, 73, 113, 115, 117
Stoller, Mike, 155

Stone Canyon Band, 178–98, 204, 268
  break-up of, 209
"Stood Up," 80
Story of Three Loves, The, 45
Strand Theater, 24, 26
Strange Agents, 267
Stray Cats, 264, 269
"String Along," 156
"Stuck in the Middle with You," 243
"Summertime," 146
Sun Records, 62, 63, 87, 103, 239, 263
Sutton, Joe, 38, 186
"Suzanne on a Sunday Morning," 172
Sweetheart of the Campus, 27
Syncopation Four, 15

"Take a City Bride," 170
"Take these Chains from My Heart," 166
Talbot, Lyle, 46
"Tale of Three Wishes, A," 251
"Tales of the Unexpected," 229
Taylor, Gene, 270
"Teen Age Idol," 146, 218
"Teenager's Romance, A," 64
Tenafly, New Jersey, 26
"Thank You Lord," 195
"That's All," 155
"That's Alright Mama," 240
"They Don't Give Medals . . . ," 169
Thornbury, Will, 37, 38, 50, 86
Three on a Date, 241
Tiomkin, Dimitri, 108
"Tired of Toein' the Line," 248–49
"Tomorrow Show," 256
"Tonight I'll Be Staying Here with You," 190
"Tonight Show," 216, 256
Torrance, Dean, 237

Toussaint, Allen, 235
Trammell, Bobby Lee, 103
"Travelin' Man," 125–29, 144–45
Travis, Merle, 65
Troubadour, 177, 180–81, 186–87, 193
"True Love," 76
"True Love Ways," 243, 276
"Try to Fall in Love," 219
"Try to Remember," 163
"Trying to Get to You," 109
Tuduri, Eddie, 219
Tulsa International Music Festival, 239
Tuttle, Lurene, 33
Two O'Clock Courage, 21
Two Sides of the Moon, 218

"Unchained Melody," 103
Universal Amphitheater, 278
Upton, Pat, 250, 284

Vallee, Rudy, 166
Van Scoyk, Randolph, 43
Vee, Bobby, 155
Venet, Nik, 112, 263–64
Venet, Ted, 113
Venetian Room, 272
Vera, Billy, 163
Verve Records, 64, 102
Very Thought of You, The, 162
"Very Thought of You, The," 157
Victor Hugo's, 23
Vincent, Gene, 111

Wackiest Ship in the Army, The, 119, 120, 122–23, 145
Wagner, Jack, 46
Waikiki shell, 119–20
"Waitin' in School," 80
Waldo, Janet, 34
Wallich's Music City, 63, 87, 218
Warford, Bob, 166

Warhol, Andy, 211
Wayne, John, 91, 92, 93
"Welcome to My World," 165
Werblin, Sonny, 21, 146
West, Red, 110, 117, 118
West, Sonny, 117
"What Is Success," 235
When the Kennedys Were in the White House, 170
White, Clarence, 166
White House, 272
White, Jay DeWitt, 211, 229, **268**
Whitney, Annabella, 149
Wilder, John, 52
William Morris Agency, 256
Williams, Andy, 190
Willie Nelson Fourth of July Picnic, 216–17
Wiltern Theater, 185
Windfall, 215, 216
Wolff, Sandy, 20
Women's Wear Daily, 216
"A Wonder Like You," 145
Woodward, Patrick, 269, 285, **289**
World War II, 28–29

Yeoman, Bob, 230
"You Are the Only One," 124
"You Can't Dance," 230
"You Don't Love Me Anymore,"**155**
"You Just Can't Quit," 164, 166, **170**
"You Know What I Mean," 274, **275**
"You Tear Me Up," 109
"Young Emotions," 123–24
Young, Skip, 51–53, 65, 70, **85**, 96, 118, 120, 121, 129, 149, 160
"Young World," 145
"Your True Love," 76, 86
"You're My One and Only Love," 64, 73, 75–76
Yours, Mine and Ours, 171

Zoom, Billy, 276